Radical Renfrew

© Tom Leonard 1990

Polygon
22 George Square, Edinburgh

Set in Linotron Sabon
by Polyprint, Edinburgh and
printed and bound in Great Britain by
Bell and Bain Limited
Glasgow

British Library Cataloguing
    in Publication Data
Radical Renfrew: poetry from
    the French Revolution to World War I.
    1. Poetry in English. Scottish writers,
    1745-1980 — Anthologies
I. Leonard, Tom, 1944-
821'.008'09411

ISBN 0 7486 6052 6
      0 7486 6028 3

The Publisher acknowledges subsidy
from the Scottish Arts Council
towards the publication of this volume

Radical Renfrew

Poetry
from
The French Revolution
to
The First World War

*by poets born,
or sometime resident in,
the County of Renfrewshire*

SELECTED, EDITED AND INTRODUCED BY

Tom Leonard

Polygon
EDINBURGH

Dedication: History & Locality

Less the childhood, more the place
and the childhood of the place;

and through the childhood of the place
the present: the present people.

T.L.

Contents

The Poems

JAMES MAXWELL 1720-1800

JOHN ROBERTSON 1767-1810

ALEXANDER WILSON 1766-1813

ROBERT BOOG 1749-1823

ALEXANDER TAIT fl. 1790

PATRICK MAGILL c. 1890-

Introduction

ANY SOCIETY is a society in conflict, and any anthology of a society's poetry that does not reflect this, is a lie. But poetry has been so defined in the public mind as usually to exclude the possibility of social conflicts appearing. The belief is widespread that poetry is not about the expression of opinion, not about 'politics', not about employment, not about what people actually do with their time between waking up and falling asleep each day; not about what they eat, not about how much the food costs. It is not in the voice of ordinary discourse, contains nothing anyone anywhere could find offensive, above all contains nothing that will interfere with the lawful exercise of an English teacher going about his or her duty in a classroom.

To an extent the connection between poetry and school has been the problem. It is not that teachers deserve any less respect than anyone else out working for a living; the trouble lies in the notion that poetry has to be 'taught' in the first place, and that there is a professional caste of people best equipped so to do. For to be 'taught' poetry has meant to be given guidance in a classroom as to how best ultimately to pass exams about it. This has had the effect of installing in people's minds certain basic ideas:

1. A 'real' poem is one that an English teacher would approve for use in an English class.
2. A 'real' poem requires some explanation and guidance as to interpretation, by an English teacher.

3. The best poems come to be set in the exams.
4. The people best able to pass these exams will be the people best able to understand and to write poetry.

The roots of all this pernicious nonsense about what a poem isn't and what it is, can be traced back to the nineteenth-century invention of Literature as a 'subject' in schools. This invention was based on certain specific principles:

1. The creation of a 'canon' of Literature, the new subject's 'set books' as it were.
2. The establishment of that canon — to be overseen by Her Majesty's Inspectorate for Schools — on the premise that Literature is a *code* embodying desirable social, moral and political values.
3. The exclusion from that canon of works that did not recognise this code, or did not see Literature as a code in the first place.
4. The exclusion from that canon of works whose main focus was thought properly to be that of another 'subject' in the curriculum.

The important word is code. To understand Literature is to understand a code, and the teacher is the person trained to possess the code that Literature is in. This has to be accepted unconditionally, as it is the sole basis of the teacher's power to grade pupils' responses. A piece of writing that does not acknowledge the code that the teacher has been trained to possess, cannot be accepted as Literature: for such writing deprives the teacher of the only basis of his power of assessment. This applies even when the 'canon' has been enlarged to 'allow' some writing about, for instance, working-class lives. The teacher's right to grade the pupils' responses must never be threatened; therefore the writing must never be such as might give the pupils the right to challenge the teacher's claim to possess it.

Literature shrinks to Teachable Literature. Taking a fairly mild and non-poetic example, the excellent prose work

Winwood Reade's *The Martyrdom of Man* is considered far
too 'literary' to be History, and far too historical to be
Literature; even more damaging, it is thought far too heretical
of orthodox beliefs to be thought an appropriate object for
pupils' potential approval. And so it cannot, as the phrase
goes, 'enter the canon'.

In fact the spread of education as a right to the mass of
people has paradoxically led to the deprivation, from them, of
much they once held to be valid literature. Generation after
generation has been 'taught' that a poem itself has as it were to
pass an exam before it can earn the right to be called a poem
in the first place; but only those people who have passed exams
about poems, can give a new would-be poem the new exam
necessary to decide whether it is a poem or not. The 'subject'
has functioned to assure the mass of people that until they have
a licence to prove otherwise, they have no public right to make,
criticise, or even claim to understand, anything that might
seriously be called Literature. This is a serious matter, and
raises the question of what is meant by democracy.

*

In the years consequent on 1792 the most influential book
circulating in Scotland besides the Bible and Burns's poems
was Tom Paine's *The Rights of Man*. This book's message was
welcomed by the Paisley poet Alexander Wilson, who was
soon, in 1794, to be forced into exile like Paine himself:

> "The Rights of Man" is now weel kenned,
>   And read by mony a hunder;
> For Tammy Paine the buik has penned,
>   And lent the courts a lounder;
> It's like a keeking-glass to see
>   The craft of kirk and statesman;
> And wi' a bauld and easy glee,
>   Guid faith the birky beats them
>   Aff hand this day . . .

The power of clergy, wylie tykes,
 Is unco fast declining;
And courtiers' craft, like snaw aff dykes,
 Melts when the sun is shining;
Auld monarchy, wi' cruel paw,
 Her dying pains is gnawing;
While Democracy, trig and braw,
 Is through a' Europe crawing
 Fu' crouse this day.

The Rights of Man, which includes practical plans for family allowance, retirement and sickness pensions, and public works for the unemployed, was a sustained argument for republican democracy centred on three principles:

1. Men are born, and always continue, free and equal in respect of their rights. Civil distinctions, therefore, can only be founded on public utility.
2. The end of all political associations is the preservation of the natural and imprescriptible rights of man; and these rights are liberty, property, security, and resistance of oppression.
3. The nation is essentially the source of all sovereignty; nor can ANY INDIVIDUAL, or ANY BODY OF MEN, be entitled to any authority which is not expressly derived from it.

Paine argued that the 'simple' democracy of ancient Athens was best replaced by the representational democracy of contemporary America:

The one was the wonder of the ancient world; the other is becoming the admiration and model of the present.

This 'simple' democracy of ancient Athens was simple in that all free citizens had the right, in common public assembly, to vote directly on the issues of government, face to face with those who carried them out. Moreover, free citizens had the right themselves to participate in government irrespective of personal wealth. Crucial to all this was the *agora*, a central area in Athens where citizens met daily and amongst other things discussed their own business and that of the state. In the sixth century BC this *agora* doubled as the assembly forum where at least forty times a year issues of governance were put to the mass vote. Later the voting assembly moved ten minutes away, but its function remained the same.

Of course it was not so simple, nor so ideal. Only about a seventh of the population were 'free citizens' to begin with: women, immigrants and their offspring, and slaves, were not. Yet this albeit restricted democracy had features not only unique in its own day, but in advance of those advocated for democracy in nineteenth-century Britain. And it contained two ideal principles which have not lost their force in two and a half thousand years: *democracy is daily dialogue,* and *true democracy lies in the equality and equal power of all parties to that dialogue.*

The enemy of democracy, Paine argued, was the mystification of government. He argued this because mystification is the device that renders equality of dialogue impossible. With mystification, one might add, comes the caste that can be called the Keepers of the Mystery. And the Keepers of the Mystery are the Keepers of the Right to Dialogue, amongst themselves.

The invention of Literature as a teachable 'subject' was the invention of Literature as a mystery — thus countering the democratic potential of the sudden expansion of literacy brought about by compulsory education. In fact the spread of the right to vote in Britain paralleled the spread of the right to literacy, in that both were allowed within formal codes whose names acknowledged the supremacy of the status quo which must not be challenged: Her Majesty's Government, Her Majesty's Inspectorate of Schools, the Queen's English. The rights and values of monarch and aristocracy were sown into the definitions of what the people's new entitlements to personal expression actually were. These rights and values were precisely those not acknowledged in the America where

Paine and Wilson were exiled. But the Queen's English had special difficulties to face in the Scotland that Wilson had left behind.

There was, in early nineteenth-century Renfrewshire, a large number of Scots words mixed in with the English vocabulary, as the poems of Alexander Wilson and others show. But by the end of the century these words had been greatly reduced in number, and poetry written in Scots was severely restricted in content. If one looks at the annual volumes of *Modern Scottish Poetry* published between 1878 and 1893 (ed. D. H. Edwards, Brechin), one gets the impression of Scots poetry as being largely a male nostalgic hymn to hearth, established religion, domestic gems of women, and fellow wee-boys-at-heart men. Contrary to the usual reasons given for this, this restriction in content was less to do with the diminution in vocabulary than with restrictions on content akin to those imposed on Queen's English. On the one hand Scots words and usages of any kind were barred from the diction of the classroom by teachers in their capacity as representatives of the diction of governance. On the other, changes in the language were seen as the result of an immigration substantially Irish Catholic as well as Highland Gaelic. There was a certain amount of looking back on what was seen as the once-dominant language of a single-religion people. This ignored certain realities, such as the fact that the written language used at the turn of the century by poets like Tannahill and Wilson in their informal letters to friends and equals, was almost exclusively English. More important, it concealed the fact that the poetry nostalgically looked back to was one stripped of anything that might challenge the contemporary status quo. *Modern Scottish Poetry*, like most late Victorian anthologies of Scots poetry, assumes a male audience not only favourable to, but members of, the established church. That tradition of Scots poetry hostile to the status quo and to clergymen of any denomination; that Protestant tradition of Scots poetry expressing conflict and difference of opinion within the church itself — all this was dropped in favour of a shy alliance of writers 'allowed' to keep their language going within the establishment as it was allowed to exist in Scotland. The angry became the pawky. It was anger at the end of a string.

Those most active in promoting this Scots were often those most opposed to what was actually happening in areas like Glasgow and Paisley. It was not a simple matter of locality and national culture. For with the industrial revolution had come the emergence in Britain of the proletarian urban dictions, and diction had become in Renfrewshire, as elsewhere in Britain, what it has never ceased to be since: not simply a matter of locality, but of class. The proletariat of the West of Scotland, Protestant or Catholic, freethinking or of any other religion, of immigrant stock or not — all could be seen as forming linguistically a colony within a colony. The new middle class of the towns and city — who identified most with Queen's English in their diction — were often those most insistent on 'good Scots' in their literary hobbies. The contempt that was heaped on the speakers of the new urban diction of the West of Scotland was based on class, and sometimes religious, prejudice as much as a desire for a return to the mythical 'pure' diction of a pure race of pre-proletarian Scottish folk.

This carried into the twentieth century, as some of it has carried to this day. In an essay on John Davidson published in 1933, T. D. Robb, teacher at Paisley Grammar and author of *Deletiae Poetarum Scotorum*, had this to say:

> Davidson, as you know, adhered to English all his life, though a Renfrewshire man for over thirty years. And well he might! For what has the Doric of the populous centres of the county become? It is not Scots at all, but a thing debased beyond tears. It is a mongrel patois due to lower class immigration from Ireland, from Lancashire mills, and the meaner streets of Glasgow. Traditional vernacular is gone. The streets are sibilant with 'huz yins', 'wis youse', 'wees wis'; ungrammatical with 'I seen', 'I done'. Bernard Shaw's immortal line of blank verse (put into the mouth of a prizefighter),

> 'he seen me comin' and he done a bunk',
> if heard in passing through the streets, would hardly raise the
> eyelid of surprise. For God's sake — to speak it with reverence —
> let such horrors cease to be printed as Doric. . . . Regret it as we
> may, the Doric of Renfrewshire is not only dead, but in an
> advanced state of putrefaction. 'An ounce of civet, good
> apothecary!'

So when one hears working-class speech, whether from
Scotland, Ireland or England, one should call for civet — i.e.
perfume. One should call for civet, because in doing so one
would be quoting from *King Lear* Act Four Scene Six — and if
you knew that, dear reader, you were as cultured a man as T.
D. Robb. One was familiar with the 'canon' of English
Literature.

But Robb was no eccentric then, as he would be no eccentric
now. The Scottish National Dictionary, in its introduction of
1936, echoed his view:

> Owing to the influx of Irish and foreign languages in the
> industrial areas near Glasgow the dialect has become hopelessly
> corrupt.

Not simply changed, but corrupted, debased. Having lost its
original value. A people, in other words, for whose words
issuing from their own lips one should have no respect. They
had lost the right to equality of dialogue with those in
possession of Queen's English, or 'good' Scots. But in fact the
urban dictions had, and have, connections not simply local,
but world-wide. To see this one has to return to America, and
Tom Paine.

*

It is no accident that the American democracy Paine so admired was made up of a mix of immigrants and their early descendants. With a new people came a new diction, and a new diction could serve as the means for an equality of dialogue. It made for an ease of conversation, one that allowed Wilson when settled in America informally to call not only on the similarly exiled author of *The Rights of Man*, but on President Jefferson himself. American society today is hardly a model of equality of wealth; but the openness of its Public Information Act, which contrasts so starkly with the obsessive Official Secrets Act in Britain, stems from the equality of dialogue on which the republic was founded. Similar contrasts can be made here between Britain on the one hand and Canada, Australia, and New Zealand on the other.

But the democracy of America, like those elsewhere, had been created at the expense of a native population. And just as in Ancient Athens, this democracy itself existed on the back of slave labour. There is an economic link, too, between these nineteenth-century American — and Caribbean and African — slaves, and the British urban proletariat: one group laboured long hours to extract raw materials which the other laboured long hours to finish into manufactured goods. This historic link survived in the language of the groups, and in the Literature of the children and grandchildren of those slaves and proletariat writing today. In Scotland the links are the more close because of the colony-within-a-colony aspect already mentioned. The language presents writers with a similar range of options, prompts similar highly political questions: whether the use of English modelled on middle-class English writers is an acceptance of colonial status; whether the use of words from the pre-colonial era is justified when the pre-colonial vocabulary is now obsolete or greatly reduced; whether a model of the language as spoken, with mainly Anglified vocabulary but non-English syntax and/or sound, is restricted to being the model of an individual speaker speaking. Always the criticism of 'provincialism': but it's an international pattern, and not just in the former English Empire. It is simply the right to equality of dialogue that is being fought for. Yet when one sees the historic connection between slave and proletariat embodied in the language, one sees more clearly the actual nature of derisive laughter at working-class speech and accent today: one sees what forces are behind the vehemence with which a child will be told to alter his or her language when addressing a superior; one sees too clearly the connection between 'lighthearted' guides to 'slang' and the lovable cheery black servants of pre-war American films.

But it isn't just the right to equality of dialogue in the present that has to be established, but equality of dialogue with the past. A person must feel free to go back into the past that is Literature, go where they like and meet equally with whom they will. If a model of Literature has been created that prevents this, that model should be removed, and with it the metaphors that restrict the open nature of people's access. There has been enough of Literature as a 'path' through the ages, as a 'course' entrusted to those appointed to 'its' charge. Let a writer have the authority to address any reader — and any reader to read any writer — without either feeling that valid dialogue can only take place in a code acceptable to a transmitter of the code of governance — in other words, within the code of governance itself. Let a writer have the authority to be nobody else but themself, if they so wish: to make direct reference to specific particulars of their own life, as lived, names and all. But the code of governance of the 'canon' specifically *excludes* any person from being 'nobody else but themself'. This is the heart of the mystery: it is the 'unwritten constitution' of what is taught as British Literature. Unwritten indeed.

The ludicrous nature of McGonagall's work, for instance. McGonagall's naivety was not in being nobody else but himself. It was in being nobody else but himself in a code that did not allow him to be nobody else but himself in the first place. But why should a code of governance exclude anyone from being nobody else but themselves? What could be the point of this? The answer, it seems to me, is that a code of Literature could not be thought desirable in which anyone might imagine that by being nobody else but themselves, they were the equal of anyone else. It would not be thought desirable, that is, to a government expressly founded on the principle that not everyone is equal to anyone else at all, but there is a 'natural' inequality which people have to be taught. One has to recognise that the concession of parliamentary democracy in Britain was not the concession that all human beings are equal. At this point I am driven to try to define what I mean by all human beings being equal. Of course to try will be an act of gross impertinence on my part, as I am a human unlicensed to define such things as what a human is. However, I will try to do so in two paragraphs, in as simple a language as I can. It isn't easy, but it is worth a try.

I would not describe myself as 'the' human being; that would mean I thought that no other human being existed, or that others weren't quite as much a human being as I am. I understand fully that I am just 'a' human being, just as anyone else is just 'a' human being as well. But of course like you the reader, whoever you are, I am *not* just anyone else — I am 'this' human being that nobody else is.

The stages can be seen like the stages between being a baby — when the universe is no more than the baby itself — and being an adult. Growing up is learning to accept you are just 'a' human being, that others are like yourself equal in that they are human and that they exist as well. The trouble starts when people are taught they can go from being 'the' human being when they open their eyes on the world, to being 'this' human being in adulthood, without having to swallow that they are just 'a' human being in between. Then they think that whatever it is makes them 'this' human being is what stops them being just 'a' human being in the first place.

This, in my opinion, is the model of the foundation of British government that has produced a specifically British model of education that has produced a specifically British model of Literature. To go simply to the model of education: a tawdry chain of privilege runs downwards from the likes of Eton and Winchester, down to the expensive private schools of Scotland and elsewhere, down finally to the less expensive schools of town and city, whose pupils, though they may not be the equal of those from Eton and Winchester, can at least know they are distinctly superior to the scruff in the free school down the road. Inequality of status of diction has been one peculiarly British way of sorting people into a hierarchy of worth. But enough of that too, it has been but one way amongst others. Sufficient to say, and to say it with double force in Scotland, that no language is more sacred than the people who speak it; more to the point, no language is more sacred than the people who don't.

A Literature in which it is possible for a writer to be nobody else but his or her own self, would not be 'an enormous extension to the present model of Literature' or some such; it can only happen within a new model of Literature altogether, one that rejects inequality as a constituent of personal being to begin with. So it isn't the addition of 'community' to 'high' culture. That assumes their separation; that is the product of the old model of 'subject', of 'path', of ownership of certain values by certain people. But if you are free to go where you like as an equal in Literature, then you don't 'cross into zones' and put on a 'serious literature' or 'local literature' hat. You don't have to give any explanations to anybody as to why you're there; nor does the writer have to give any explanation to you. It's all one Literature, as it is all one world.

This is what makes the use of *King Lear* for instance as a way of putting people 'in their place' so awful: *King Lear* is among other things about a monarch's coming to terms with the fact that he's a human being the equal, no more, of all others, having to face the reality of his place in a world where dogs, horses and rats can have life when his own daughter can't. This recognition of the equality of human beings is part of what makes it impossible for the play to be seen as the 'property' of any particular person or class. In this anthology James Thomson's poem 'The City of Dreadful Night' also takes such equality as given, which is why it connects as easily with 'community' as with 'high' art.

The full poem, by some Community versus High Art ways of looking at things, might be thought ripe for the 'élitist' tag. It has subtitle quotes from Dante and Leopardi, and links with other European writers such as Novalis; it can even be seen, in terms of its underlying shape and tone — its long circular movements of thought, its building up of counterpointed blocks of logic, its brooding seriousness throughout; its pauses, its final climaxes presenting images that summarise the preceding themes — as being organised like a 'typical' symphony of Thomson's Austrian contemporary, the composer Anton Bruckner.

But even my discussing this might be thought 'élitist' to some and a bit uppity to others. To the latter in one way I am 'breaking the code' of Literary Criticism by moving from Literature into Music, but as it's Classical Music I've moved into, that's probably alright. But it wouldn't be alright for me to say that it doesn't actually matter whether you the reader like Bruckner or not; that it doesn't matter a damn whether you've even heard of him. To say so would be me being nobody else but myself, telling you that you have the right to be nobody else but yourself as well: this, at the expense of the authority of 'the canon' of classical music. But whether or not Bruckner ever wrote a note of music doesn't matter in the sense that it has nothing to do with the value of you — or me — as human beings. Neither Music nor Literature, nor any other art, *puts* value into people. Yet it's because of that very fact as a given (though we have been taught to assume the opposite) that I claim the freedom to mention Bruckner if I want to, without being called 'élitist': I happen to like his music a lot, that liking has led me to see a connection with Thomson that might interest you, and my liking for Bruckner is part of 'this' human being that is me and nobody else. Which is partly the way that James Thomson proceeds in 'The City of Dreadful Night'.

It's not the place here to start a technical analysis of the poem. But two important things are worth adding. One is that the narrator directly addresses the reader, and presents an image that can be thought of as an image of his own existence; but half the poem is in the present tense, and if the reader finds the image relevant to their own existence, this strange thing happens, that you suddenly find that the 'present' the narrator is speaking in, seems your own present time, that you're sitting in reading the poem. But. The image that Thomson presents is not simply an image of a peculiar despair; it is also a vivid image of the material conditions of his time: the Victorian city with its perpetual fog, the despair of lonely people in crowds, death-dealing open sewers in the streets spreading infection. So 'The City of Dreadful Night' links directly with the poem that happens to come before it chronologically in *Radical Renfrew*, the poem written by the Paisley town gardener William Elder, who attacks the complacency of clergy and the greed of the profit motive which was behind much of the despair of those cities that Thomson's poem images. And the fact that Thomson's poem ends with a rejection of the role of women as saviour of men, means that it naturally links with the radical feminist poetry of Marion Bernstein which follows, though her work also is placed where it is simply through chronological sequence. Bernstein's work, like Elder's, connects naturally onward to other poetry in the anthology: poetry about politics, poetry about work; temperance songs and poems, and poems about alcoholism — from which temperance movement songs should be distinguished — like John Mitchell's long narrative *Cautious Tam*.

Once you accept that the model of Literature is based on universal equality of human existence, past and present, then you can travel in Literature, as a writer or as a reader, wherever you like. And it is not a 'broad-based subject' — 'Open Literature' or 'Social Studies' — with a new caste charged to grade the responses of those who approach 'it', that I'm talking about; for it is that very system of grading and exams which turns the living dialogue between writer and reader into a thing, a commodity to be offered in return for a bill of exchange, i.e. the certificate or 'mark'. But no caste has the right to possess, or even to imagine it has the right to possess, bills of exchange on the dialogue between one human being and another. And such a dialogue is all that Literature is.

*

The place where a democratic freedom of encounter with Literature has occurred is in the free public libraries. It is not that they haven't operated censorship, but the public libraries have remained the one place where anyone can build his or her own relation with the literary world. It was in the public library in Pollok that I built mine. The five-to-seven department, just a green tin cupboard with about eight shelves, and the books facing out the way. You had to wrap your books in newspaper, and you had to show your hands. Then the day when I could use the Junior Department for the 7-14s, a whole wall under the window. Real books at last, that wouldn't be finished as soon as you got home. Of course the time came when the Junior Department wasn't what I wanted, but I wasn't old enough yet for the adult. I got to know the names of the authors in the A to C section of the adult section that adjoined the Junior wall at the far end. The adult fiction went right round two walls of the building, with non-fiction in standing shelves between. What a day that would be, when you could get into that. My mother let me take the bus to Govan to use the Junior Department at Elder Park. It seemed enormous, as big as Pollok's adult section; it had a very quiet atmosphere I'll never forget, with really heavy stone walls, and the pillars you went in at the entrance. It was there I got to know Dickens. Then the adult section at Pollok. Then the Stirling, the Mecca of them all.

The public libraries gave me the education I wanted. Like most Scottish writers I know of my generation, I went to school and got British — mainly English — Literature. I went to the library and borrowed American, Russian and European. And these were the ones that mattered as far as I was concerned. When the hero of *Crime and Punishment* ran down the stairs of a close after the murder, I knew what it was he ran down. All the poetry that meant anything to me in my middle teens, when I first got to like poetry — all of it that meant anything to me, I got out the library. You could choose what you wanted there, read it in your own house, say exactly what you wanted about it, or — most precious right of all — you could say absolutely nothing about it whatever.

In my early twenties I worked in a university bookshop. I hated it. You might as well have been selling bananas, and the pay was rubbish. A non-union place, I was young, and it took the work inspectorate to call and pin up the minimum workshop rates for me to find out I was being paid less than the legal minimum for shopworkers. I decided to try to get to university, and studied at night to make up my Highers. At dinner time I would sometimes make it to the library at St George's Cross, and get a quick half hour in in the reading room. Other times in the Mitchell Library at Charing Cross not getting on with my Highers but sitting with a book called *The Annotated Index to the Cantos of Ezra Pound*, writing in tiny pencil in the margin of my own copy of Pound's poems the references from the index. This was my education.

I did get in to university, and at the second attempt got the degree in English and Scottish Literature that gave me the bit of paper that now matters to me. That paper I renew every year for £5: the membership card to Glasgow University Library. That Library is specialised, and offers a specialised view of the world. Its filters have excluded literature by working-class people, though there are books in plenty about 'them'. You have to go elsewhere for original literature itself.

In some ways it's here that the public libraries come into their own, and in others it's where they have been most frustrating. The public libraries have been where millions including myself have received that education beyond basic literacy that actually mattered to them; but while the public has been out front borrowing the books, through the back there has always been that world you see over the librarian's shoulder when they go to the phone, those rooms with half-open doors marked Private that they put the light on when they go through. Always when I have requested a book at the issue desk of the Mitchell Reference Library in Glasgow, and when someone has later appeared to hand the book over at the counter, there has been that pleasant smile between us as if isn't it lucky a wee fairy turned up with the right book just out of sight round the corner. And always I've thought at the back of my mind, I wonder what it looks like where you've been.

It was therefore a great thing to me when I was given the job as 'Writer in Residence' at Paisley Central Library. Besides running writers' groups and meeting people who wanted a response to their writing, I was given the freedom to go wherever I wanted behind the counter, and unlike the staff who were always busy having to be librarians, I could stop wherever I wanted and read whatever I liked. Paisley, besides being a public lending library, holds the main large collection of non-borrowable books in Renfrew District Libraries: books that are too rare or flimsy to be going in and out on public loan. They are all available for the public to read though in the reference section — but like any other reference library, you can't really get to know the collection from a cabinet index. You don't feel like asking the librarian to fetch you up twenty books to see what ones you like. It's only by physically having them in your hand you can get to know the range of them. That privilege was given to me in my job, and this anthology from the local poetry collection in the reference room gallery is the result.

TOM LEONARD

I didn't have any particular plan in mind when I started on this anthology, not in the sense of trying to look for specific themes. Certainly whenever I came on a biographical reference that would say something like 'Unfortunately his poems of this period show his extreme radical views' I would be on the lookout for that poet's poems during the period referred to. But in general that was not my way of doing things. Basically I just read the poetry collection from A to Z, together with other anthologies in the gallery, and the collections of mainly nineteenth-century 'Paisley Pamphlets' that have been bound in leather volumes. The selection I have made, allowing for the fact that some of the poets are represented by groups of poems written over a number of years, still follows a chronological forward progression. The poets were either born in the County of Renfrewshire — which during the period extended from what is now south-west Glasgow, to Greenock — or spent a period of their life there. I have added a few poems not to be found in the Paisley collection, and the county border has been stretched about a mile to take in Marion Bernstein's house in Paisley Road, Glasgow.

The main forerunner to the present anthology is David Brown's two-volume *Paisley Poets* of 1889 and 1890, and the two volumes of *The Harp of Renfrewshire* published in 1819 and 1876. A good deal of biographical information came from David Brown, some came from David Semple's centenary edition in 1875 of Tannahill's poems, some from the introductions to the individual books, some from the newspaper cuttings and handwritten entries put inside the books by librarians or the original owners who donated them. I have done a lot of work, sometimes in other libraries, to extend the notes that introduce each poet's contribution to the anthology. Paisley is not a town that I feel has suffered chiefly from a dearth of historians; I am not one of these, and mistakes and omissions will no doubt be found.

If the reader has read this far, he or she will understand that I do not intend either to discuss 'the path' of Renfrewshire

Poetry through the nineteenth century, or to suggest that this anthology is such a path. It is an area, through which you make your own paths. But the anthology is large, and for those who want them I have suggested some short thematic journeys in the *Guide to Themes* that immediately follows this introduction. At least as useful as this, I hope, will be the *List of Sources* at the back of the anthology. If any poems interest you enough to make you want to see more of the writer's work, you will find, listed under author, the name of the book from which the poem was taken together with the book's reference number in Paisley Central Library. Of course Glasgow and Edinburgh people interested in this way will get most of the books in the Mitchell and the National Library of Scotland. At the time of writing — with the possible exception of John Davidson — all the poets are out of print; the majority have been so for over a hundred years.

I am grateful to J. D. Hendry, Director of Arts and Culture for Renfrew District, for not only welcoming the proposed project but making sure I had all the time and any facilities needed to complete it. All the staff at Paisley Central Library I thank for their consistent friendly help during my erratic comings and goings. Of the many individuals who have been of help, I want to thank especially my friend the writer James Kelman. At times his words of encouragement have been crucial.

Tom Leonard
Paisley Centre Library
November 1988

A guide to the location of some different themes

The aim of this section is not to categorise the contents, but to give the reader the chance to look in one 'dip' at how some common themes are differently treated, and how the treatment developed over the period of time covered by the anthology. Many of the poems listed under one heading would appropriately also appear under others (or the reader after reading a poem might disagree with its particular placing here) and many new headings might have been added, for example 'Domestic Politics', or 'Children'. But though loose, the guide is inserted in the hope that some will find it of practical value.

The poems under the various headings are listed in groups. Italic subheadings give the reasoning behind the groupings.

The number beside each poem is its page number.

*

RELIGION

favourable

Maxwell	The Divine Attributes of God (p.4)
Pollok	The Course of Time (pp.104-5)
Richmond	Subject Matter of the Books of the Bible (pp.232-3)
Thomson	Anniversary Lines on the Death of My Only Son (pp.239-40)

critical of sectionalism

Mitchell	A Braid Glower at the Clergy (pp.146-156)
Hamilton	The Lay of the Bogle Stone (pp.271-274)

hostile

Elder	To the Defenders of Things As they Are (pp.278-80)
Thomson	The City of Dreadful Night (pp.284-295)
Davidson	A Ballad in Blank Verse (pp.355-9)
McGilvray	What Deil Has Gane Wrang with the True Holy Kirk (pp.174-5)

ALCOHOL

EMIGRATION

EMPLOYMENT

REPUBLICAN

Wilson   Lines on Looking at the Picture of a King (p.118)
Anon   Lorne and Louise (pp.262-5)

FEMINIST

Bernstein   Woman's Rights and Wrongs; A Rule to Work Both Ways; Wanted a Husband; Manly Sports; Human Rights; A Dream; Married and 'Settled'; A Song for the Working Man (pp.297-305)
Picken   An Auld Friend Wi' A New Face (pp.189-191)
Anon   Jenny — A Love Lay (p.234)
Russell   Women's Rights *versus* Women's Wrongs (pp.306-7)

SOLDIERING AND POLICE

Anon   The Renfrew Volunteers (pp.205-6)
Magill   La Basée Road; The Listening-Patrol; Marching (pp.364-6)
McGilvray   When I Wi' the Laird Did Enlist (pp.168-9)
Lorimer   Instructions for the Police (pp.275-7)

LITERATURE AND REPUTATION

Maxwell   The Divine Origin of Poetry (pp.1-3)
Tannahill   Ode to Jealousy (p.46)
Crichton   The Library (pp.53-4)
Webster   Droll Will Dunbar (pp.101-2)
Pollok   The Course of Time (pp.105-9)
Motherwell   I Am Not Sad! (pp.114-6)
Wingate   The Sin O Sang (pp.256-8)
Davidson   From Grub Street (pp.349-351)

TOWN AND CITY

not critical
Tait   A Ramble Through Paisley (pp.36-7)
Wilson   Daybreak (pp.16-7)
Smith   Glasgow (pp.207-10)
critical
Thomson   The City of Dreadful Night (pp.284-95)
Bernstein   A Song of Glasgow Town (p.304)

James Maxwell

Born in 1720 at Auchenblack near Pollok House. He worked as a hardware pedlar, weaver, school usher and, for a short while, as a schoolmaster. The last eighteen years of his life he sold his pamphlets of his own prolific verse in Paisley. He died in 1800, and his unsold pamphlets were auctioned to pay for his burial. Brown (Vol. 1 pp. 17-23) mentions 59 of Maxwell's publications, this not taking into account 'an infinite number of things, comprising elegies, panegyrics, satires, squibs, epigrams, acrostics etc., etc.' Much of Maxwell's rhyming couplets are moral and religious; the rest includes topical and personal material such as a verse autobiography, a description of Paisley, descriptions of the manufacture of cotton and of paper, verses on the usefulness of the Forth and Clyde Canal, and a celebration of Nelson's victory at the Battle of the Nile.

*

from The Divine Origin of Poetry Asserted and Approved

Thousands of years had they no written word,
To teach them how they aught to serve the Lord.
Yet were they never left without a light,
To understand his holy will aright.
Till Moses' time, when men were multiplied,
Then writings did the Lord for them provide.
And ever since have books been more and more,
Diffusing learning from shore to shore.

Now Moses was a Poet most sublime,
Much Poetry he wrote; of blank or rhyme

1

No matter which; it surely was divine,
And will for ever with bright lustre shine.
Then is it not a most enormnous crime,
To prostitute the Muse in prose or rhyme?
To make her speak a language that's profane,
Or any thing in a lascivious strain?
The greatest sacrilege this sure must be,
And aggravated to the last degree.
This ought to be by all mankind abhor'd,
Who are the true subjects to our rightful Lord.
Most daring sure, to take the gifts of Heav'n,
Which were to men for God's own glory giv'n,
To make them instruments for use of hell,
To teach mankind against him to rebel.
Their heinous guilt is of the deepest dye,
That can be offer'd to the Lord Most High:
Which if not cancel'd ere their breath expire
Their portion must be everlasting fire.
Their crime is taking things that are divine,
And casting them before the dogs and swine.

Nor only such as write and publish these
Vile trumpery, the carnal mind to please;
But all who purchase such audacious things,
Are open rebels to the King of kings.
Their guilt will not be found a whit the less
Than those who dare such noxious things express.
Nay these perhaps may deemed be the chief,
As the receiver's blacker than the thief.
They take the things they had in trust from God,
Which for his glory were to be bestow'd,
To raise rebellious arms against his throne,
What more enormous crime was ever known?
O with what trembling! with what gloomy fear,
Must they before his judgment seat appear!
Prepost'rous wretches! ah, how they will stand,
With dire despair! assign'd to his left hand!
And with what horror! with what trembling heart,
Hear their dire sentence, 'Hence from me depart,
With devils go eternally and dwell,
Amidst the black infernal lake of hell!
Prepar'd for Satan and his cursed crew,
This is the portion that remains for you!

Who have embezzl'd what you had in trust,
To gratify the flesh and please the lust.
Thus have you wasted all my trusted store,
Which was to aid my cause, and feed my poor.'

   Thus all base scribblers, who with hellish wit,
Have things profane, or things lascivious writ;
And those who them encouragement have giv'n,
To raise rebellion 'gainst the Pow'rs of Heav'n
Let such consider this their certain doom,
Who wealth and wit on wickedness consume.
Yea, let such wanton wits, of hellish flame,
Who glory only in their open shame,
Consider this their dire destructive end,
While they the great Almighty God offend.
Now they may laugh and please themselves betimes
And their companions, with audacious rhymes,
Until they plunge together down to hell,
Where they for ever must with devils dwell.

   This friendly warning they may ridicule,
And call the author but a crazy fool.
Well, be it so, if you be truly wise,
And count the truths of God but flatt'ring lies;
This is no doubt what some of you believe,
And credit freely to the devil give.
Well, you may take his counsel; trust his lies,
And all reveal'd religion now despise:
And think, when you resign your mortal breath
There will be no more reck'ning after death.*
But tho' this age is now so wicked grown,
That few, too few, against such jargon frown;
But give encouragement to such gross lies,
While those who write the truth they quite despise.

   Yet time will come, perhaps 'tis not far off,
When you, who now at all religion scoff,
Shall weep and howl; by God and men abhor'd,
And none will think you worth one flatt'ring word;
Or if your names should be at all exprest,
'Twill be with detestation, not in jest.

* See R. Burns' pretended paraphrase on the xcth Psalm [Maxwell's note]

Introduction to On the Divine Attributes of God

Say whence came this sublime, this glorious frame,
And how all matter into being came?
Matter could not eternally subsist,
Then must a God eternally exist:
Or we must say, the origin of man,
By his own pow'r from nothing first began.
Absurdity, devoid of common sense!
Could man from nothing make himself commence?
To say from nothing all things came by chance,
Who can such gross absurdity advance?
One being therefore must for ever be,
Quite self-existent from eternity!
Divinely perfect, and but only one,
For equal, or superior could be none.
But some may say, if one could only be,
Whence comes the doctrine of the Trinity!
One must be greater and the other less
Or must we reason totally suppress?
To this we answer, Three consists in One,
And yet superior or inferior none.
Tho' one in essence, yet in persons Three,
Thus they subsist, and all in One agree,
Tho' our weak reason cannot comprehend,
Nor fully understand this to defend.
Tho' this above our reason is we own,
Yet contradiction herein can be none.
For sure that Being infinite must be,
That has existed from eternity:
Nor does this myst'ry reason overthrow,
Altho' it be above its pow'r to know.
We must allow that Being infinite,
Tho' finite reason cannot see aright.
Therefore our faith hereon we safely build,
Since it is what he hath to us reveal'd.
Canst thou by searching find out God? canst thou
Make infinite to finite reason bow!
Cease then, vain man, presumptiously to pry
Into the depths of God's infinity.

John Robertson

Born in Paisley, the son of a grocer, in 1767. He was well educated and expected to enter a profession, but his father's business collapsed and John took up weaving. In 1803 he was driven by poverty to join the Fifeshire Militia, where he was given the job of regimental clerk. By this time he had already become known as a poet, 'The Toom Meal Pock' having been a very popular song after its publication during an economic depression in 1800. Robertson was sent south with his regiment. While stationed near Portsmouth in 1810 he committed suicide outside the barracks, being buried on the unmarked spot where his body had been found.

*

The Toom Meal Pock

Preserve us a'! what shall we do,
    Thir dark unhallowed times;
We're surely dreeing penance now,
    For some most awfu' crimes.
Sedition daurna now appear,
    In reality or joke,
But ilka cheil maun mourn wi' me,
    O' hinging toom meal pock.
                And sing, Oh waes me!

When lasses braw gaed out at e'en
    For sport and pastime free,
I seem'd like ane in paradise
    The moments quick did flee.

Like Venuses they a' appeared,
　　Weel pouther'd were their locks,
'Twas easy dune, when at their hame,
　　Wi' shaking o' their pocks.
　　　　　　　And sing, Oh waes me!

How happy past my former days,
　　Wi' merry heartsome glee,
When smiling fortune held the cup,
　　And peace sat on my knee:
Nae wants had I but were supplied,
　　My heart wi' joy did knock.
When in the neuk I smiling saw,
　　A gaucie weel fill'd pock.
　　　　　　　And sing, Oh waes me!

Speak no ae word about reform,
　　Nor petition parliament,
A wiser scheme I'll now propose,
　　I'm sure ye'll gie consent—
Send up a cheil or twa like me,
　　As sample o' the flock,
Whase hallow cheeks will be sure proof,
　　O' a hinging toom meal pock.
　　　　　　　And sing, Oh waes me!

And should a sicht sae ghastly like,
　　Wi' rags, and banes, and skin,
Hae nae impression on yon folk,
　　But tell ye'll stand ahin!
O what a contrast will ye shaw
　　To glowring Lunnon folk,
When in St James's ye tak' your stand,
　　Wi' a hinging toom meal pock.
　　　　　　　And sing, Oh waes me!

Then rear your hand, and glow'r and stare,
　　Before yon hills of beef,
Tell them ye are frae Scotland come,
　　For Scotia's relief;
Tell them ye are the vera best,
　　Wal'd frae the fattest flock,

JOHN ROBERTSON

Then raise your arms, and oh! display
  A hinging toom meal pock.
               And sing, Oh waes me!

Tell them ye're wearied o' the chain
  That hauds the state thegither,
For Scotland wishes just to tak'
  Gude nicht wi' ane anither.
We canna thole, we canna bide,
  This hard unwieldy yoke,
For wark and want but ill agree,
  Wi' a hinging toom meal pock.
               And sing, Oh waes me!

Alexander Wilson

Born in Seedhills, Paisley, in 1766. After some education at Paisley Grammar he was apprenticed when aged thirteen to a weaver, and lived and worked some time near Lochwinnoch as well as in Paisley. In 1789 he accompanied his brother-in-law on his travels as a packman, Wilson the while writing poems, and in 1789 Wilson made a tour as a pedlar alone in East Scotland, trying to raise subscribers for a projected collection of poems. This appeared in 1790. A reprint of this work in 1791 contained a journal made while on his 1789 wanderings.

In 1790, besides his collection *Poems*, Wilson published 'The Hollander, or Lightweight' (pp. 13-16), attacking a local silk manufacturer, William Henry — late of Holland — for the cheating of weavers by charging them for discrepancies in the weight and holes made by himself in the cloth. The poem was widely circulated, and Henry took out summons for criminal libel and incitement to unrest. He asked for £60 plus costs. The trial, though set for November 1790, did not take place.

Wilson wrote another attack on cheating of weavers by a local manufacturer, 'Hab's Door', then in 1792 a warrant for Wilson's arrest was issued after he had sent the Paisley manufacturer William Sharp a copy of a poem called 'The Shark' together with a letter saying that five guineas, if paid within three hours, would ensure the poem's suppression. The poem accused Sharp of cheating by altering his machinery to make returned weavers' work seem smaller than it was. It included a description of Sharp being flogged through the streets by the public hangman (p. 18). Sharp immediately sought Wilson's arrest, stating that Wilson was well known for such publications 'some of which are this moment subject of enquiry'. Wilson was described as the author of 'highly libellous, incendiary and dangerous publications', and in

Wilson's absence £50 costs were granted to Sharp and a fine of £10 Scots imposed in June 1792.

In August Wilson was arrested and imprisoned until his fine was paid, then in January 1793 he was again jailed in the Tolbooth for 14 days and fined 300 Scots merks as a warranty of good behaviour for two years. He was ordered to destroy all copies of 'The Shark', two of which he had publicly to burn on the steps of the Tolbooth at 11 a.m. on February 6th. But not everything he wrote in 1792 brought him trouble. 'Watty and Meg' (pp. 24-25) reputedly sold 100,000 copies throughout Scotland, many believing at first that the anonymous poem was by Burns. Yet in May 1793 Wilson was back in the Paisley Tolbooth, further damages were awarded to Sharp, and Wilson had to borrow money to pay the fine that brought his release.

In January 1794 Wilson was once more in jail for what was to be the last time, and this time the possible consequences of his arrest were much more serious than before. He was charged with 'being concerned in framing and industriously circulating an advertisement addressed to The Friends of Liberty and Reform. Calling a General Meeting of the Friends of Reform to have been held this night in Falconer's Land, Stories Street at five o'clock. Said to be by order of a committee and of having John Neilson printer in Paisley to print the said advertisement.'

Wilson managed for a third time to borrow enough money to pay for his release from prison, this time for bail. In May he walked to Portpatrick with his nephew William Duncan, sailed for Belfast, and changed ship there on May 23rd for a vessel sailing to Philadelphia.

The reasons for Wilson's flight — for such it was — are not hard to understand. It occurred only a few months after the transportation, for 14 years, of Thomas Muir, one of the founders of the Friends of the People in 1792. Again in December 1793 five of the leading members of the 'British Convention of the Delegates of the Friends of the People

9

associated to obtain Universal Suffrage and Annual Parliaments' were arrested after the convention had met in Edinburgh; three of the five arrested were subsequently, like Muir, sentenced to fourteen years' transportation. The government's attitude to Parliamentary Reform was summed up by Lord Braxfield during Muir's trial:

> A government in every country should be just like a corporation, and in this country it is made up of the landed interest which alone has a right to be represented. As for the rabble, who have nothing but personal property, what hold has the nation of them?

It was the exclusive presumption of such 'landed interest' that Wilson had lampooned in his 'The Insulted Pedlar'. He was never to feel thus hemmed in again, once arrived in America. He worked in a printer's office, then as a weaver, and travelled as a pedlar once more, raising subscriptions for another volume of poetry. For some years he worked as a teacher, and while such in 1801 he describes in a letter his visit to the local Falls of Paterson, which William Carlos Williams was to describe in his poem *Paterson* a century and a half later. Wilson did not like teaching, as his letters and the poem 'The Teacher' included here show.

In 1806 Wilson obtained a job editing *Ree's Encyclopaedia* and managed to interest the publishers in his projected magnus opus, *American Ornithology*. The scope of this work he outlined in the first of nine volumes, published in 1808:

> As to the nature of the work, it is intended to comprehend a description and representation of every species of our native birds from the shores of St Lawrence to the mouths of the Mississippi, and from the Atlantic Ocean to the interior of Louisiana. These will be engraved in a style superior to anything of the kind hitherto published; and colored from Nature, with the most scrupulous adherence to the true tints of the original.

Wilson made six main journeys between 1804 and 1812 in

the preparation of this work, and covered several thousand miles by foot, horse and canoe. Among the many meetings described in his letters are those with Jefferson and with Thomas Paine. Distributing Paine's works had been one of the charges against Thomas Muir, and *The Rights of Man* had been a primary source of inspiration to the Friends of the People. It was chiefly to obtain subscriptions to his ornithological work that Wilson visited Paine and President Jefferson; but two verses from Wilson's satiric 'The Aristocrat's War-Whoop' — the supposed pre-election speech of an anti-Democrat bemoaning the power of common people in America — shows that Wilson did not lose his awareness of why he had had to emigrate to America:

> As Heav'n's my judge, I owe them a grudge,
>   And vengeance and hate in my heart is a-hovering;
> To think that such wretches, escap'd from the clutches
>   Of George, our most gracious, omnipotent Sovereign, —
> To see his dominions, by Paine's curst opinions,
>   Cut up and controul'd by mechanics and farmers;
> Without noble blood, and bespattered with mud, —
>   It drives me to madness, and well may alarm us.
>
> O, England, thou glory and pride of a Tory!
>   Blest country, where riches and rank have the pref'rence;
> Where crowds at the sound of 'My Lord' kiss the ground,
>   Or sink, in his presence, with honour and rev'rence.
> Where are you now, rabble, that dare not to babble,
>   Are ty'd neck and heels at the nod of their judges;
> For all without riches are ignorant wretches,
>   Ordained to believe, and submit to be drudges.

Wilson died in 1813 of dysentry, aged 47. He developed the illness from a cold caught after swimming a river in pursuit of a bird he had noticed passing the window where he sat. He was buried in the Swedish Church in Southwark, Philadelphia. A statue of him was erected in Paisley in the corner of Paisley Abbey grounds in 1877.

A copy of the now rare and very valuable *Birds of America*

is held by Renfrew District Library Service, and applications can be made to inspect it by arrangement. Occasionally it is put on display. Wilson's journal of his travels in Scotland together with his letters and prose describing his life and travels in America, give a compelling account of the most varied and independent life of any Renfrewshire poet not only of the nineteenth, but of any other century. These can be read in Volume One of the two-volume *Poems and Literary Prose of Alexander Wilson* (ed. Rev. A. B. Grosart, Alex Gardner, Paisley 1876). (PCL Ref: B/WILS PC 8052)

Hollander

or

LIGHTWEIGHT

> *—unheard of tortures*
> *Must be reserved for such, these herd together;*
> *The common damn'd shun their society,*
> *And look upon themselves as fiends less foul.*
>
> Blair

Attend a' ye, wha on the loom,
   Survey the shuttle jinking,
Whase purse has aft been sucket toom
   While Willie's scales war clinkin'.
A' ye that for some luckless hole
   Ha'e paid (though right unwillin')
To satisfy his hungry soul,
   A saxpence or a shillin'
         For fine some day.

Shall black Injustice lift his head,
   An cheat us like the devil,
Without a man to stop its speed,
   Or crush the growin' evil!
No — Here am I, wi' vengeance big,
   Resolv'd to calm his clashin';
Nor shall his cheeps or powder'd wig,
   Protect him frae a lashin'
         Right keen this day.

See! cross his nose he lays his specks,
   And o'er the claith he glimmers,
Ilk wee bit triflin fau't detects
   And cheeps, an' to him yammers,
Dear man! — that wark'll never do;
   See that: — ye'll no tak' tellin';
Syne knavish chirts his fingers through,
   An' libels down a shilling
         For holes that day.

13

Perhaps the fellows needin' clink,
  To calm some threatnin' beagle,
Whilk mak's him at sic baseness wink,
  And for some siller wheedle.
In greetin, herse, ungracious croon,
  Aul' Willy granes, 'I hear ye,
But weel! a wat our siller's done,
  We really canna spare ye
            Ae doyt this day.

Health to the brave Hibernian boy,
  Who when by Willy cheated,
Cock'd up his hat, without annoy,
  An' spoke wi' passion heated;
'Upon my shoul I have a mind,
  Ye old deceiving devil,
To toss your wig up to the wind
  And teach you to be shevil,
            To me this day.'

But see! anither curtain's drawn,
  Some chiel his web has finish't,
An Willy on the tither han'
  The price o't has diminisht.
But brought before the awfu Judge,
  To pay the regulation;
Will lifts his arm, without a grudge,
  An' swears by his salvation
            He's right that day.

Anither's been upon the push,
  To get his keel in claith,
In certain hopes to be sure flush,
  O' notes an' siller baith.
Returnin' for his count at night,
  The poor impos'd on mortal
Maun pay for pounds o' clean light weight,
  Tho' he's maist at the portal
            O' want that day.

In vain he pleads — appeals to God,
  That scarce he lost an ounce;
The holy watcher o' the broad
  Cheeps out that he's a dunce.

Out frae the door he e'en must come
  Right thankfu' gin ye get
Some counterfeits, a scanty sum
  Brought frae the aul kirk yate
               Yon preachin' day.

O sirs! what conscience he contains,
  What curse maun he be dreein'!
Whase every day is mark'd wi' stains
  O' cheatin' an' o' leein'!
McK———l, H—b, or throwther O—r,
  May swear an' seem to fash us,
But justice dignifies their door
  An' gen'rously they clash us
               The clink each day.

Our Hollander, (gude help his soul)
  Kens better ways o' workin',
For Jock an' him has aft a spraul
  Wha'll bring the biggest dark in.
Weel, Jock, what hast thou skrewt the day?
  'Deed father I'se no crack o't,
Nine holes, sax ounce, or there a way
  Is a' that I could mak' o't
               This live lang day.

Sic conversation aft taks place,
  When darkness hides their logic;
Like Milton's De'l and Sin, they trace
  For some new winning project;
Daft though they be, and unco gloits,
  Yet they can count like scholars,
How farthings, multiplied by doits,
  Grow up to pounds and dollars
               Some after day.

Forbye, to gie the deil his due,
  I own, wi biggest won'er,
That nane can sell their goods like you,
  Or swear them up a hun'er.
Lang hacknied in the paths o' vice,
  Thy conscience nought can fear her;

And tens and twals can, in a trice,
Jump up twa hun'er far'er
                On any day.

What town can thrive wi' sic a crew
   Within its entrails crawlin',
Muck-worms, that must provoke a spew
   To see or hear them squalin'!
Down on your knees, man, wife, an' wean —
   For ance implore the Deevil
To haurl to himsel his ain,
   And free us frae sic evil
                This vera day.

Daybreak

SCENE: *The Town*

Now darkness blackens a' the streets,
   The rowan e'e nae object meets,
      Save yon awl cawsey lamp
That has survived the dreary Night,
An' lanely beams wi' blinkin' light,
      Right desolate an' damp.

Fore-doors an' winnocks still are steeket,
An' Cats, wi' silent step, and sleeket,
      Watch where the rattons tirl;
Or met in yards, like squads o' Witches,
Rive ither's hair out wi' their clutches,
      An' screech wi' eldritch skirl.

Now mony a ane, secure frae harm,
Lies row't in blankets snug, an' warm,
      Amus'd wi' gowden dreams;
While others scart their sides an' lugs,
Tormentet' wi' infernal bugs,
      Thick swarmin' frae the seams.

Some sunk amid their kimmer's arms,
Are huggin' matrimonial charms,
     In bliss an' rapture deep.
Some turnin', curse the greetin' wight
For skirlin a' the live-lang night,
     An keepin' them frae sleep.

Some weary Wight perhaps, like me,
Doom'd, Poverty's distress to dree,
     Misfortune's meagre brither;
Now dauners out beneath the starns,
Wi' plans perplexing still his harns,
     To keep his banes thegither.

Now lasses start, their fires to kin'le,
An' load the chimly wi a tanle
     O' bleezin' coals an cin'ers;
Syne scowr their stoups, an' tankar's clear,
An' glasses dight, wi' canny care,
     To grace the Gentry's dinners.

Wi' clippet feathers, kame, an' chirle,
The Gamester's Cock, frae some aul' burrel,
     Proclaims the Morning near;
Ilk chiel now frae his hammock jumps,
The floor receives their lang bare stumps,
     An' wives an' a's asteer.

Now reek rows briskly out the lums;
Loud thro' the street the Piper bums,
     In Highlan' vigour gay.
Doors, hatches, winnock-brods are steerin',
An ev'ry ane in short's preparin',
     To meet the toils o' Day.

from The Shark

Wha could believe a chiel sae trig
   Wad cheat us o' a bodle?
Or that sae fair a gowden wig
   Contain'd sae black a noddle?
But SHARK beneath a sleekit smile
   Conceals his fiercest girning,
And, like his neighbours of the Nile,*
   Devours wi' little warning
      By night or day.

O happy is that man and blest
   Wha in the Canal gets him!
Soon may he cram his greedy kist
   And dare a soul to touch him;
But should some poor aul wife, by force
   O' Poortith, scrimp her measure,
Her cursed reels, at Paisley Corse,
   · Wad bleeze wi' meikle pleasure
      To them that day.

Whiles, in my sleep, methinks I see
   Thee marching through the City,
And Hangman Jock, wi' girnan' glee,
   Proceeding to his duty.
I see thy dismal phiz, and back,
   While Jock, his stroke to lengthen,
Brings down his brows at every swack,
   'I'll learn you' frien to lengthen
      Your Mills the day.'

Poor wretch! in sic a dreadfu' hour,
   O' blude and dirt and hurry,
What wad thy saftest luks or sour,
   Avail to stap their fury?
'Lang Mills,' wad rise around thy lugs
   In mony a horrid volley,
And thou be kickest to the dugs,
   To think upon thy folly
      Ilk after day.

* crocodiles

from Rab and Ringan

There liv'd in Fife, an auld, stout, warldly chiel,
Wha's stomach kend nae fare but milk and meal;
A wife he had, I think they ca'd her Bell,
And twa big sons, amaist as heigh's himsel.
Rab was a gleg, smart cock, with powder'd pash,
Ringan, a slow, fear'd, bashfu', simple hash.

Baith to the College gaed. At first spruce Rab
At Greek and Latin, grew a very dab;
He beat a' round about him, fair and clean,
And ilk ane courted him to be their frien';
Frae house to house they harl'd him to dinner,
But curs'd poor Ringan for a hum-drum sinner.

Rab talked now in sic a lofty strain,
As tho' braid Scotland had been a' his ain;
He ca'd the Kirk the Church, the Yirth the Globe,
And chang'd his name, forsooth, frae Rab to Bob.
Whare'er ye met him, flourishing his rung,
The haill discourse was murder'd wi' his tongue.
On friends and faes wi' impudence he set,
And ramm'd his nose in ev'ry thing he met.

The College now, to Rab, grew douf and dull,
He scorn'd wi' books to stupify his skull;
But whirl'd to Plays and Balls, and sic like places,
And roar'd awa' at Fairs and Kintra Races:
Sent hame for siller frae his mother Bell,
And caft a horse, and rade a race himsel;
Drank night and day, and syne, when mortal fu',
Row'd on the floor, and snor'd like ony sow;
Lost a' his siller wi' some gambling sparks,
And pawn'd, for punch, his Bible and his sarks;
Till, driven at last to own he had eneugh,
Gaed hame a' rags to haud his father's pleugh.

Poor hum-drum Ringan play'd anither part,
For Ringan wanted neither wit nor art:
Of mony a far-aff place he kent the gate;
Was deep, deep learn'd, but unco, unco blate;

He kend how mony mile 'twas to the moon,
How mony rake wad lave the ocean toom;
Where a' the swallows gaed in time of snaw;
What gars the thunder roar, and tempests blaw;
Where lumps o' siller grow aneath the grun',
How a' this yirth rows round about the sun;
In short, on books sae meikle time he spent,
Ye cou'dna speak o' aught, but Ringan kent.

Sae meikle learning wi' sae little pride,
Soon gain'd the love o' a' the kintra side;
And Death, at that time, happ'ning to nip aff
The Parish Minister — a poor dull ca'f, —
Ringan was sought: he cou'dna say them nay,
And there he's preaching at this very day.

The Insulted Pedlar

A POETICAL TALE RELATED BY HIMSELF

Honi Soi Qui Mal y Pense

O Ye, my poor sca't brethren a',
Wha mony a time wi' hungry maw,
Implore the beild o' some barn wa'
        Wi' hurdies sair;
Now to the deil your boxes blaw,
        And beg nae mair.

I've seen the day, but faith it's gane,
When roun' farm-towns, frae ane to ane,
The shortest cut we might have ta'en,
        Nor been molested;
But now wi' stabs, an' lime, an' stane,
        We're vext an' pested.

The deil a fit ye owre dare set,
But trudge lang twa mile to the yett,
Or by the Lord ye'll aiblins get
                        Your legs in chains;
Or skelpit back wi' haffits het,
                        And broken banes.

Ae nicht short syne as hame I trampit,
Beneath my pack, wi' banes sair crampit,
But owre a wee bit dyke I lampet
                        And trottin burn;
There to do for my ain bethanket,
                        A needfu' turn.

Aweel, I scarcely had begun
To ope the evacuating gun,
I'll swear they hadna reached the grun,
                        When frae the wud
A bellied gent, steps owre the run,
                        Wi' 'Dem your blood!

'By whose authority or order,
Came ye upon this corn-rig border,
To rowe your filth and reeking ordour
                        On me a Bailie?
Hence wi' your dirt, else by the Lord, or
                        Lang, I'll jail ye.'

I glowert a wee, syne fetch'd a grane,
'Deed sir, through mony a lane I've gane,
An' gin ye raise me frae this stane,
                        Ne'er laird or lady
Attempted such a job their lane,
                        Till I was ready.

'Gin ye can prove, by pen or tongue,
That lan' ne'er profited by dung,
That by its influence corn ne'er sprung,
                        Though I should lumple,
I'se thole a thump o' that hard rung,
                        Out owre my rumple.

'My order, sir, was Nature's laws,
That was the reason, and because
Necessity's demands and ca's
     War very gleg,
I hunkered down 'mang thir hard wa's
     To lay my egg.

'And sir, I'm seeking naething frae ye;
My offering here I freely lea you,
Sic presents ilka ane wont gie you,
     Tak' ye my word,
Ye're richer since I first did see you,
     That reeking turd.'

Scarce had I spoke, when owre he sprung,
And rais't a yellow knotted rung,
And aim't at me a dreadfu' fung,
     Wi' foaming spite;
But owre my head it suchin swung,
     Dash on the dyke.

I started up an' lap the dyke
'Now, curse ye, sir, come when you like,
I'll send this stick, armed wi' a pike,
     Amang your painches;
Ye ugly, greasy, girnin' tyke,
     Now guard your hainches.'

He roared a most tremendous oath,
That Satan's sell wi' shame wad loath,
While frae his devilish mouth the froth
     Flew aff wi' squatter;
Then raised a stane, as dead's a moth
     My brains to batter.

When at this instant o' the faught,
A gentleman came belly-flaught,
And in his arms the tiger caught,
     Wi' frighted tone;
Exclaiming, 'Lord's sake, Mr L———
     What has he done?'

Here I stood forth to bring't to a bearing,
'Please, sir, to grant a patient hearing,
An' I'll unravel what your speering,
      To your contentment;
Let go the bitch, don't think I'm fearing
      The fool's resentment.'

Sae I related a' the matter,
That raised between us sic a clatter;
At which he laughed till fairly water
      Reliev'd his e'en;
While the grim wretches baith did clatter
      Wi' malice keen.

'Now, sir, compose yoursel' a wee;
Tak' aff your hat an' join wi' me,
While for this sinner black I gie
      My earnest prayer;
Whilk frae my very saul on hie
      I here uprear.

'Great Jove! before thee here is seen,
A human bear, a speakin' swine,
Wha wi' dread oaths, and fiery e'en,
      An' devilish feature,
Has dared to curse a work o' Thine
      For easing nature.

'On him pour plagues without restraint,
Wi' restless buneuchs him torment,
Till through fierce purgin' he be spent
      As tume's a blether;
And that big wame that's now sae bent,
      Be a' lowse leather.

'And when he limps wi' gout and spavie,
Thro' jaunering crowds, held as a knave aye,
There may't attack him, while a privie
      In vain he seeks,
Till he be forc'd to blowt the gravie
      Just in his breeks!

'Whene'er he drinks to raise the flame,
Syne hurries hame to Venus' game,
May cauld yill clankin' in his wame
   Wi' hurlin' rum'le,
Aft force him to forsake the dame
   Wi' spoulin' whum'le.

'Then may he rue (although owre late
To stop the yellin' roarin' spate)
That e'er he curst, or vicious flate
   On pedlar Sawney;
And e'en envy his blessed fate
   Wha sat sae canny.

'And Lord! an answer soon sen' back,
And let him see Thy han's na slack.
Amen, amen, — Put on your hat,
   An' haud the bear in.'
So up I swung my verdant pack,
   And left him swearin'.

Watty and Meg or The Wife Reformed

A TALE

We dream in courtship, but in wedlock wake.
Pope

Keen the frosty winds were blawin'
 Deep the sna' had wreath'd the ploughs,
Watty weary't a' day sawin',
 Daunert down to Mungo Blew's.

Dryster Jock was sitting, cranky,
 Wi' Pate Tamson o' the hill,
Come awa', quo Johnny, Watty,
 Haith we'se ha' anither jill.

Watty, glad to see Jock Jabos,
  And sae mony neibours roun',
Kicket frae his shoon the sna ba's,
  Syne ayont the fire sat down.

Owre a board, wi' bonnocks heapet,
  Cheese an' stowps and glasses stood;
Some war roaring, ithers sleepet,
  Ithers quietly chewt their cude.

Joke was selling Pate some tallow,
  A' the rest a racket hel',
A' but Watty, wha, poor fellow,
  Sat an' smoket by himsel'.

Mungo hil't him up a tooth-fu',
  Drank his health an' Mag's in ane,
Watty puffin' out a mouthfu',
  Pledg't him wi' a dreary grane.

What's the matter, Watty, wi' you?
  Trouth your chafts are fa'ing in
Something's wrang — I'm vext to see you —
  Gude sake! but ye're desp'rate thin!

Aye, quo' Watty, things are alter't,
  But it's past redemption now,
Lord, I wish I had been halter'd
  When I marry'd Maggy How.

I've been poor, an' vext, and raggy,
  Try't wi' troubles no that sma',
Them I bore — but marrying Maggy
  Laid the cap'stane o' them a'.

Night an' day she's ever yelpin,
  Wi' the weans she ne'er can gree;
When she's tired wi' perfect skelpin',
  Then she flees like fire on me.

See you, Mungo, when she'll clash on,
  Wi' her everlasting clack,

Whyles I've had my nieve, in passion,
    Liftet up to break her back!

O, for gudesake, keep frae cuffets,
    Mungo shook his head and said,
Weel I ken what sort o' life it's;
    Ken ye, Watty, how I did?

After Bess and I was kippl't,
    Fact she grew like ony bear,
Brak' my shins, and when I tippl't,
    Harl't out my verra hair!

For a wee I quietly knuckl't,
    But when naething wad prevail,
Up my claes and cash I buckl't,
    Bess for ever fare ye weel.

Then her din grew less and less aye,
    Fact I gart her change her tune;
Now a better wife than Bessy
    Never stept in leather shoon.

Try this, Watty — When ye see her
    Raging like a roaring flood,
Swear that moment that ye'll lea' her;
    That's the way to keep her gude.

Laughing, sangs, and lasses' skirls,
    Echo'd now out thro' the roof,
Done! quo Pate, and syne his airls
    Nail't the Dryster's wauket loof.

In the thrang o' stories-telling,
    Shaking hauns, and ither cheer,
Swith! a chap comes on the hallen,
    Mungo, is our Watty here?

Maggy's weel-kent tongue and hurry
    Dartet thro' him like a knife,
Ope the door flew — like a fury
    In came Watty's scawlin' wife.

Nasty, gude-for-naething being!
    O ye snuffy, drucken sow!
Bringan wife and weans to ruin,
    Drinkin' here wi sic a crew!

Devil nor your legs were broken!
    Sic a life nae flesh endures —
Toilan like a slave, to slocken
    You, ye divor, and your whores!

Rise! ye drucken beast o' Bethel!
    Drink's your night and day's desire:
Rise this precious hour, or faith I'll
    Fling your whisky in the fire.

Watty heard her tongue unhallow'd,
    Pay't his groat wi' little din,
Left the house while Maggy follow'd,
    Flytin' a' the road behin'.

Fowk frae every door cam' lampin,'
    Maggy curs't them ane and a',
Clappit wi' her hauns, and stampin',
    Lost her bachals i' the sna.

Hame at length, she turn'd the gavil,
    Wi' a face as white's a clout,
Ragin' like a verra devil,
    Kitchen stools and chairs about.

Ye'll sit wi' your limmers round you!
    Hang you, Sir, I'll be your death!
Little hauds my hauns, confound you!
    But I cleave you to the teeth.

Watty, wha, 'midst this oration,
    Ey'd her while but daurna speak,
Sat like patient resignation,
    Trem'lan by the ingle cheek.

Sad his wee drap brose he sippet,
    Maggy's tongue gaed like a bell,
Quietly to his bed he slippet,
    Sighen aften to himsel'.

Nane are free frae some vexation,
· Ilk ane has his ills to dree;
But through a' the hale creation,
    Is a mortal vext like me!

A' night lang he rout and gauntet,
    Sleep nor rest he cou'dna tak!
Maggy, aft wi' horror hauntet,
    Mum'lin started at his back.

Soon as e'er the morning peepet,
    Up raise Watty, waefu' chiel,
Kist his weanies while they sleepet,
    Waukent Meg, and sought farewell.

Farewell, Meg! — And O! may heav'n
    Keep you aye within his care,
Watty's heart ye've lang been grievin',
    Now he'll never fash you mair.

Happy cou'd I been beside you,
    Happy, baith at morn and e'en;
A' the ills did e'er betide you,
    Watty aye turn't out your frien'.

But ye ever like to see me,
    Vext and sighin', late and sair,
Fareweel, Maggie, I've sworn to lea' thee,
    So thou'll never see me mair.

Meg a' sabbin', sae to lose him,
    Sic a change had never wist,
Held his haun close to her bosom
While her heart was like to burst.

O my Watty, will ye lea' me,
    Frien'less, helpless, to despair!
O! for this ae time forgie me,
    Never will I vex you mair.

Aye! ye've aft said that, and broken
    A' your vows ten times a week:
No, no, Meg! See there's a token,
    Glittering on my bonnet cheek.

Ower the seas I march this morning,
    Listet, testet, sworn an' a',
Forc'd by your confounded girning;
    Fareweel, Meg! for I'm awa'.

Then poor Maggy's tears and clamour
    Gusht afresh, and louder grew,
While the weans, wi' mournfu' yaummer,
    Round their sabbin' mother flew.

Through the yirth I'll wander wi' you —
    Stay, O Watty! stay at hame,
Here upon my knees I'll gie you
    Ony vow you like to name.

See your poor young lammies pleading?
    Will you gang and break our heart!
No a house to put our head in!
    No a friend to tak our part?

Ilka word came like a bullet!
    Watty's heart begoud to shake!
On a kist he laid his wallet,
    Dightet baith his een and spake.

If ance mair I could, by writing,
    Lea' the sogers and stay still,
Wad ye swear to drop your flyting?
    Yes, O Watty, yes I will.

Then, quo Watty, mind, be honest;
    Aye to keep your temper strive;
Gin ye break this dredful promise,
    Never mair expect to thrive.

Marget Howe! this hour ye solemn
    Swear by every thing that's gude,
Ne'er again your spouse to scol' him,
    While life warms your heart and blood.

That ye'll ne'er in Mungo's seek me,
    Ne'er put drucken to my name,
Never out at e'ening seek me
    Never gloom when I come hame.

That ye'll ne'er, like Bessy Miller,
   Kick my shins, and rug my hair;
Lastly, I'm to keep the siller
   This upo your soul you swear?

O--h! quo' Meg, 'Aweel,' quo Watty,
   Fareweel! faith, I'll try the seas,
O stan still, quo Meg, and grat aye
   Ony ony way ye please.

Maggy syne, because he prest her,
   Swore to a' thing owre again,
Watty lap, and danc't, and kist her;
   Wow! but he was wondrous fain.

Down he threw his staff victorious;
   Aff gaed bonnet, claes, and shoon;
Syne below the blankets, glorious,
   Held anither Hinny-Moon.

The Teacher

Of all professions that this world has known, —
From humble Cobblers upwards to the throne,
From the great Architects of Greece and Rome
Down to the maker of a farthing broom, —
The worst for care and undeserv'd abuse,
The first in real dignity and use
(If kind to teach, and diligent to rule)
Is the learned Master of a little school.
Not he who guides the legs, or fits the Clown
To square his fists and knock his fellow down;
Not He whose arm displays the murd'rous art
To parry thrusts, and pierce th' unguarded heart:
But that good man, who, faithful to his charge,
Still toils the op'ning Reason to enlarge,
And leads the growing mind through every stage,
From humble A, B, C, to God's own page;
From black rough pot hooks, horrid to the sight,
To fairest lines that float o'er purest white;
From Numeration thro' an op'ning way,
Till dark *Annuities* seem clear as day;
Pours o'er the soul a flood of mental light,
Expands its wings, and gives it power for flight,
Till Earth's remotest bounds, and Heaven's bright train,
Are trac'd, weigh'd, measur'd, pictur'd, and explain'd.
      If such his toils, sure honour and regard,
And wealth of fame, will be his sweet reward;
Sure, every mouth will open in his praise,
And blessings gild the evening of his days!
Yes, blest, indeed, with cold ungrateful scorn,
With study pale, by daily crosses worn;
Despis'd by those, who to his labour owe
All that they read, and almost all they know;
Condemn'd each tedious day, such cares to bear,
As well might drive even Patience to despair.
The partial parents taunt the Idler dull,
The Blockhead's dark, impenetrable skull;
The endless sound of A, B, C's dull train,
Repeated o'er ten thousand times in vain.
Placed on a point, the object of each sneer,
His faults enlarge — his merits disappear.

If mild — 'Our lazy Master loves his ease,
He lets his boys do anything they please.'
If rigid — 'He's a stern, hard-hearted wretch,
He drives the children stupid with his birch.
My child with gentleness will mind a breath,
But frowns and floggings frighten him to death.'
Do as he will, his conduct is arraigned,
And dear the little that he gets is gain'd;
E'en that is given him on the Quarter-Day,
With looks that call it money thrown away.
   Great God! who knows the unremitting care
And deep solicitude that Teachers share,
If such our fate by Thy divine control,
O give us health and fortitude of soul:
Such that disdain the murd'ring tongue of Fame,
And strength to make the sturdiest of them tame!
Grant this, O God! to Dominies distrest;
Our sharp-tailed Hickories will do the rest.

Robert Boog

Born in Edinburgh, he became minister at Paisley Abbey in 1774, assumed first charge there eight years after his appointment, and remained such until his death in 1823.

*

from Excursion Through the Starry Heavens

Where yonder radiant host adorn
    The northern evening sky,
Seven stars, a splendid waving train,
    First fix the wondering eye.

To deck Great Ursa's shaggy form
    These brilliant orbs combine;
And where the first and second point,
    There see the North Pole shine.

The third looks 'twixt the fourth and fifth
    To silver Vega's light;
The sixth and seventh point near to where
    Arcturus cheers the night.

Arcturus first to Vega join,
    The Northern Crown you'll spy;
And join'd with Ursa's second star
    He marks Cor Caroli.

Thro' Ursa's second, from her third,
    You reach the Charioteer;
Preceding whom, above her Kids,
    Capella shines so clear.

Capella, from the Charioteer
  Will nearly shew the place
Where Algol shines 'bove three faint stars
  In fell Medusa's face.

A ray from Algol to the Pole
  With accuracy guide,
Near, but behind it, Algenev,
  Beams bright in Perseus' side.

*

If during Winter's bright domain
  You range the southern sky,
The great Orion's splendid form
  Will fill your wondering eye.

With brilliant gems his belt, his sword,
  His broad-spread shoulders blaze;
While radiant Rigel, at his foot,
  Pours forth his silver rays.

The glittering belt from Taurus' eye
  Guides down to Sirius bright;
The spreading shoulders shove you east
  To Procyon's pleasing light.

And Rigel, cross by 's shoulder, where
  Betelgeux burns so red,
Thro' Pollux' toe, will point the light
  That flames on Castor's head.

Thro' Cancer's sign, whence no bright stars
  Distinguished light impart;
Castor, thro' Pollux, sends you down
  To hideous Hydra's heart.

From Hydra's and thro' Leo's heart,
   (It marks the Ecliptic line,)
You rise to where, in Ursa's great,
   The third and fourth stars shine.

*

Cassiopeia, spangled Queen,
   All seated in her chair,
Precedes Camelopardalus,
   As that the greater bear.

Betwixt the Great and Lesser Bears
   The monstrous Draco twines
His writhing tail; his sparkling crest
   'Twixt Vega and Kokab shines.

The ever-watchful Kokab guards,
   While Dubhe points, the Pole;
The Pole at rest sees Heaven's bright host
   Unwearied round him roll.

Alexander Tait

A tailor who worked in Castle Street, Paisley, though he lived in Tarbolton before and sometime after publication of his 1790 *Poems and Songs*. He knew Robert Burns, and wrote some derogatory verses about him after Burns allegedly slighted Tait in verses no longer extant. There is a hostile chapter on Tait in *The Contemporaries of Burns and the More Recent Poets of Ayrshire* (Hugh Paton, Carver & Gilder, Edinburgh 1840).

*

from A Ramble Through Paisley

> The Paisley folk, they may be bold,
> Their Main Street sides is worthy gold,
> Their price can by no man be told
>   That's new come forth,
> Their masters' pockets canna hold
>   What they are worth.
>
> In Incle Street they knittings twine,
> In Cotton Street work muslins fine,
> Into Silk Street the silk-gauze shine
>   In mirk mid-night,
> In Back-raw Street they drink at wine
>   In fair day-light.
>
> In Fisher-row Street's Tam and Johnny,
> In Main Street, O! the maids they're bonny!
> In oxter, oxter, joins each crony,
>   And their gear sort,
> In high crown'd hats, high cockernony,
>   O man, fine sport.

In Smithhills sure they're at nae loss,
In comes the maids of Abbey Close,
In Water Wynd they mind the gloss,
   And candle doups,
In Causeyside they like the dross
   O' the pint stoups.

In Storie Street they're a' sae kind
Unto the trade they were design'd,
In at your spare they'll tell their mind
   Right plain wi' ease,
In at your mouth comes out behind
   Fruit o' their cheese.

In New Street tightly they toil on,
In Cow Street too, and Lady's Loan;
In comes the cadger they ca' John
   To Wane-gate end,
In Grammar-school Close draws his drone
   For Dyster's Wynd.

In Old Sneddon the sailors skip,
In New Sneddon the ladies trip,
In Croft they pair and tightly clip
   These jolly souls,
In Brick Lane sit at others' hip
   Wi' flowing bowls.

Robert Tannahill

Born in what later became Castle Street, Paisley, in 1774, and moved with his family a year later to a house in Queen Street. At the age of twelve Robert was apprenticed to his father, a weaver, and it was as a weaver in Paisley that the poet spent his working life. He did travel to England with his brother Hugh at the time of the depression of 1799/1800, and worked for two years in Bolton. But learning of the terminal illness of his father in 1801 he returned to Paisley, where he lived alone with his mother after his brother's marriage in 1802.

He taught himself how to arrange airs on a German flute, and began to be known in the town as a poet and songwriter. He helped found the local Literary and Political Club in 1803, and the Paisley Burns Club two years later. He befriended the composer R. A. Smith who in time set some of Tannahill's most popular songs. In 1807 the poet obtained enough subscribers for his first and only book. Printed in Paisley, it contained a verse-drama, 'The Soldier's Return', and 33 of his poems. The 900 copies sold out within weeks. In March 1810 Hogg came to visit Tannahill in Paisley, showing clearly how high Tannahill's reputation had become.

But as some of his work shows, Tannahill could be prone to depression and a sense of being the butt of negative remarks. Perhaps his retiring manner together with distaste for the literary drinking scene did not help with some locals. At any rate by May 1810 some of his friends were worried about his behaviour. Then a projected new collection by Tannahill was rejected first by the publisher Thomas Stewart of Greenock, then by Archibald Constable of Edinburgh (the latter returning the parcel apparently uninspected, saying his publications list for the season was full). On May 17th Tannahill committed suicide. He left his mother's house some time around 3 a.m., and his body was found soon after in a culvert of the Candren Burn, his coat and silver watch on the ground nearby.

Tannahill began the preface to his 1807 book as follows:

> The author of the following Poems, from a hope that they possess some little merit, has ventured to publish them; yet, fully sensible of that blinding partiality with which writers are apt to view their own productions, he offers them to the Public with an unfeigned diffidence. When the man of taste and discrimination reads them, he will no doubt find many passages that might have been better, but, his censures may be qualified with the remembrance that they are the effusions of an unlettered Mechanic, whose hopes, as a poet, extend no further than to be reckoned respectable among the minor Bards of his country.

Of this same edition, he wrote in a letter of April 1807:

> I hate dependence on printers, paper-folks, or anybody. On inquiry, they found I was poor. Nothing could be done without I found security. That was easily procured; *then*, they were most happy to serve me in any thing I wanted. 'Tis the way of the world! Self-interest is the only passion. Merit might pine in obscurity for ever, if Pride, or Interest, for their own gratification, were not to hand the lone sufferer into public notice.

In 1883 a statue of Tannahill was unveiled in the grounds of Paisley Abbey, facing the entrance to the Town Hall and a few yards from the statue of Alexander Wilson that had been unveiled in 1874.

Ten of the twelve poems used follow the text printed in the 1807 collection. 'The Simmer Gloamin' is from the *Scots Magazine* of January 1810. 'Gloomy Winter's Now Awa'' is from an undated songsheet of R. A. Smith's setting, dated in the National Library of Scotland catalogue as c. 1810.

The Braes O' Gleniffer

TUNE: *Bonny Dundee*

Keen blaws the win' o'er the braes o' Gleniffer,
    The auld castle's turrets are cover'd wi' snaw;
How chang'd frae the time when I met wi' my lover,
    Amang the broom bushes by Stanely green shaw:
The wild flow'rs o' simmer war spread a' sae bonny,
    The mavis sang sweet frae the green birken tree;
But far to the camp they hae march'd my dear Johnnie,
    An' now, it is winter, wi' nature an' me.

Then ilk thing around us was blithsome an' cheery,
    Then ilk thing around us was bonny an' braw:
Now naething is heard but the wind whistlin' dreary,
    An' naething is seen but the wide-spreading snaw:
The trees are a' bare, an' the birds mute an' dowie,
    They shake the cauld drift frae their wings as they flee,
An' chirp out their plaints, seeming wae for my Johnnie,
    'Tis winter wi' them, an' 'tis winter wi' me.

Yon cauld sleety cloud skiffs alang the bleak mountain,
    An' shakes the dark firs on the stey rocky brae,
While down the deep glen bawls the snaw-flooded fountain,
    That murmur'd sae sweet to my laddie an' me:
It's no its loud roar on the wint'ry win' swellin',
    It's no the cauld blast brings the tears i' my e'e,
For, O gin I saw but my bonny Scots callan,
    The dark days o' winter war' simmer to me!

O Are Ye Sleepin', Maggie

TUNE: *Sleepin' Maggie*

O are ye sleepin', Maggie,
O are ye sleepin', Maggie!
Let me in, for loud the linn
Is roarin' o'er the warlock craggie.

Mirk an' rainy is the night,
    No' a starn in a' the carry,
Lightnings gleam athwart the lift,
    An' winds drive wi' winter's fury.

O are ye sleepin', Maggie,
O are ye sleepin', Maggie!
Let me in, for loud the linn
Is roarin' o'er the warlock craggie.

Fearfu' soughs the boor-tree bank,
    The rifted wood roars wild an' dreary,
Loud the iron yate does clank,
    An' cry o' howlets mak's me eerie.

O are ye sleepin', Maggie,
O are ye sleepin', Maggie!
Let me in, for loud the linn
Is roarin' o'er the warlock craggie.

Aboon my breath I daurna' speak,
    For fear I rouse your waukrife Daddie,
Cauld's the blast upon my cheek,
    O rise, rise my bonny lady!

O are ye sleepin', Maggie,
O are ye sleepin', Maggie!
Let me in, for loud the linn
Is roarin' o'er the warlock craggie.

She opt the door, she let him in,
    He cuist aside his dreepin' plaidie;
'Blaw your warst, ye rain an' win',
    Since Maggie now I'm in aside ye,

Now since ye're wauken Maggie,
Now since ye're wauken Maggie!
What care I for howlet's cry,
For boor-tree bank, or warlock craigie?

[The version published in the 1806 anthology *The Nightingale* (A. & G. Leslie, Glasgow), has 'craigie' as last word of the chorus; but it lacked the farewell chorus added above. The 1807 version here changed 'craigie' to 'craggie' in the main chorus, then reverted to 'craigie' in the new chorus added at the end. As the words 'craigie' and 'craggie' were interchangeable, it doesn't really matter which one sings. 'Craigie' has been used throughout in printings since, though a change in the sound of the last word as above might be used for effect. One certainly can't assume 'craggie' was a mistake — it does rhyme better, and had the same meaning.]

Lang Syne, Beside the Woodland Burn

Lang syne, beside the woodland burn,
    Amang the broom sae yellow,
I lean'd me 'neath the milk-white thorn,
    On nature's mossy pillow;
A' 'round my seat the flow'rs were strew'd,
That frae the wild wood I had pu'd,
To weave mysel' a simmer snood,
    To pleasure my dear fellow.

I twin'd the woodbine round the rose,
    Its richer hues to mellow,
Green sprigs of fragrant birk I chose,
    To busk the sedge sae yellow,

The crow-flow'r blue, an' meadow-pink
I wove in primrose-braided link;
But little, little did I think
 I should have wove the willow.

My bonnie lad was forc'd afar,
 Tost on the raging billow,
Perhaps he's fa'n in bludy war,
 Or wreck'd on rocky shallow.
Yet, ay I hope for his return,
As round our wonted haunts I mourn,
And often by the woodland burn
 I pu' the weeping willow.

W. ————'s Recipe

For Attaining A Character

If thou on earth wouldst live respecket,
In few words, here's the way to make it —
Get dog-thick wi' the Parish Priest,
To a' his foibles mould thy taste,
What he *condemns*, do thou condemn,
What he *approves*, do thou the same;
Cant scripture words in *every* case,
'Salvashion, saunt, redemshion, grace,'
But controverted points forbear,
For, thou may'st shew thy *weakness* there;
Look grave, demure, as any owl,
A cheerful look might d—— the whole,
Gang rigid to the kirk on sunday,
With face as lang's a gothic window,
But from these maxims should'st thou sever,
Poor profligate! *thou'rt lost for ever.*

Song: When John an' Me war' Married

TUNE: *Clean Pea Strae*

When John an' me war' married,
  Our haudin' was but sma',
For my Minnie, canker't carlin,
  Wou'd gie us nocht ava';
I wair't my fee wi' canny care,
  As far as it wou'd gae,
But, weel-I-wat, our bridal bed
  Was clean pea-strae.

Wi' wurkin' late an' early,
  We're come to what ye see,
For fortune thrave aneath our han's,
  Sae eydent ay war' we;
The lowe o' luve made labour light,
  I'm sure ye'll find it sae,
When kind ye cudle down at e'en,
  'Mang clean pea-strae.

The rose blooms gay on cairny brae,
  As weel's in birken shaw,
An' luve will lowe in cottage low,
  As weel's in lofty ha':
Sae lassie tak' the lad ye like,
  Whate'er your Minnie say,
Tho' ye soud mak' your bridal-bed
  O' clean pea-strae.

The Moralist

'Barb'rous!' cried *John* in humanizing mood,
To *Will* who'd shot a blackbird in the wood;
'The savage Indian pleads necessity,
But thou, barbarian wretch! hast no such plea.'
Hark! —— click the ale-house door — *his wife* comes in —
'Dear, help's man *John*! — preserve me, what d'ye mean!
'Sax helpless *bairns* — the deil confound your drouth!
'Without ae bit tae stop a single mouth.'
'— Get hame,' cried *John*, 'Else, jade! I'll kick your a—!'
Sure such humanity is all a farce.

A Resolve

*Written on hearing a fellow tell some stories, to the hurt
of his best friends*

As secret's the grave be the man whom I trust,
    What friendship imparts still let honour conceal,
A plague on those Babblers, their names be accurs'd!
    Still first to *enquire*, and the first to *reveal*.
As open as day let me be with the man,
    Who tells me my failings, from *motives* upright,
But when of those gossiping fools I meet one,
    Let me fold in my soul and be close as the night.

Ode to Jealousy

Mark what *daemon* hither bends,
Gnawing still his finger-ends,
Wrapt in contemplation deep,
Wrathful, yet inclin'd to weep.
Thy wizard gait, thy breath-check'd broken sigh,
Thy burning cheeks, thy lips, black, wither'd, dry;
Thy side-thrown glance, with wild malignant eye,
Betray thy foul intent, infernal Jealousy.

Hence thou self-tormenting *fiend*,
To thy spleen-dug cave descend,
Fancying wrongs that never were,
Rend thy bosom, tear thy hair,
Brood fell hate within thy den,
Come not near the haunts of men.

Let *man* be faithful to his brother *man*,
Nor guileful, still revert kind heaven's plan,
Then slavish fear, and mean distrust shall cease,
And confidence, confirm a lasting mental peace.

The Trifler's Sabbath Day

Loud sounds the deep-mouth'd parish-bell,
    Religion kirkward hies,
John lies in bed and counts each knell,
    And thinks 'tis time to rise.

But, O how weak are man's resolves!
    His projects ill to keep,
John thrusts his nose beneath the clothes,
    And dozes o'er asleep.

Now fairy-fancy plays her freaks
    Upon his sleep-swell'd brain;
He dreams — he starts — he mutt'ring speaks,
    And waukens wi' a grane.

He rubs his een — the clock strikes TWELVE —
    Impel'd by hunger's gripe,
One mighty effort backs resolve —
    He's up — at last he's up!

Hunger appeas'd — his cutty pipe
    Employs his time till TWO,—
And now he saunters thro' the house,
    And knows not what to do.

He baits the trap — catches a mouse —
    He sports it round the floor —
He swims it in a water tub —
    Gets *glorious* fun till FOUR!

And now of cats, and mice, and rats,
    He tells a thousand tricks,
Till even dulness tires herself,
    For hark — the clock strikes SIX!

Now view him in his easy chair
    Recline his pond'rous head;
'Tis EIGHT — now Bessie raiks the fire,
    And *John* must go to bed!

Bonny Wood of Craigie-Lee

TUNE: *Gang to the deil an shake yoursel'*

Thou bonny wood of Craigie-lee,
Thou bonny wood of Craigie-lee,
Near thee I past life's early day,
And won my Mary's heart in thee.

The broom, the brier, the birken bush,
Bloom bonny o'er thy flow'ry lea,
An' a' the sweets that ane can wish,
Frae nature's han' are strew'd on thee.

Thou bonny wood of Craigie-lee,
Thou bonny wood of Craigie-lee,
Near thee I past life's early day,
And won my Mary's heart in thee.

Far ben thy dark green plantin's shade,
The cushat croodles am'rously,
The mavis down thy bughted glade,
Gars echo ring frae ev'ry tree.

Thou bonny wood of Craigie-lee,
Thou bonny wood of Craigie-lee,
Near thee I past life's early day,
And won my Mary's heart in thee.

Awa' ye thoughtless murd'ring gang,
Wha tear the nestlings ere they flee!
They'll sing you yet a canty sang,
Then, O in pity let them be!

Thou bonny wood of Craigie-lee,
Thou bonny wood of Craigie-lee,
Near thee I past life's early day,
And won my Mary's heart in thee.

When winter blaws in sleety show'rs,
Frae aff the norlin' hills sae hi',
He lightly skiffs thy bonny bow'rs,
As laith tae harm a flow'r in thee.

Thou bonny wood of Craigie-lee,
Thou bonny wood of Craigie-lee,
Near thee I past life's early day,
And won my Mary's heart in thee.

Though fate should drag me south the line,
Or o'er the wide Atlantic sea,
The happy hours I'll ever min',
That I in youth hae spent in thee.

Thou bonny wood of Craigie-lee,
Thou bonny wood of Craigie-lee,
Near thee I past life's early day,
And won my Mary's heart in thee.

The Simmer Gloamin'

TUNE: *Alex Donn's Strathspey*

The midges dance aboon the burn,
　　The dew begins to fa',
The pairtricks down the rushy howm,
　　Set up their e'ening ca':
Now loud and clear the blackbird's sang
　　Rings through the briery shaw,
While fleeting gay, the swallows play
　　Around the castle wa'.

Beneath the gowden gloamin' sky
　　The mavis mends his lay,
The redbreast pours its sweetest strains,
　　To charm the lingering day:
While weary yeldrins seem to wail
　　Their little nestlings torn,
The merry wren, frae den to den,
　　Gaes jinkin' through the thorn.

The roses fauld their silken leaves,
　　The foxglove shuts its bell,
The honey-suckle and the birk
　　Spread fragrance through the dell:
Let others crowd the giddy court
　　Of mirth and revelry,
The simple joys that nature yields
　　Are dearer far to me.

Gloomy Winter's Now Awa'

Gloomy winter's now awa',
Saft the westlin breezes blaw;
'Mang the birks o' Stanly shaw
    The Mavis sings fu' cheery O;
Sweet the crowflow'rs early bell
Decks Gleniffer's dewy dell;
Blooming like thy bonnie sel',
    My young, my artless dearie O.
Come my lassie let us stray
O'er Glenkilloch's sunny brae,
Blythly spend the gowden day,
    'Midst joys that never weary O.

Tow'ring o'er the Newton woods,
Lav'rocks fan the snaw-white clouds,
Siller saughs, wi' downy buds,
    Adorn the bank sae briery O;
Round the the sylvan fairy nooks,
Feath'ry breckans fringe the rocks,
'Neath the brae the burnie jouks,
    And ilka thing is cheery O;
Trees may bud, and birds may sing,
Flow'rs may bloom, and verdure spring,
Joy to me they canna bring,
    Unless wi thee my dearie O.

Thomas Crichton

Born Paisley, 1761, he was appointed in 1791 schoolmaster and clerk to the Paisley Managers of the Poor, and became subsequently Governor to the Town's Hospital for the Poor. He wrote memoirs of Alexander Wilson (q.v.) and of a number of local clergymen. He died in 1844 aged 83.

'The Library' was his best known poem, dedicated 'to the President and Curators of the Paisley Library Society' when their library opened in 1802. It was the first library in Paisley, its 138 subscribers paying three guineas on joining and half a guinea per year thereafter. A committee of twelve elected annually were empowered to buy books to the value of a third of the library's income, 'purchases to be confined to such books as were of high character and general utility, and excluding all those that were merely professional'. By 1812 there were 200 subscribers and 3,000 books.

In 1867 proposals for a Free Library and Museum were raised by the Paisley Philosophical Society, and a donation of £3,000 by Peter Coats towards its building led to the formal opening to the public of this institution on April 11th 1871. The building was extended in 1882 to include the area now occupied by Paisley Central Library, whose stock includes those volumes transferred from the library of Crichton's poem to the Free Library and Museum in 1871.

Crichton's poem is more than 4,000 lines long and contains reflections on Shakespeare, Milton, Cowper, Hume, Voltaire, Sir William Jones, 'Parliamentary Eloquence', Hope-Temple Gardens Paisley, missionaries to Greenland, Bengal etc.

from The Library

Dedicated to the President and Curators of the Paisley Library Society

Hail! friends of Science! friends of human kind!
Yours is the noblest task t'improve the mind;
To form, mature, to execute a plan
Design'd to rouse the latent powers of man;
To teach the Youth, within his studious bower,
To spend, improv'd, his idle, vacant hour.
'Tis yours, to chase the mental fogs away;
Conduct from Error's night to Truth's bright day;
Reclaim from Vice's dark, entangling snare,
Lead smoothly on to Virtue's temple fair;
Prepare for action, on Life's bustling stage,
By all the wisdom of the letter'd page.
To place before the mind a world all new;
Designs like these, ye friends of Man, pursue.

How many, sunk on Sloth's ignoble bed,
Doze their dull hours away, nor think, nor read;
Ne'er wish to range the fields of Knowledge o'er,
Nor add one mite to their ideal store.
With them, Retirement's listless moments steal
With leaden feet along, nor ever feel
Those pleasures, rational, felt by the few
Who thirst for Science, and her paths pursue.
What numbers down the streams of Pleasure fail,
Wasted by flatt'ring Fortune's fav'ring gale,
Neglect t'employ the golden hours of youth,
In quest of physical, divine or moral truth;
And, when decrepid Age, with all his cares,
Steals on, their mental poverty appears.
The poor old man, with converse light and vain,
Can only catch the ear of Folly's train.
His wond'ring stare of Ignorance displays
The slothful trifling of his earlier days;
His mind appears a dreary desert bare;
If aught springs up, 'tis only weeds are there.

The hoary Sire, plac'd on his restful chair,
Whose mind is fraught with knowledge, I revere,
And listen to the venerable sage,
Tho' wrinkled o'er his brow, tho' bent with age;
Attend the prudent dictates of his tongue,
Resolv'd, like him, to read and think, when young.

George MacIndoe

Born Partick 1771. Worked in Paisley as a silk weaver, then became a hotel keeper in King Street, Glasgow, for 21 years. He returned to Paisley to resume weaving. He also ran a public house, was a popular violin player, and 'invented a machine for figuring on muslin, which secured to him rewards from the Board of Trustees and the Corporation of Glasgow'. He died in Glasgow in 1848.

'Nelson's Monument' appears as printed here, in a satirical poem 'The Vision of Inanimates' in which the narrator describes a dream in which he finds himself on Glasgow Green listening to an argument between the Herdshouse, the Washing House and the Dead House (The Humane Society House) about the proposed building of a monument to Nelson beside them on the Green. The poem carries the subcaption 'Dreamed, the night after the foundation stone of Lord Nelson's monument, at Glasgow, was laid; on having heard it disputed, "whether the old Herdshouse, if allowed to stand, would not disgrace its appearance"'. The buildings are more concerned with the monument's likely effect on them and their Green, than their possible effect on it:

> Besides the hourly mischief it will cause
> By gazing strangers treading down the grass —
> Our bleaching green, the brag o' town an shire
> Will soon be left a paste o' mud an mire.

Then in the narrator's vision the future monument (in shape as it now stands in 1988) appears beside the arguing buildings. It so startles him that he wakes up:

> The dream evanish'd like a Hamlet's ghost,
> And left the monument a — bare bed-post.

f
the
rim
y cl
ouds
ascen
d,——
Rend
ye po
rtals o
f the s
ky,——
Flee to
every d
istant la
nd,—T
o celebr
ate his m
emory! -
Trump-
ets blow
from pol
e to pole!
——Rocks
& woods
your ech
oes join;
——Thro'
the vallies
make the
m roll,——
And wrea
ths of mus
ic for him
twine.——
See! the HE-
RO mounts aloft,
Palms and gar
lands Angel's
bring;——Tune your tim
brels sweet and soft,
Of the SEAS pro
claim him KING:
——Tho' no mort
al crown he wo
re,——*Nelson* no
w immortal rei
gns,——Travers
ing winds the deeps expl
ore,——And strew his GLO
RIES o'er the plains.——And when Hi
storians' pages cease—To tell of mighty
deeds in war,—My never-ending theme is this,—
THE GLORIOUS VICTORY OF TRAFALGAR!

William Finlayson

Born Pollokshaws 1787, became secretary to the weavers' union sometime after 1810. In 1822 he became an exciseman and worked as such for fifty years. He died in Leith in 1872, aged 86.

The background to 'The Weaver's Lament' is as follows. The weavers' union attempted to have weavers' rates established by magistrates at a rate agreed to be reasonable to prevent manufacturers driving wages down. The advocates Henry Cockburn and Francis Jeffrey (of the *Edinburgh Review*) took their case, based upon old Scottish Statutes, before the Justices of the Peace, who found the weavers' claims 'moderate and reasonable'. The Court of Session affirmed the right of the Justices of the Peace to set wage rates, but the Supreme Court of Session did not include any compelling clauses in its decision. The manufacturers therefore simply ignored the ruling and carried on as before.

Acting again on the basis of a ruling by the Lord Justice Clerk in another case (that if paper-makers had had their prices sanctioned by Justices of the Peace they had a right to strike if these were not paid) a strike of weavers was called and spread throughout Scotland until 40,000 took part. But the strikers were not entitled to Poor Relief, the Combination Act was brought into force in Scotland, making not only 'secret oaths' but strikes illegal, and the strike committee was arrested, seven were jailed, and the committee members made liable for legal costs of 30 shillings to two pounds each. In Paisley rewards of twenty pounds were offered by the magistrates for information against the strikers and intimidation of strike-breakers. The strike collapsed after twelve weeks, and the weavers starved back to work where they had to accept the old rates.

See Murray, Norman; *The Scottish Hand Loom Weavers 1790-1850: A Social History*, John Donald, Edinburgh 1978; pp. 186-190. Also P. M. Kemp-Ashraf's discussion of the weaver-poet John Chirrey in his essay 'The Vernacular Poet Faces Reality', to be found in *Essays in Honour of William Gallacher*, Humboldt University, East Berlin, 1966.)

Weaver's Lament

ON THE FAILURE OF THE CELEBRATED STRIKE OF WEAVING, FOR A MINIMUM OF WAGES, IN 1812

Ye Weavers cease to mourn an' grieve,
Can bitter sighs your case relieve?
Nae mair let hope your hearts deceive,
      Fix'd is your fate;
Be thankfu' ye're allow'd to weave
      At ony rate.

Deaf to your earnest cries, an' pray'rs,
Against you ilka door declares,
Nor King, nor Parliamentar cares,
      Nor local pow'rs,
A' busy wi' their ain affairs,
      They mind not ours.

For refuge whither can we fly?
What ither schemes of succour try?
Where'er we sen' the sorrowing eye,
      Or turn the head,
Wives, weans, an' aged parents die,
      For lack o' bread.

Alas! that any 'ministration
Should glory to involve a nation,
In ruin, horror, an' starvation,
      An' even disdain
To make the slightest reparation,
      Tho' it complain.

When wealth to poortith spurns concession,
Each rank receding in progression;
When the bien, rural, mid condition,
      O' life is past,
The *ne-plus-ultra* o' oppression,
      Approaches fast.

An' soon may it approach — blest time!
Desire o' mony a fervent rhyme!
Then seeking Right shall be nae crime
            i' the law's esteem;
Then happiness owre Scotia's clime,
            Again shall beam —

The sturdy tiller o' our plains,
Whose work demands nae scowth o' brains,
A competence frae labor gains,
            That in auld age
Ensures a beild for crazy banes,
            Frae poortith's rage.

Whilst we tho' patient, an' alert
In mastering an ingenious art;
Tho' conscious we hae done our part,
            Some gear to gain,
Perceive wi' sad foreboding heart,
            Each effort vain.

The manufact'rers strongly feel,
Our lack o' murphies, an' pease-meal,
An' as a proof they wish us weil
            Some mae potatoes,
Add twa three yards to our thrum-keel
            To work at gratis.

What tho' they brav'd the pains o' law,
An' thol'd baith meikle shame an' jaw,
Their knaverie past, as they were a'
            Rich wealthy Reivers;
An' justice thought the crime was sma'
            To gull poor weavers.

Wi' mounds o' auld contracted debt
On ilka side, we are beset;
In nae man's beuk we'll farther get,
            Tho' life to save,
For what we owe, they gie us het
            Fu' mony a crave.

For me, I daurna tak' the street,
For fear some creditor I meet;
Even when I chance to hear strange feet
        Upon the stair,
I'm in a heavy, deadly sweat,
        To ken wha's there.

Hence we are a' sae shifty grown,
There's scarce a House in Glasgow town,
That pays seven shillings in the poun',
        (A common case)
But may itself inferior own
        To our sly race.

In correspondence wi' our betters,
Respecting sundry money-matters,
They aften ca' us 'Men o' Letters',
        By way o' jeering;
Few wad believe how muckle debtors
        Are daily bearing.

Were never wretches sae forlorn!
Were never wrangs sae meekly born!
From us by violence is torn,
        Each dear-won blessing!
Our Calling has become a scorn —
        — Ourselves a hissing!

O! Scotia, thy spring is past,
Thy Simmer but a blink did last,
Thy leaves are strewing on the blast,
        O' Autumn snell!
Thy Winter is approaching fast,
        Dark, dowr, an' fell!

Geordie's Marriage

O! Ken ye that Geordie and Jean,
   Are cry'd in the Chapel on ither;
And that we are a' to convene
   On Friday, to loop them together?
The lassie is handsome an' fair,
   Has plenty o' beauty an' braw-things;
The Villager Gossips declare,
   To plenish a house, she has a' things.

Tho' Geordie has little laid by,
   To serve the important occasion,
Nane need to gang hungry, or dry,
   Gin they hae a stout inclination.
His mither, a pensie auld wife,
   Has vow'd to preside at the table,
And she can plan things to the life,
   When willing, she's hearty, an' able.

Of haggises, lang-kail, an' pies;
   And birsled sheep-heads, there is plenty;
Wi' a patfu' o' guid monie-plies,
   To taste ony mouth that is dainty.
Then, Fiddler, your fiddle-string stent,
   An' play us up *Scamber-come-scratch me*;
This e'enin' on dancing I'm bent,
   Gin the Bridegroom's guid-mother will match me.

Sae the Fiddler he lilted an' play'd,
   An' the young anes I wat werena idle;
While the Auld Bodies tippled, an' pray'd
   For a blessing to follow this bridal!
But the *Young Folk* deserted the fiel',
   An' skulked unseen frae the Weddin';
Sae some think they'll never do weil,
   As naebody witness'd the Beddin'!

On Three Children in the
Eastwood Churchyard — 1814

Here lie the mouldering remains
O' three unkirsent guiltless weans;
Wha never underwent that rite
Maks sinners mystically white;
Will ony zealot e'er presume
These early dwellers in the tomb
Wad nae admission gain in Heaven
Or that their sins were unforgiven?
Let him wi' care his Bible read,
An' to this precious text gie heed,
'Wha wad the bliss o' Heaven attain
Maun enter like a little wean.'

James Yool

Born in Moss Street, Paisley, in 1792. He worked as a weaver and after publishing 'The Rise and Progress of Oppression' when he was 21, he was one of the founders of the Paisley Literary and Convivial Club the following year. Active politically, he had temporarily to go into hiding during the Radical agitation and rising of 1820. When the Weavers' Union was formed in 1832 he was elected to the central committee. For the background to 'The Rise and Progress of Oppression' see the notes on William Finlayson, p. 57. He worked some time with the Paisley printer J. Neilson, and edited several local literary journals — *The Caledonian Lyre* (three issues, 1815), *The Gaberlunzie* (twelve issues, 1825) and *The Paisley Literary Miscellany* (three issues, 1853-54). He died in 1860.

*

The Rise and Progress of Oppression

A Tale

Dedication: To the Weavers

> HECH! what a race? my sides are sair,
> The dribblin' sweat fa's frae my hair;
>   I fear I'll yet repent it.
> But fo'k, that's writin' things that's new,
> An' thae things too, sae unco true,
>   Wad fain hae them presentit.
>   An' that's the way I've come hale sale,
>   Thro' dub an' mire a splashin';

To dedicate to you my tale,
   Because it's grown a fashion.
     An' now Sirs, adieu Sirs,
      I'll tell without a swither;
     Your servant, most fervent,
      By trade's a weavin' brither.

*

Oppression; hell born cursed pest!
   Wi' dire destructive grapple,
Scours up an' down, frae east to west,
   To cut auld freedom's thrapple.

But freedom, haith's a sturdy tyke,
   An' he has muckle need o't;
If they forgether 'hint a dyke,
   He'll aiblins break the head o't.

Oppression, when a wee bit bairn,
   The throne gat for a craddle;
An' teeth it gat like rods o' airn
   Before it weel cou'd striddle.

It kookit out, frae neth a crown,
   E'er crowns were weel in fashion:
An' fo'k were fear't to venture near't,
   For fear they'd get a thrashin'.

An' then, baith friends an' flatt'rin' foes,
   Sae puft it wi' oblations,
That pride flew up the young thing's nose,
   An' haith! 'twad thrash the nations.

It's sceptre gumstick it flang down,
   O' glitt'rin' toys grown weary,
An' lash't the nations roun', an' roun',
   As weans wad skelp a peery.

Frae less to mair, it rax't an' grew,
   A great big bully giant;
An' now it's grown sae big that few
   Dare think about defyant.

Langsyne I min', when young an' daft,
  A raw bain't playrife laddy,
A braw gowd giltet beuk I caft,
  To read wi' my auld daddy.

An' there I read, I min' it weel,
  O thrawn hard-heartet Pharaoh,
A sort o' cruel heath'nish deil,
  Wha' scarce had e'er a marrow.

Guide's! how I've seen me girn, an' chirt
  My teeth wi' rage thegither,
To see him use the Jews like dirt;
  Ilk father, man, an' mither.

Syne 'mang the rest o's cursed tricks,
  He slew their helpless bairnies;
An' vex't their daddy's makin' bricks,
  To bundle up in cairnies.

But O! what joy flew to my e'e,
  When proud oppression's churls;
Horse, gigs, an' a', plung'd in the sea,
  Like bungs an' staves o burrels.

Then, then, I thought, oppression's wings,
  For ever mair were pouket;
An' thought, that tyrant lords and kings,
  Should a' like them be drouket.

Yet, though oppression gat a fell,
  In chosen Israel's quarrel;
It's now grown like a sea itsel',
  An's co'ert maist a the warl'.

In rapid stream, or petty brook,
  Thro' Europe wide it sweepet;
An' ay whare e'er its course it took,
  That course it still hath keepet.

An' now, alas! its cursed waves,
   Flow in on trade an' commerce;
An' a' to feed some blasted knaves;
   Wha maun hae wine an' limmers.

Short syne wi' rapid sweep it brings
   (As if it meant to scour us)
A spate o' blastit corks an' things,
   That's liken to devour us.

They say we're fit eneuch to live
   On meal an' water drummock;
L—d keeps! I daresay they believe,
   That we hae lost our stomach.

An' now, sae far they hae us brought,
   Dear me, we're fit for naething;
Our fleshless bains sae toil'd an' wrought,
   Keeks through our tatter'd claithing.

Yet still, it's a' their hale delight,
   To mak', an' keep us hum'le;
An' what's the warst confoundet spite,
   It's needless e'er to grum'le.

But now some wabsters up hae bang't,
   Wha're no that easy frightet;
They're sure, they say, they hae been wrang't,
   An' vow they shall be rightet.

For while oppression rade like fire,
   Out owre our necks triumphan';
An' us wi' noses in the mire,
   Our base-like wrangs were grumphan.

We fan 'mang Scotland's lumber acts,
   Some statutes queer in diction;
Whilk gar't oppressors claw their backs,
   An' laid on them restriction.

Some curs't, an' swore, by gude an' a',
  Sic acts were stupit blethers;
An' ithers swore they baith were law,
  An' proud oppression's tethers.

The weavers syne fell hard to wark,
  Their task, self-preservation;
An' how they best could hit the mark,
  To work their trade's salvation.

A short petition they drew up,
  Wharein the wrangs were written;
That pointed out the smartin whip,
  By whilk they lang were smitten.

Before the Glasgow Magistrates,
  Their paper they presentet;
Wha promis'd for to rax their pates,
  To study cures anent it.

They promis'd fair, that a' their pow'r
  They'd stretch, if 'twad redress them;
Ev'n while they mean't to gar them cour,
  An' a' their pith oppress them.

The corks wad fain tane wabster Jock,
  An' by the neck a hung him;
The Magistrates got in a flock
  O' sodger scums to bung him.

Sae, Sirs, frae him wha fills a throne,
  To him wha rules a city;
Ye see, there's nae sweet mercy show'n;
  Nae tricklin' tear for pity.

Theirs is the lifeless heart o' stane.
  Theirs is the sleepin' conscience;
Their ears are shut to misery's grane,
  An' all but wealth is nonsense.

Then how frae sic a rotten crew,
    Cou'd ought else been expected:
Than, that our claims, tho' just an' true,
    Wad be wi' pride rejected.

Yet hope sat smilin' on the cause,
    By petty pow'r deserted;
An' forward prest wi' Scotland's laws,
    By Scotia's kings concerted.

Syne frae auld Embro raise a chap,
    A sly glib-gabbet billy;
Wha took oppression by the tap,
    An haith he wasna silly.

He open'd out the fankl't law,
    His tale o' truth like thun'er
Cam rattlin' out, till great an' sma',
    Were gapin' a' wi' won'er.

Then let his name, the world round,
    By fame's loud trump be soundet;
Till proud aggressors at the sound,
    Start back wi' fear confoundet.

To Jamfray's patriot worth alone,
    Ye owe your sanction'd table;
'Tis he who made your cause his own,
    An' cut oppression's cable.

Now like a vessel tempest-tost,
    By jarin' billows driven;
The corks rave for the pow'r they've lost,
    An' curse the verdic' given.

Yet aft on nettle cover't fiels,
    Spring up sweet smellin' daisies;
Sae 'mang the corks, some feelin' chiels,
    Deserve our warmest praises.

But, hark! what thun'rin' voice was yon?
  L—d! what an awfu' crisis?
The Paisley weavers too, come on,
  To bark for muckle prices.

But see their masters, gen'rous band!
  'Gude guide us but they're frien'ly!
They winna for a trifle stand,
  They winna skulk it meanly:

Hoot no'; they're o' anither cast,
  'Let's glint lads at your table;
'An' hear ye, Sirs, our word we've past,
  'We'll help you if we're able.'

O glorious friendly feelin' few!
  Wha here on earth can match you?
Yet lest our fingers ye slip thro',
  We'll aiblins better watch you.

Your smile's ower like a brussen chirt;
  Your sudden change sae funny;
But short syne, ye were sour as dirt,
  An' now ye're sweet as honey.

I fear it's but a specious snare,
  To catch poor thoughtless creatures,
Wha by themsel's your conduct square;
  Wha judge but by the features.

Or like the rose which cheers the shade,
  That 'neath its smilin' blossom
Conceals a thorn, to pierce the maid,
  Wha places't in her bosom.

But, hush! what rumour's this I hear?
  A ball an' pouther breakfast!
Faith, if they try't, I vow an' swear,
  We'll try them wha can kick best.

They'll try, the scums, to fankle a'
  Our yet ungotten mercies;

An' sodgers bring to deal club law,
 An' riddle a' our arses.

But aiblins that may be a lie,
 'Bout giein' us our millin's;
I hear they're willin' yet to gie
 A wage a' saxteen shillin's.

They've pledg'd their word, their honour's pawn'd,
 They'll surely no negleck it,
For honour's tie's a gowden band,
 An' nane but rogues 'ill break it.

But, what is honour, worth, or fame,
 To rogues wha herd thegither;
Wha's cheeks ne'er glow'd wi' honest shame;
 Wha'd ruin e'en their brither.

What's honour, but an empty soun',
 A spur for rotten courage,
A glit'ren gem to deck a crown,
 A puff to cool your porrage.

It hath at least been sae wi' them,
 For a' their promis'd favours
Hae turn'd out naething but a name,
 Or bunch o' idle clavers.

They got indeed a wee bit hitch,
 A self-wrought extrication;
I dinna say, they brought the bitch
 That ca'd it combination.

Nor do I say, 'twas but a scheme,
 To get us a' hood-winket;
Hoot, that wad be a filthy shame;
 Yet, aiblins, Sirs, I think it.

I never spake o' ill win gear,
 Nor said, ye wrang't the poor o't;
But let me whisper in your ear,
 I whiles was geyan sure o't.

But yet, before I tak' fareweel,
   I'll be sae condescendin',
As wish you routh o' milk an' meal,
   If ye wad think o' mendin'.

Now, fare-ye-weel, ye rich, adieu;
   The lave o' my bit story,
Ye weaver tribe, is meant for you;
   Sae dinna look sae sorry.

I'm gaun to turn a spaewife loon,
   An' try to spae your fortune;
But dinna sleep before I'm doon,
   An' fright me wi' your snortin'.

We're tauld that poets hae a gift
   O tellin things that's comin';
Then, why deny puir me that shift,
   While owre my rhymes I'm hummin'.

Now for a wee, my e'en I'll steek,
   An' backlin's throw them blinkin',
To keek through the prophetic reek,
   That roun' my brains is jinkin'.

I see auld freedom's god-like ban',
   Wi' satisfaction smilin';
A horn o' plenty in ilk han',
   To scatter owre this islan'.

I see oppression's lang airn rods,
   For whilk the tear now dribbles,
Made into braw new sturdy shods,
   To co'er potato dibbles.

I see, tho' geyan dark, the gloom,
   The hawks that's at us tearin',
Driven back for shelter to the loom,
   For a' their noise an' swearin'.

Now, should I be for ance mista'en,
  My hopes are no ungroundet;
For God ance heard his people's grane,
  An' a' their foes counfoundet.

Then, if the thing I should mistak',
  Kind Sirs, O! spare my blushes;
An' let me quietly turn the tack,
  To croon o'er twa-three wishes.

May troubles cease thro' Europe wide,
  Nae mair in bluid let's welter;
Be smilin' peace, our country's bride,
  An' weary't warrior's shelter.

May little Britain's hardy sons,
  Nae mair 'bout wars be speirin';
May they get routh o' cakes an' buns,
  To had their chafts a' steerin'.

May he wha has a groat to spen';
  To him wha may hae naething,
Be willin' aye to gie or len';
  As lang's he's fit for breathing.

An' O! frae ilka couthie pair,
  Wha's hearts by fate are linket,
Gude Lord dash down the cup o' care,
  Before they need to drink it.

Anither wish, then, I'll hae done,
  Tho' maybe no the brawest,
I'm free to swear by a' aboon,
  It winna be the sma'est.

May proud oppression, freedom's fae,
  In this bit faught be slain;
Gude Lord, do thou but grant it sae,
  An' I'll be pleas'd. *Amen.*

O! If Ye Hae A Heart To Spare

TUNE: *Duncan Davieson*

O! if ye hae a heart to spare,
    And yet refuse that heart to gie,
It will but gart me try the mair
    To wile awa that heart frae thee.
For thou has stown into my breast,
    And thou has ta'en my heart awa';
Wi' thoughts o' thee I've tint my rest,
    And yet I pardon thee for a'.

I canna want thee out my sicht,
    I weary for thee nicht and day;
'Tis thee I think o' aye at nicht,
    When I gae ben the hoose to pray.
A youthfu' life's a sinfu' time,
    I've heard my eldrin mother say;
But oh! if love be made a crime
    Then I hae cause to be richt wae!

For I'm sae caucht wi' Cupid's snare,
    That if by chance I hear thy name,
My heart plays dunt ere I'm aware,
    And sets my bosom in a flame.
Sae, if ye're willing, here's my hand,
    And dinna think me pert or bauld,
Though young and daft, yet wedlock's band,
    Will wear me wise as I grow auld.

There's Andrew o' the Bramble-knowe,
    He vows and swears he'll hae me soon:
I'll gie his rock anither tow,
    And gar the body change his tune.
For I hae sworn a holy aith,
    And mair than that, this very day
I tauld my mam and daddie baith,
    Nae ither lad than you I'd hae.

Three Radical Poems: Introduction

An overall — as distinct from detailed local — context to the three Radical poems on pp. 77-91 follows.

After the collapse of the strike of 1812-13, weavers' wages during the following ten years were the lowest of the period 1800-1850. Destitution and unemployment were widespread at the end of the Napoleonic Wars in 1815. Government policy worsened the situation. Direct taxation that had financed the war was abolished in favour of indirect taxes on goods, thus transferring the burden to the poorer mass of the people. The Corn Law introduced restriction on wheat import until an artificially sustained price was first reached: the price decided priced bread beyond the purchase of many.

Military policing, what would now be called 'intelligence gathering', and the close conjunction between cabinet will and judicial action were the means used to fight attempts at what was necessarily extra-parliamentary organisation. Reformers such as William Cobbett, 'Orator' Hunt and Major Cartwright sought to change the nature of the law by changing the nature of parliament. Cartwright included Renfrewshire in his tour of Britain in which he advocated annual parliaments, equal electoral districts, vote by ballot and payment of MPs. Petitions from Paisley, Glasgow and elsewhere in Britain produced no result; reform societies, necessarily secret, were riddled with the forerunners of today's Special Branch, and Glasgow magistrates had 26 radicals arrested in 1817. That year Habeus Corpus was suspended.

The 1819 'Peterloo Massacre' — the wounding of 400 and the killing of 11 people by the military, breaking up a public outdoor meeting in support of parliamentary reform and the repeal of the Corn Laws — intensified protest in Renfrewshire as elsewhere. The arrest of 'Orator' Hunt at Peterloo — whilst

74

the military were considered beyond the law — emphasised the injustice. A month before Peterloo, 30,000 had attended a similar reform meeting at Meikleriggs outside Paisley. A protest meeting after Peterloo that was held in Paisley on September 11th led to troops being poured into the town, the Riot Act being read, and after days of clashes between troops and protestors, and of imposed curfews, the council decided to ask the government to build barracks in the town — though these were not established until 1822.

The 'Six Acts' of 1819 further extended local magistrates' powers to restrict radical meetings and close meeting-places; now private premises could be searched, drilling was expressly forbidden, and magistrates had the power of summary conviction. Again, repression produced stronger reaction, including the continued manufacture of pikes and secret drilling by a minority of radicals. During the night of April 2nd 1820 a handbill proclamation calling for the establishment of a provisional government was posted up in many public places in the West of Scotland. Once again troops poured into Paisley. There was no mass response to the proclamation's call for action. Some radical Stirlingshire weavers did attempt to march to Falkirk to commandeer an ironworks, but they were stopped at Bonnymuir by the 10th Hussars and the Stirlingshire Yeomanry, who took nineteen of the weavers prisoner. Similarly Strathaven radicals marching to Cathkin Braes where they mistakenly expected others to be assembling, found they were alone; of those subsequently arrested, James Wilson was executed, as were Andrew Hardie and John Baird who had been taken at Bonnymuir.

The extent to which the rising was driven on by government *agents provocateurs* is disputed. Evidence is hard to weigh because of the undoubted widespread use of spies: their role may have been no more than infiltration and reporting of organisations that definitely would have been active without them. The fullest account of the 1820 rising is *The Scottish Insurrection of 1820* by P. B. Ellis and S. Mac a' Ghobhainn

(Gollancz, London 1970: PCL REF. R. 941-1074). Norman Murray's *The Scottish Handloom Weavers: 1790-1850* (John Donald, Edinburgh 1978: PCL REF. R. 338.47677) summarises on pp. 214-227 the events of 1813 to 1822 with particular regard to weavers' involvement; it also — in conjunction with the research indicated in its bibliography — disagrees with Ellis and Mac a' Ghobhainn in interpretation.

A memorial to Hardie, Baird and Wilson was erected in Thrushgrove Cemetery, Paisley, in 1867. Verses carved include:

> Our heath-clad hills and lonely mountain caves
> Are marked by battle-fields and martyrs' graves,
> This stone records the last embattled stroke
> Which Scotchmen struck at vile oppression's yoke.
> At Bonnymuir, they trod their native heath,
> And sought a warrior's or a martyr's death,
> Sad choice! for there they found their enterprise
> To claim or force Reform, by arm'd surprise,
> Was circumvented and betrayed by spies,
> And, thus ensnared in Treason's feudal laws,
> Their personal honour in the people's cause
> Compelled the fight which claims our pity and applause.

*

The anonymous dialogue opposite refers to the poverty at the end of the Napoleonic wars. The dismissive attitude of Pate can be aligned with that of Charles Marshall in 'Stick To Your Last' (pp. 200-1). The verse dialogue-dispute is a form that appears in one of the earliest extant Renfrewshire poems, 'The Packman's Pater Noster', written by Robert Sempill of Beltrees and his son Francis, in the seventeenth century. In that poem a priest has the worse of a theological dispute with a Protestant pedlar. It can be found in *The Harp of Renfrewshire* (2nd Series), Alex Gardner, Paisley 1873, pp. 1-27.

Paisley Politics; or, Rab and Pate

A Dialogue

Pate

Guid help me, Rab, whaur hast tu been?
Its a full towmont out, I ween,
Since I thy auld blythe face hae seen,
      An' something mair,
Safe's! I can scarce believe my een,
        Thou's turn'd sae spare.

Rab

Nane at my spareness, won'er, Pate,
Working richt sair, baith soon an' late,
An' little gaun, whiles caul, whiles het,
      And sometimes nane,
Sic is the way to drown the fat
      An' save the bane.

An' seest thou, Pate, I've just been down,
Lifting my week's wage, that puir crown,
The fam'ly's cares awee to drown,
      Wi' some hue livin',
And keep them ae day mair aboon
      The need o' thieving.

We're laught at by oppressors vile,
Our spirits sunk wi' care and toil,
Yet pinch'd wi' a' our pains and skill,
      To mak' a meal o't,
Lord, I the rascals would impale,
      Had I my will o't.

Afflictions hard upon us press,
Our days are blank and comfortless;
Wi' Knaves who do our souls oppress,
      The lan' is swarmin',
Lord, stretch thy haun', an' us release
      Frae the vile vermin.

Pate

Stop there now, Rab, thou's rather fast,
I grant our sky is overcast,
I grant the whirlwind's ruthless blast
      Now sweeps the plain,
But binna flee'd, our Sun at last
      Will shine again.

This sudden hitch frae war to peace,
Is the sole cause o' our distress,
An' tho' some sumphs set up their face,
      An' daur dispute it,
Believe me, Rab, the bleth'rin geese
      Ken nought about it.

What! will a base illit'rate rabble,
Set up their rank seditious gabble,
An' signify that they are able
      To rule a lan';
Vile trash! scarce fit to clean a stable,
      Or yet a straun'.

They rage and rave about taxation,
A weak an' corrupt 'Ministration,
'Bout charters, richts, and reformation,
      Yet the vile fien's
Cou'dna, by Jove, for their salvation,
      Tell what it means.

They'll count you up the war's expences,
A statement gie o' our finances,
An' a' the bits o' wee mischances,
      We hae sustain'd;
Yet they ne'er think, the silly dunces,
      On what we've gain'd.

O! if they knew the *honours* vast
Which, in these twice ten towmonts past,
This happy nation hath amass'd,
      They'd drap declaiming,
An' think the ills with which they're press'd
      Scarce worth the naming.

War hath at last her red flag furl'd,
Which long hath wav'd o'er half the world;
The base Usurper now is hurl'd
      Frae aff his hicht,
There to deplore that e'er he snarled
      At Britain's micht.

What then is nakedness and famine?
Are not our brows with laurels streaming?
Our far-fam'd land with glory beaming,
      Burns like a star,
While Afric's dark-hued sons a'hymning
      Our praises are.

'Tis true, the Protestants they've brunt them,
What then, to heaven they hae sent them,
We needna, faith, I think, anent them
      Mak' sic a sang;
L—d Rab, there's plenty mair ahint them,
      E'en let them gang.

O! if the Rabble had the wit
Down on their hams content to sit
Till a kin' Providence thought fit
      To cure their ailings,
But na, they'll growl, an' girn, an' fret,
      At His wise dealings.

But Rab, we winna langer thole it,
Your pow'r to gab, we shall control it;
Too lang our honour hath been sullied
      Wi' your curs'd havers;
We may gie up, faith, if we're bullied
      By a wheen starv'd weavers.

Rab

Rab drew the cutty frae his cheek,
He near haun chokit wi' the reek:
L—d blast you, Pate, just hear me speak,
      An', by my conscience,
I'll prove that a' this rhetoric
      Is downricht nonsense.

The hale force o' thy sneers an' snash
Is levell'd at our want o' cash;
But Pate, my man, thou needna fash,
      That's nae dispute;
Is't truth we speak, ye senseless hash,
      Or is it not?

I don't deny that we are poor,
That's granted, as I've said afore;
But is a man on that same score
      To haud his tongue,
Nor tell the knaves who pinch him sore
      They do him wrong?

No:—Dire misfortune's bitter blast
May beat against the poor man's breast,
His body may to earth be prest
      'Neath mis'ry's load,
But the free soul will still resist
      The oppressor's rod.

O Britain! what accursed scenes
Of fraud an' blood thy hist'ry stains!
How many thousands of thy swains
      Have bled and died
To nurse Ambition's dark designs
      An' feed her pride!

But to the point:—If a' this bluid
In which our hauns have been imbru'd
Hath only serv'd to bring a load
      O' Debt upon us,
Then, Pate, I fain would ask what guid
      The war hath done us?

The *Hope o' France* is now restor'd,
And *Ferdinand* by Spain ador'd;
The *Pope*, that servant o' the Lord,
      Now sits secure;
Monks, Friars, an' *Nuns,* an' a' the herd
      O' *Bab'lon's Whore.*

In France reigns fiery persecution,
In Spain is reared the Inquisition,
An' the black limmer, Superstition,
                    Trots at her tail;
While here, beneath a curs'd Taxation
                    We weep an' wail.

See *Pleasure's* hair-brain'd airy band,
Wi' our wise R****t hand in hand,
At Balls an' Routs, an' Galas grand,
                    Regaling w——s,
While a poor famish'd, weepin', land
                    His aid implores.

But, Pate, we needna rin to Lon'on,
Even here are rascals muckle run on;
An' faith, it is my fix'd opinion,
                    A baser breed
The sun o' heav'n never shone on
                    Sin' he was made.

Our B——s, mercenary wretches,
Hing heavy loads on us poor b——s;
Our thin lank sides they suck like leeches,
                    An', what is worse,
To the last doit they've drain'd our poutches,
                    Without remorse.

The Town's Supremacy, they've sold it;
The mouth o' Cart, wi' dirt they've filled it;
Our sair won gear, awa' they've dealt it,
                    As they thought fitting;
In short, our ruin they hae seal'd it
                    Wi' their d——d eating.

But faith, Sir M—— I gart them stare
That day he shook wee S——h B—r sair,
Sent B——y foaming like a bear
                    Out o' the kirk,
While big B——n i' the chair
                    Sat like a stirk.

Our Clergy, too, a snivling pack,
Amidst a nation's general wreck;
Na, though our ain toom tripes hing slack
      Wi' bitter want,
Set up their vile insulting clack,
      An' preach content.

That minion B——g wi' pois'nous breath
Tells us, though we're oppress'd to death,
Tho' we're wrought sair, an' hunger'd baith
      On puir thin kail,
We've reason to be thankfu', faith,
      That we're sae weel.

An' Willy S——t, that *man o' feelin'*,
He talks o' *worth* an' *honest dealin'*,
Yet taks a puir man's hinmost shilling
      To pay his debt;
He's done't, an' I'se be sworn he's willing
      To do it yet.

Ilk virtue frae our lan' hath fled,
Honour is sick, an' Truth is dead,
Justice has broke her sword, the Jade,
      An' brunt her scales,
An' Liberty, like ane afraid,
      Has tane her heels.

John MacGregor

Born 1790, Paisley, ran a business as embroiderer of Canton crepe in Kilbarchan. He lived some time in Paisley, being elected to the town council in 1855. After serving three years there he returned to live in Kilbarchan where he died in 1870.

John MacGregor's song below was published after he attended the unveiling ceremony in 1867 of the memorial to Hardie and Baird. An editor's preface to the poem, titled 'A Radical Ballad of 1819', states:

> Our veteran friend, Mr John MacGregor, has sent us the following ballad, which he says, was written by him in 1819, with a view of being sung in the streets to the violin, and which, he thinks, may now be interesting as an illustration of the feelings of reformers in those dark days of Castlereagh and Sidmouth, — when men were in danger who advocated political changes far less sweeping than those now proposed by a Tory government.

The poem is printed at this chronological point in the book as it deals with the rising of 1819-20. However, it is difficult not to see the poem as having been considerably enlarged by MacGregor from whatever he had actually written nearly half a century before. Much of the poem, such as the statement that people 'will be' sent abroad, suggests hindsight rather than foresight. MacGregor, as one of the old survivors of the time, was treated with some deference at the unveiling. The poem's exhortation for people not to flee might seem a bit opportune given MacGregor's continued local presence since the time; but his suggestion that any unconstitutional behaviour would be the behaviour of people duped by spies, his statement that those subsequently arrested therefore 'may have erred', his ascription to the Radicals of an ultimate wish to behave 'like

the saints above', and his concluding imperialist two lines —
all these would have made many of the Radicals turn in their
graves. In fact the poem as published in 1867 seems as much an
indication of the use to which the Rising was later put, as an
expression of the feelings of the time. In 1867, as far as many
were concerned, the Great Reform Bill would achieve most of
what had been needed in 1820. It was time to put up
monuments to revolutionaries, and sit down to a knife-and-
fork tea. A different perspective can be had by reading Edward
Polin's 'John Henderson, My Jo' (pp. 164-5) or Marion
Bernstein's 'Woman's Rights and Wrongs' (p. 297). A report
on the ceremony and speeches at the unveiling of the Hardie
and Baird memorial, together with MacGregor's poem, is
amongst the cuttings bound in Paisley Central Library as
Fugitive Pieces Chiefly Local (941.41 REN 1 PC 2174).

JOHN MacGREGOR

The Tories Treat Us With Disdain

The Tories treat us with disdain,
   Have done, and will do so!
State, if we don't our voice restrain,
   To prison we must go.
And many jails are in repute,
   Our bodies to secure,
Until State Trials come about,
   And punishment made sure.

The Habeus Corpus Safety Act
   Is now, alas! suspended;
And many of our dearest friends
   Are daily apprehended.
Tread mills, and other cruel schemes,
   Are brought in operation,
To torture those who plead our cause —
   The bulwarks of the nation.

Spies with impunity now urge
   Rebellious movements on,
And teach the doctrine, to destroy
   The altar and the throne,
And rouse the multitude to act
   In a tumultuous way,
Led from a virtuous prudent path,
   By villains who betray.

They speak in language very strong,
   And well we know the reason:
They want the people to go wrong,
   Then charge them with high treason.
They would make dupes of simple men,
   And place them in affliction,
That they may get a high reward
   On criminal conviction.

And some will be condemned to die,
    And others sent abroad,
And many more immured in jail,
    To feel the tyrant's rod.
All victims of a dreadful time,
    With mercy little shown;
Our rulers are submerged in crime,
    And justice overthrown.

Lords Sidmouth, Castlereagh, and Co.
    Would work the nation's ruin;
We ne'er had statesmen so obtuse,
    So bent on evil doing.
We find them mad — so very bad,
    So worthless every way —
That they may fail, both one and all,
    We most devoutly pray.

We have no voice to make a choice
    Of those who rule the nation,
And do abhor, and must deplore,
    This want of toleration.
They, haughty knaves, would make us slaves,
    Alive to their dictation;
We can't submit, and won't permit,
    This moral degradation.

They won't relax our bread to tax,
    A crime felt deep and sore
Grant no redress for our distress,
    A want we much deplore.
And when we meet to state our woe,
    Fresh hardships we endure;
Oppression strikes another blow —
    More guilt the only cure.

The Tories call us rogues and fools,
    Condemn and shun our creed;
And would presume to take our lives
    And glory in the deed.
They would imprison pensive men,
    Who differ in opinion;
And make our friends submissive tools,
    Whilst they would hold dominion.

Such is their wanton arrogance, —
    Their wild and mad ambition;
And if we dare to mourn our fate,
    They charge us with sedition.
They would, with domineering pride,
    Promote a civil war;
And hang us up till we were dead,
    Or banish us afar.

We must be brave, ourselves to save,
    From trials so severe;
And not incline to emigrate,
    In consequence of fear, —
Though Brother Cobbett he has fled,
    Who thought he was in danger,
While sterling good Americans
    Make him a welcome stranger.

They know the value of the man
    Our Tories would expel;
And they will strive to judge aright,
    That they may use him well.
They know his genius and his power
    In giving illustration
Of those political events
    That agitate our nation.

And Major Cartwright, honest man,
    With every good intention —
And others of a similar worth —
    Command our grave attention;
If they are put in durance vile,
    Then what are we to do?
We must prepare the toil to share,
    Whatever may ensue.

A host of spies are now engaged
    To spread about sedition,
And get the public men inflamed
    To do some violation;
And then commitments will take place
    Of those who may have erred;
And vain the voice to plead the case
    That they had been ensnared.

The gallows, dungeons, and the lash
    Are all brought into play,
To keep the voice of suffering down,
    And drive complaints away.
Bad laws are formed by callous men,
    And demons bear the sway;
And we are taught to murmur not,
    But tremble and obey.

Amidst this melancholy gloom,
    Who will our minds console —
Who will arise to vanquish spies,
    And bear a just control?
A speedy and effectual change
    We earnestly desire;
To live in love, like saints above,
    Are feelings we admire.

Though doomed to suffer many woes,
   We will not nurse despair;
Our cause is just, in God we trust,
   To dissipate our care;
And bring relief for all our grief —
   Rear virtue to excel;
And level low the daring foe
   Who would doom us to Hell.

O may fair Liberty expand
   And spread her pleasure's round;
And sweet contentment bless our land,
   And righteousness abound.
May Britain claim a precious fame
   For all that's great and grand;
And nation's found in intercourse,
   Obey her just command.

Anon

This song again refers to Radical frustration at the entrenchment of ruling-class power after the end of the Napoleonic Wars. It was sung on October 22nd 1822 at a soiree held in the Saracen's Head Inn, Paisley, to celebrate the release from Ilchester Jail of Orator Hunt. The song was also sung at the soiree for Patrick Brewster (see p. 119) so it was evidently popular at radical occasions for at least twenty years.

*

Song: The Deluge of Carnage at Length has Subsided

TUNE: *Jamie, The Glory and Pride of the Dee*

The deluge of carnage at length has subsided,
And Peace found her way to this ark on the sea,
But a bramble she's brought, and our fond hopes derided,
Not a branch being left on fair liberty's tree.
For kings have resolved that in Europe for ever,
The tocsin of freedom shall sound again never,
But power shall be law, and the flaming sword sever
'Twixt man and the path to fair liberty's tree.

From slavery's long slumber, when Gallia upspringing,
Bade a crown-scourged world be equal and free,
Then hail'd we the dawn the bright summer day bringing,
The lovers of man beneath liberty's tree.

But soon sceptred locusts congressing together,
In the first spring of bliss bent their blasting march thither:
While budding in glory, alas, we saw wither,
The goodliest blossom on liberty's tree.

What land has not seen Britain's crimson flag flying,
The *meteor of murder, but justice the plea,*
Has the blood of her sons, in her ruthless wars dying,
Been the warm showers! to nourish fair liberty's tree.
Yes! if placemen and paupers in myriads unceasing
If nations degraded, white slave trade increasing,
If scorn with oppression be reckon'd a blessing,
Then Britain has nourish'd fair liberty's tree.

Why lingers the blow which with vengeance deserved
Strikes once that whole millions may sparkle with glee,
Far better that life, than to woe still reserved,
Expire in the shade of fair liberty's tree.
Then let those disturbers of this social world;
The oppressors of man, in one vast ruin whirl'd,
From the necks of mankind to the trodden dust hurl'd,
Manure the blest soil, where stands liberty's tree.

Too long has the palace with sighs fill'd the cottage,
Too long to proud despots we've bended the knee,
Let their old guilty empires, already in dotage,
Give the verdure immortal to liberty's tree.
May the time soon arrive when the tyrant and minion
Shall be heard of no more save in tales of the evening,
When freemen from labour in circle conveying,
Tell them o'er, in the shade of fair liberty's tree.

David Webster

Born in Dunblane in 1787, he came early to Paisley where he worked his life as a weaver. Brown notes that 'He was fond of company, and frequently, with his companions he joined in the public-house, indulged to excess. I remember seeing him more than once in a very bad condition on the street, with scarcely a coat on his back.' He died in 1837.

*

Song

AIR: *Contented wi' little, and cantie wi' mair*

> Wha wadna be blyther o'er a cogie o' ale,
> Wha wad luik sour at a humorous tale,
> And wha when his neebour was dowie and sad,
> O wha wadna strive to make his heart glad.
> Wha wadna be cheer'd wi' an auld Scottish sang,
> And wha wi' gude fellows, O wha wad think lang;
> And wha when we wish the downfa' o' our faes,
> O! wha wadna join us wi' hearty huzzas.
>
> Awa ilka camseugh and hard-hearted loun,
> Ye fretfu' ye calous wi' hearts ne'er in tune;
> Awa' ye unsocial — ye misers awa',
> Ye're strangers to pleasure to friendship and a'.
> Let luxury flow in the ha's o' the great;
> Let the hearts o' ambition gang wrestle wi' fate;
> Tho' course be our fare, and tho' humble our shed,
> O'er the fruits of our labour we'll ever be glad.

The gentry may slight us, and say that we're rude,
And ca' us the rabble — the ignorant crowd;
But where comes their riches, their learning, and shaw,
It's the poor working body wha pays for it a'.
Gude kens we hae teachers and preachers enou',
Wha wi' dreepends and steepends are a' het and fu;
But what wad they do for a kirk or a creed,
Giff it werena wark bodies wha gie them their bread.

When the tree o' corruption shall wither and fa',
When oppressors shall fail to haud us at the wa';
O'er our tithes and our taxes we'll cease to repine,
And be blythe brave and free like our daddies lang-syne.
Then let us be blythe o'er a cogie o' yill,
Round the stoup and the cappy let friendship prevail;
May the sunshine o' freedom shame tyrants awa,
Soon to gladen the hearts wha maun slave for them a'.

Tak It Man, Tak it

TUNE: *Brose and Butter*

When I was a Miller in Fyfe,
    Losh! I thought that the sound o' the happer,
Said tak hame a wee flow to your wife,
    To help to be brose to your supper.
Then my conscience was narrow and pure,
    But someway by random it rackit;
For I lifted twa neivefu' or mair,
    While the happer said, tak it man, tak it.
        Hey for the mill and the kill,
            The garland and gear for my cogie,
        Hey for the whisky and yill,
            That washes the dust frae my craigie.

Altho' it's been lang in repute,
    For rogues to mak rich by deceiving;
Yet I see that it does not weel suit,
    Honest men to begin to the thieving.
For my heart it gaed dunt upon dunt,
    Od! I thought ilka dunt it would crack it;
Sae I flung frae my neive what was in't,
    Still the happer said, tak it man, tak it.
                Hey for the mill, &c.

A man that's been bred to the plough,
    Might be deav'd wi' its clamerous clapper;
Yet there's few but would suffer the sough,
    After kenning what's said by the happer.
I whiles thought it scoff'd me to scorn,
    Saying shame, is your conscience no checkit;
But when I grew dry for a horn,
    It chang'd aye to tak it man, tak it.
                Hey for the mill, &c.

The smugglers whyles cam wi' their pocks,
  'Cause they kent that I liked a bicker;
Sae I bartered whyles wi' the gowks,
  Gied them grain for a soup o' their liquor.
I had lang been accustom'd to drink,
  And aye when I purpos'd to quat it,
That thing wi' its clappertie clink,
  Said aye to me tak it man, tak it.
              Hey for the mill, &c.

But the warst thing I did in my life,
  Nae doubt but ye'll think I was wrang o't,
Od, I tauld a bit bodie in Fyfe
  A' my tale, and he made a bit sang o't.
I have aye had a voice a' my days,
  But for singing I ne'er got the knack o't:
Yet I tried whyles, just thinking to please
  The greedy, wi' tak it man, tak it.
              Hey for the mill, &c.

Now, miller and a' as I am,
  This far I can see through the matter;
There's men mair notorious to fame,
  Mair greedy than me or the muter.
For 'twad seem that the hale race o' men,
  Or wi' safety that half we may mak it,
Had some speaking happer within,
  That said to them, tak it man, tak it.
              Hey for the mill, &c.

Paisley Fair

Serenely the morning was dawning,
   The suny beams raise ow'er the hill;
Our beasts stood a' rowting and yawning,
   By the side of a summer dry'd rill.
The larks in the lift they were singing,
   In notes baith harmonious and shrill;
And round me the woodlands were ringing,
   To the clack of a neebouring mill.

Then quoth I to my auld aunty Peggy,
   The morning's sae bonny and clear,
Troth I'll e'en gang and saddle my naigie,
   And ride in to see Paisley Fair.
But quo' she man ye're lucky light headed,
   Or else ye've grown lazy and slack;
Kens thou that at hame thou'll be needed,
   To help us to big the peat stack.

But quo' I, the hearst on us is drawing,
   We'll be toiling frae morning till dark,
Trouth its either aye sawing or mawing,
   A young cheil gets naething but wark.
Then I drew frae the boost the bit kibbock,
   And took to mysel' a bit whang —
Wi' some bannocks weel baked by Tibbock,
   Wha's e'en been our servant sae lang.

Then I gied my beast wat'ring and corning,
   Wi' twa heaped hanfu' o' beans —
Hae, quo' I, tak thee that for thy coming,
   'Twill help to put strength in thy banes.
Then aff I cam cheery and merry,
   I galloped down the lang lone —
And soon met wi' mae in a hurry,
   A' makin' best speed to the town.

There was Tam that wins down in the hallow,
    Wi' haveral Jock Hodge frae Brae Side;
Wi' their doxes of intellects shallow,
    Mair scrimpit o' sense than o' pride.
There was Peggy wi' een aye sae pawky,
    That bides at the head o' the glen;
And Nelly that thriftless gowky
    Wha's siller entices the men.

Then quo' Tammy, quo' he, quo' Tammy,
    How's a' the day, Willie M'Nair?
I thank thee, quo' I to Tammy,
    And thou'll be for seeing the fair.
And then, quo' Jock Hodge, quo' Johnny,
    As he turn'd round is red face —
And thou'll be for trying thy pouney,
    Nae doubt at the thirty pound race.

Now frae ilka by road they were thranging —
    Baith blind folk and lame, folk and weans;
And straight to the fair they were ganging,
    And striddlen o'er hillocks and stanes.
Then some o' them thought on their duddies,
    And ithers o' them on their crimes —
But the maist thing that troubled the bodies,
    I think was their hungry wames.

We arriv'd man and stabled our horses —
    Syne a luncheon we took for support;
Then securing our lang necked purses,
    Took a dauner to see a' the sport.
And while we stood gaping and staring,
    To a poor bodie singing a sang,
Quo' a hizzie, Will buy me my fairing —
    Losh! thou kens thou has promised it lang.

But the Corse it was a' in a hubble
   O' confusion and perfect uproar;
Sae wi' punch man we push'd thro' the rabble,
   Till we cam' the length o' the score —
There were dolts man and dinsome deceivers,
   Wha like statesmen impose upon man;
And some silver-hunting believers,
   Wha catch a' the cash that they can.

Now one by the wa'-side was wailing,
   'Gude christians, help an auld man;'
While M'Adam was rantin' and railing,
   The cheapest goods under the sun.
Here's veils for auld maids wrinkled faces,
   The cheapest and best here awa;
With Waterloo ribbons and laces,
   And penknives for naething ava.

There was darners and clippers, and flowerers,
   Wi' bleachers fu' trig frae the braes —
Wi' scogies, and cooks, and tambourers,
   Wha's clatter was a' on their claes.
Braw lasses — but losh man their faces,
   We scarce got a peep o' ava;
Sae hidden they were in big cases,
   Or capes made o' strae, some said straw.

But some roar'd the race was beginning —
   Hech Sirs sic a hullibaloo;
Frae taverns and tents they were rinning
   Some sober, and ithers blin fou.
Then some roar'd the hindmost was foremost,
   And roos'd a Kilbirnie bit beast;
But I swore the first wad be foremost,
   Or that he wad be second at least.

Neist we heard the wild beasts all a howling,
   And wild fools beginning to squake;
There a gowk 'bout the elephant was bawling,
   That it could do a' things but speak.
Sae Nanny was oxter'd wi' Tammy,
   And Nelly wi' muckle Jock Hodge;
Sae we drew out our siller fu' canny,
   And paid to win in wi' a grudge.

The elephant stood in a closet,
   And whether for hunger or greed
I kentna, but ay the big nose o't
   Was wagging for bawbees and bread.
Now as we stood staring and glowring,
   The lasses were shaking wi' fear;
Losh to see the big servant devouring
   As meikle meat's sairt for a year.

There were fiddlers, and fifers, and drummers,
   Wha play'd for bawbees in a neuk;
With pipers, and droners, and bummers,
   And dogs that could dance by the beuk.
But quo' Tam, as we stood wi' the tawpies,
   And leugh at the merryman's tale,
Deed, lassies, I'm e'en growing gawpish,
   We maun hae some buns and some ale.

Syne resolved on a bit and a drappie —
   And be blythe as our daddies of yore,
We daunert to mak oursels happy,
   Into wee Jamie Smith's at the Score.
There ae core was hauding a loudey,
   What neist they wad hae for to drink;
While some o' the tousy and tawdry,
   Were schemin' the way to get clink.

At length we fell a' to the prancing,
    And louping like fools in the floor;
Sae wi' fiddling and diddling, and dancing,
    The house was in perfect uproar.
But the sun in the west now was sinking,
    And gloamin' began for to fa';
Grown tired wi' their daffing and drinking,
    Deed I thocht man I'd just come awa.

Sae now I'm come hame, gude be thanket,
    To tak tent o' my grandmother's gear;
I had but sax groats, tho' I drank it,
    Od, I'll surely win ow'rt in a year.
But the first time I gang to the smiddie,
    As on Saturday teen I'll be there;
Gosh I'll gar them a' laugh round the study,
    Wi' the humours o' Paisley Fair.

Droll Will Dunbar

Droll Will Dunbar was a rhymer they say,
Whas hurdies were happit wi' gude howden grey,
Some ca'd him a stirk, ithers ca'd him a star—
But a' bodies kent him by droll Will Dunbar.
Tho' Willie was comely, his manners were odd,
Grew aulder and dafter like whalps o' the tod;
But wha in a satire wad wage wi' him war—
Were sure to be licket by droll Will Dunbar.

      Cuplets, treeplets, Willie Dunbar,
      Treeplets, cuplets, Willie Dunbar,
      Jingle awa without jum'le or jaur,
      Ay sleeket and witty was droll Will Dunbar.

To mak a bit sonnet cost Willie nae fash,
For his verses cam readier to him than the cash;
Whene'er he took haud o' the scrunt o' a pen,
Lines lampin like maukins cam doun frae his brain.
When a lilt he fell till't, as if nature he law'd,
He ordered his muse to awake for a jade;
Then red wud for fame like a bold British tar,
In raptures she sang wi' her droll Willie Dunbar.

'Tis said that his fancy was ever in flight,
In the shine of the day and the shade of the night;
And like a' ither rhymers, as bodies remark,
He was lazy at naething but prayers and wark.
Willie lo'ed a bit spark o' the stark usquebey,
It put his sad heart in a happier key,
For he thocht that his roundels cam readier far,
When hauf capernuitie, this Willie Dunbar.

Sometimes when he spoke ye wad thocht him a clown
As vulgar as any in kintry or town;
Other times ye wad thocht by his style sae complete,
He had soar'd like a lark frae Gamalial's feet.
This moment and Willie was modest and mild,
But sting him like Boreas his raging was wild;
Ye wad thocht in a court he might done for a scar
To our gentlemen liars, this droll Will Dunbar.

Droll Will Dunbar he could philosophize,
Could measure the karry, the earth, and the seas;
Nae hist'ry, nor myst'ry, but Willie could scan,
Bamboozled wi' nought but the roguery o' man.
Will was friendly to man yet was jimp in belief,
For he watched their drift as he watched a thief,
And when they in their reveries began for to jaur,
That was balm to the bosom of droll Will Dunbar.

Of astronomy Will had a kind o' a nack,
The height o' the stars he could tell ye correct,
The number of planets, their distance, and whar
They sail'd round the sun on their aerial car.
He could pointed ye out by the system in vogue,
As clear as a glutton could empty a cog;
And how a roun' moon made a daft body waur,
Could be clearly described by droll Will Dunbar.

Will could tell ye o' tykes wha had travell'd sae far,
That they saw a new heaven and a new set o' stars;
They doubted a wee if it was the same moon,
But wad freely gie aith it was roun like our ain.
Will could tell ye o' seamen who sailed sae far north,
That gude sooth they ran out o' baith water and earth;
A' had grown into ice by the force o' the air—
That's waur yet than Scotland, quoth Willie Dunbar.

That Willie had merits his friends a' confess'd,
Tho' his poverty hid them like gowd in a kist;
But Willie had ay a bit glimpse of a hope,
And nae langer at hame the rhymer wad stop.
He gaed into Auld Reekie to shew what he wrote,
And thus spake the spenticle gentry I wot,
'Man ye're liker a stirk than a poetic star,'
Maist dumfunert the feelings o' droll Willie Dunbar.
                    Cuplets, treeplets, &C.

Robert Pollok

Born at North Moorhouse in the Parish of Eaglesham in 1798. Graduated M.A. from Glasgow University in 1822, he studied for five years for the ministry at the Divinity Hall of the United Secession Church, Glasgow, being licensed to preach in May 1827.

He published 'Tales of the Covenanters' in 1826, and two months before he received his licence to preach he published what was seen as his masterpiece, the ten-canto *The Course of Time*, a Calvinistic story of the Fall modelled upon Milton's 'Paradise Lost'. But Pollok's health deteriorated with consumption shortly after his poem's publication. In September of 1827 he was persuaded to travel to Italy for the sake of his health, but he got no further than Southampton, where he died and was buried.

By 1868 Blackwood's edition of *The Course of Time* claimed 'seventy-eighth thousand' on its title-page, and Eyre-Todd in his *The Glasgow Poets* wrote that at one time it was the book that would be found beside the Bible and Burns in cottages throughout Scotland. The poem tells how a soul travelling from his 'native land' to Heaven, comes by the perimeter of Hell on his journey. When he gets to Heaven, he asks what the place he saw was, and why it's there. The reply is given from Canto Two onward by a particularly favoured inhabitant of Heaven, the Bard. He tells how once, a long time ago, there was a planet called Earth — and so on.

The selection here from Book Four onwards shows how Pollok treated literature.

*

The Course of Time

from Book One (A DESCRIPTION OF HELL)

        . . . and far as sight could pierce,
Or down descend in caves of hopeless depth,
Through all that dungeon of unfading fire,
I saw most miserable beings walk,
Burning continually, yet unconsumed;
For ever wasting, yet enduring still;
Dying perpetually, yet never dead.
Some wandered lonely in the desert flames.
And some in fell encounter fiercely met,
With curses loud, and blasphemies that made
The cheek of darkness pale; and as they fought,
And cursed and gnashed their teeth, and wished to die,
Their hollow eyes did utter streams of woe.
And there were groans that ended not, and sighs
That always sighed, and tears that ever wept,
And ever fell, but not in Mercy's sight.
And Sorrow, and Repentance, and Despair
Among them walked, and to their thirsty lips
Presented frequent cups of burning gall.
And as I listened, I heard these beings curse
Almighty God, and curse the Lamb, and curse
The earth, the resurrection morn; and seek,
And ever vainly seek, for utter death.
And to their everlasting anguish still,
The thunders from above responding spoke
These words, which, through the caverns of perdition
Forlornly echoing, fell on every ear—
'Ye knew your duty, but ye did it not:'
And back again recoiled a deeper groan.

*

from Book Four

One glance of wonder, as we pass, deserve
The books of Time. Productive was the world
In many things, but most in books. Like swarms
Of locusts, which God sent to vex a land
Rebellious long, admonished long in vain,
Their numbers they poured annually on man,
From heads conceiving still. Perpetual birth!
Thou wonderest how the world contained them all?
Thy wonder stay. Like men, this was their doom:
'That dust they were, and should to dust return.'
And oft their fathers, childless and bereaved,
Wept o'er their graves when they themselves were green.
And on them fell, as fell on every age,
As on their authors fell, oblivious Night,
Which o'er the past lay darkling, heavy, still,
Impenetrable, motionless, and sad,
Having his dismal leaden plumage stirred
By no remembrancer, to show the men
Who after came what was concealed beneath.

     The story-telling tribe alone outran
All calculation far, and left behind,
Lagging, the swiftest numbers. Dreadful, even
To fancy, was their never-ceasing birth;
And room had lacked, had not their life been short.
Excepting some, their definition take
Thou thus, expressed in gentle phrase, which leaves
Some truth behind: A Novel was a book
Three-volumed, and once read, and oft crammed full
Of poisonous error, blackening every page;
And oftener still, of trifling, second-hand
Remark, and old, diseased, putrid thought,
And miserable incident, at war
With nature, with itself and truth at war;
Yet charming still the greedy reader on,
Till, done, he tried to recollect his thoughts,
And nothing found but dreaming emptiness.

These, like ephemera, sprang in a day
From lean and shallow-soiled brains of sand,
And in a day expired; yet while they lived,
Tremendous, ofttimes, was the popular roar;
And cries of — Live for ever! struck the skies.

*

　　Take one example, to our purpose quite.
A man of rank, and of capacious soul,
Who riches had, and fame, beyond desire;
An heir of flattery, to titles born,
And reputation, and luxurious life.
Yet, not content with ancestorial name,
Or to be known because his fathers were,
He on this height hereditary stood,
And, gazing higher, purposed in his heart
To take another step. Above him seemed
Alone the mount of song, the lofty seat
Of canonised bards; and thitherward,
By nature taught, and inward melody,
In prime of youth he bent his eagle eye.
No cost was spared. What books he wished, he read;
What sage to hear, he heard; what scenes to see,
He saw. And first in rambling schoolboy days
Britannia's mountain-walks, and heath-girt lakes,
And story-telling glens, and founts, and brooks,
And maids, as dewdrops pure and fair, his soul
With grandeur filled, and melody and love.
Then travel came, and took him where he wished.
He cities saw, and courts, and princely pomp;
And mused alone on ancient mountain-brows;
And mused on battle-fields, where valour fought
In other days; and mused on ruins grey
With years; and drank from old and fabulous wells;
And plucked the vine that first-born prophets plucked;
And mused on famous tombs, and on the wave
Of ocean mused, and on the desert waste.
The heavens and earth of every country saw.

Where'er the old inspiring Genii dwelt,
Aught that could rouse, expand, refine the soul,
Thither he went, and meditated there.
He touched his harp, and nations heard, entranced.
As some vast river of unfailing source,
Rapid, exhaustless, deep, his numbers flowed,
And opened new fountains in the human heart.
Where Fancy halted, weary in her flight,
In other men, his, fresh as morning, rose,
And soared untrodden heights, and seemed at home
Where angels bashful looked. Others, though great,
Beneath their argument seemed struggling whiles;
He, from above descending, stooped to touch
The loftiest thought; and proudly stooped, as though
It scarce deserved his verse. With Nature's self
He seemed an old acquaintance, free to jest
At will with all her glorious majesty.
He laid his hand upon 'the Ocean's mane,'
And played familiar with his hoary locks;
Stood on the Alps, stood on the Apennines,
And with the thunder talked, as friend to friend;
And wove his garland of the lightning's wing,
In sportive twist, the lightning's fiery wing,
Which, as the footsteps of the dreadful God,
Marching upon the storm in vengeance, seemed;
Then turned, and with the grasshopper, who sang
His evening song beneath his feet, conversed.
Suns, moons, and stars, and clouds, his sisters were;
Rocks, mountains, meteors, seas, and winds, and storms,
His brothers, younger brothers, whom he scarce
As equals deemed. All passions of all men,
The wild and tame, the gentle and severe;
All thoughts, all maxims, sacred and profane;
All creeds, all seasons, Time, Eternity;
All that was hated, and all that was dear;
All that was hoped, all that was feared, by man,
He tossed about, as tempest, withered leaves;
Then, smiling, looked upon the wreck he made.
With terror now he froze the cowering blood,
And now dissolved the heart in tenderness:

Yet would not tremble, would not weep himself;
But back into his soul retired, alone,
Dark, sullen, proud, gazing contemptuously
On hearts and passions prostrate at his feet.
So Ocean from the plains, his waves had late
To desolation swept, retired in pride,
Exulting in the glory of his might,
And seemed to mock the ruin he had wrought.

As some fierce comet of tremendous size,
To which the stars did reverence as it passed,
So he, through learning and through fancy, took
His flights sublime, and on the loftiest top
Of Fame's dread mountain sat; not soiled and worn,
As if he from the earth had laboured up;
But as some bird of heavenly plumage fair
He looked, which down from higher regions came,
And perched it there to see what lay beneath.

The nations gazed, and wondered much, and praised.
Critics before him fell in humble plight,
Confounded fell, and made debasing signs
To catch his eye; and stretched and swelled themselves
To bursting nigh, to utter bulky words
Of admiration vast; and many, too,
Many that aimed to imitate his flight,
With weaker wing unearthly fluttering made,
And gave abundant sport to after days.

Great man! the nations gazed, and wondered much,
And praised; and many called his evil good.
Wits wrote in favour of his wickedness;
And kings to do him honour took delight.
Thus, full of titles, flattery, honour, fame,
Beyond desire, beyond ambition, full,
He died — he died of what? — of wretchedness;
Drank every cup of joy, heard every trump
Of fame, drank early, deeply drank, drank draughts
That common millions might have quenched; then died
Of thirst, because there was no more to drink.

His goddess, Nature, wooed, embraced, enjoyed,
Fell from his arms abhorred; his passions died;
Died all but dreary, solitary pride;
And all his sympathies in being died.
As some ill-guided bark, well built and tall,
Which angry tides cast out on desert shore,
And then retiring, left it there to rot
And moulder in the winds and rains of heaven;
So he, cut from the sympathies of life,
And cast ashore from pleasure's boisterous surge,
A wandering, weary, worn, and wretched thing,
A scorched, and desolate, and blasted soul,
A gloomy wilderness of dying thought —
Repined, and groaned, and withered from the earth.
His groanings filled the land his numbers filled;
And yet he seemed ashamed to groan. Poor man!
Ashamed to ask, and yet he needed help.

Proof this, beyond all lingering of doubt,
That not with natural or mental wealth
Was God delighted, or his peace secured;
That not in natural or mental wealth
Was human happiness or grandeur found.
Attempt how monstrous, and how surely vain,
With things of earthly sort, with aught but God,
With aught but moral excellence, truth, and love,
To satisfy and fill the immortal soul!
Attempt, vain inconceivably! attempt,
To satisfy the ocean with a drop,
To marry Immortality to Death,
And with the unsubstantial shade of Time
To fill the embrace of all Eternity!

William Motherwell

Born Glasgow, 1797. Educated three years in Edinburgh then in Paisley Grammar, taking classes in Greek and Latin at Glasgow University. At fifteen he was apprenticed to the Sheriff-Clerk's office in Paisley, becoming at twenty-one the Sheriff-Clerk Depute for Renfrewshire. His job brought him into the thick of military suppression of the Radical risings and civil disturbances around 1820; in 1818 he was knocked unconscious by an angry crowd and narrowly escaped being thrown into the River Cart. The author of the memorial prefacing his *Poetical Works* has it that 'Motherwell was instinctively a Tory — all the tendencies of his mind gravitated towards the creed of that old and respectable party — and I am satisfied that his monarchical principles would have been just as high after he escaped from mere nonage had he never handled a truncheon in defence of the public peace on the streets of Paisley.'

It was Motherwell who was responsible for completion of the first anthology of Renfrewshire poetry, *The Harp of Renfrewshire*, in 1819. Two editors had failed to complete the job before the work was given to Motherwell, who wrote the introduction quoting some of the most interesting of the older Renfrewshire works as a kind of prefatory anthology to the work proper. His ballad collection (containing a number of versions gathered locally), *Minstrelsy Ancient and Modern*, was published in 1827. The following year he founded the *Paisley Magazine*, then assumed editorship of the *Paisley Advertiser* in 1828. He then moved to the *Glasgow Courier* which he edited for five years until his death in 1835. He was at a dinner with dancing on October 31st at a friend's house in a Glasgow suburb, 'and it was observed that he bled freely at the nose, which was attributed to the heated state of the apartments. On going into the open air for a short time the bleeding stopped. . . . At 4 o'clock on the morning of the 1st of November he was suddenly struck while in bed with a violent shock of apoplexy, which almost instantly deprived him of consciousness. He had simply time to exclaim "My Head! My Head!" when he fell back on the pillow and never spoke more.'

His grave is in the Glasgow Necropolis.

The sentimental 'Jeanie Morrison' was once an anthology piece.

*

Jeannie Morrison

I've wandered east, I've wandered west,
    Through mony a weary way;
But never, never can forget
    The luve o' life's young day!
The fire that's blawn on Beltane e'en,
    May weel be black gin Yule;
But blacker fa' awaits the heart
    Where first fond luve grows cule.

O dear, dear Jeanie Morrison,
    The thochts o' bygane years
Still fling their shadows ower my path,
    And blind my een wi' tears:
They blind my een wi' saut, saut tears,
    And sair and sick I pine,
As memory idly summons up
    The blithe blinks o' langsyne.

'Twas then we luvit ilk ither weel,
    'Twas then we twa did part;
Sweet time — sad time! twa bairns at scule,
    Twa bairns, and but ae heart!

'Twas then we sat on ae laigh bink,
　　To leir ilk ither lear;
And tones, and looks, and smiles were shed,
　　Remembered evermair.

I wonder, Jeanie, aften yet,
　　When sitting on that bink,
Cheek touchin' cheek, loof lock'd in loof,
　　What our wee heads could think?
When baith bent doun ower ae braid page,
　　Wi' ae buik on our knee,
Thy lips were on thy lesson, but
　　My lesson was in thee.

Oh, mind ye how we hung our heads,
　　How cheeks brent red wi' shame,
Whene'er the scule-weans laughin' said,
　　We cleek'd thegither hame?
And mind ye o' the Saturdays,
　　(The scule then skail't at noon),
When we ran aff to speel the braes —
　　The broomy braes o' June?

My head rins round and round about,
　　My heart flows like a sea,
As ane by ane the thochts rush back
　　O' scule time and o' thee.
Oh, mornin' life! oh, mornin' luve!
　　Oh lichtsome days and lang,
When hinnied hopes around our hearts
　　Like simmer blossoms sprang!

Oh mind ye, luve, how aft we left
　　The deavin' dinsome toun,
To wander by the green burnside,
　　And hear its waters croon?
The simmer leaves hung ower our heads,
　　The flowers burst round our feet,
And in the gloamin o' the wood,
　　The throssil whusslit sweet;

The throssil whusslit in the wood,
　　The burn sang to the trees,

And we with Nature's heart in tune,
    Concerted harmonies;
And on the knowe abune the burn,
    For hours thegither sat
In the silentness o' joy, till baith
    Wi' very gladness grat.

Aye, aye, dear Jeanie Morrison,
    Tears trinkled doun your cheek,
Like dew-beads on a rose, yet nane
    Had ony power to speak!
That was a time, a blessed time,
    When hearts were fresh and young,
When freely gushed all feelings forth,
    Unsyllabled — unsung!

I marvel, Jeanie Morrison,
    Gin I hae been to thee
As closely twined wi' earliest thochts,
    As ye hae been to me?
Oh! tell me gin their music fills
    Thine ear as it does mine;
Oh! say gin e'er your heart grows grit
    Wi' dreamings o' langsyne?

I've wandered east, I've wandered west,
    I've borne a weary lot;
But in my wanderings, far or near,
    Ye never were forgot.
The fount that first burst frae this heart,
    Still travels on its way;
And channels deeper as it rins,
    The luve o' life's young day.

O dear, dear Jeanie Morrison,
    Since we were sindered young,
I've never seen your face, nor heard
    The music o' your tongue;
But I could hug all wretchedness,
    And happy could I die,
Did I but ken your heart still dreamed
    O' bygane days and me!

I Am Not Sad!

I am not sad, though sadness seem
   At times to cloud my brow;
I cherished once a foolish dream—
   Thank Heaven, 'tis not so now.
     Truth's sunshine broke,
     And I awoke
   To feel 'twas right to bow
To fate's decree, and this my doom,
The darkness of a Nameless Tomb.

I grieve not, though a tear may fill
   This glazed and vacant eye;
Old thoughts will rise, do what we will,
   But soon again they die;
     An idle gush,
     And all is hush,
   The fount is soon run dry:
And cheerly now I meet my doom,
The darkness of a Nameless Tomb.

I am not mad, although I see
   Things of no better mould
Than I myself am, greedily
   In Fame's bright page enrolled,
     That they may tell
     The story well,
   What shines may not be gold.
No, no! content I court my doom,
The darkness of a Nameless Tomb.

The luck is theirs — the loss is mine,
  And yet no loss at all;
The mighty ones of eldest time,
  I ask where they did fall?
    Tell me the one
    Who e'er could shun
  Touch with Oblivion's pall?
All bear with me an equal doom,
The darkness of a Nameless Tomb.

Brave Temple and huge pyramid,
  Hill sepulchred by art,
The barrow acre-vast, where hid
  Moulders some Nimrod's heart;
    Each monstrous birth
    Cumbers old earth,
  But acts a voiceless part,
Resolving all to mine own doom,
The darkness of a Nameless Tomb.

Tradition with her palsied hand,
  And purblind History, may
Grope and guess well that in this land
  Some great one lived his day;
    And what is this,
    Blind hit or miss,
  But labour thrown away,
For counterparts to mine own doom,
The darkness of a Nameless Tomb?

I do not peak and pine away,
   Lo! this deep bowl I quaff;
If sigh I do, you still must say
   It sounds more like a laugh.
     'Tis not too late
     To separate
   The good seed from the chaff;
And scoff at those who scorn my doom,
The darkness of a Nameless Tomb.

I spend no sigh, I shed no tear,
   Though life's first dream is gone;
And its bright picturings now appear
   Cold images of stone;
     I've learned to see
     The vanity
   Of lusting to be known,
And gladly hail my changeless doom,
The darkness of a Nameless Tomb!

O That This Weary War of Life!

O that this weary war of life
    With me were o'er,
Its eager cry of woe and strife
    Heard no more!
I've fronted the red battle field
    Mine own dark day;
I fain would fling the helmet, shield,
    And sword away.
I strive not now for victory—
    That wish hath fled;
My prayer is now to numbered be
    Among the dead—
All that I loved, alas!—alas!
    Hath perished!

They tell me 'tis a glorious thing,
    This wearing war;
They tell me joy crowns suffering
    And bosom scar.
Such speech might never pass the lips
    That could unfold
How shrinketh heart when sorrow nips
    Affections old:
When they who cleaved to us are dust,
    Why live to moan?
Better to meet a felon thrust
    Than strive alone—
Better than loveless palaces
    The churchyard stone!

William Wilson

Born Paisley 1817, he became a weaver, settling in Elderslie where he died in 1850. The title page of the copy of his *Poetical Pieces* in Paisley Central Library is inscribed under 'Composed by a Young Author', 'Wm Wilson, Elderslie'. Above the publication details is added in the same hand, 'The author is 25 years of age — a weaver. Married with two children — and lives at Elderslie'.

*

Lines on Looking at the Picture of a King

If kings were just a harmless thing like thee,
    A form on paper, not in real life,
Then would this suffering world be free
    From many a bloody scene of strife.

Their power is guarded by a gaudy force
    Of legal murderers, their gilded throne
Emanates from heaven's righteous curse,
    Reason and justice they have seldom known.

The blood of millions lave their royal track,
    The wail of nations mingle with the slain;
Wild deeds of darkness make the scene more black,
    Woe, want, and ruin, follow in their train.

Soon may their power by reason's voice be stem'd,
    With all its pomp, and pride, and wealth,
A power by heaven and earth condemn'd,
    A power invented by the devil himself.

Song sung at a Soiree for Patrick Brewster, 1838

Patrick Brewster, minister at Paisley Abbey, became a focus and spokesman for the 'moral force' faction of those chartists who considered it essential to pledge not to use physical force in pursuit of their aims. Brewster's views were still radical enough to have him eventually suspended from his ministry for a year. That and his welcoming to Paisley of Daniel O'Connel — also opposed to physical force in Ireland — are recounted in John Mitchell's poem 'A Braid Glow'r at the Clergy' (pp. 146-156). Brewster's eloquence was recorded at a soiree held in his honour on November 12th 1838:

> . . . I know not the day when I was not a liberal — a radical in opinion. [*Cheers.*] I had almost said that I inherited radical opinions, but you know I am not an admirer of inherited wisdom. [*A laugh and cheering.*] I imbibed in part, however, those principles from the lips of a venerated parent, with some of that love of freedom and hatred of oppression which I have often heard him express, and which I am doing my best to transmit unimpaired to my own children — a legacy, and it may be the only legacy which many of us will have to leave to our children, [*hear, and great approbation*] but a legacy — an inheritance far better, and far more honourable, with the blessing of God, than those usurped rights — those gewgaw titles and those accumulated thousands wrung from the hard earnings of an over-toiled people — branded and blighted with a nation's tears and a nation's curse. [*Cheers.*] You ask me to persevere in this good cause. By every effort which may avail I will do so. [*Cheers.*] It is a cause to which my heart and life are devoted, and I can well sacrifice all personal consideration in this cause. [*Cheers.*] I will live and die the supporter of this cause. [*Cheers.*] No man will I call enemy who is the friend of this cause, and no man will I call friend — though certainly I cannot cease to love many a dear friend who differs from me — yet no man will I call friend in the deepest sympathies of my heart who is an enemy of this cause. [*Great cheering.*] When I cease to be a friend to this cause I will cease to be a friend to

truth, justice, humanity, — to the cause of God and God's oppressed people throughout the world. [*Great cheering.*] Some of us were lately addressed on this subject by one of the most eloquent of living preachers. He told us not to meddle with politics. He told us to leave politics to the potsherds of the earth, and to look to our safe landing in another world, for that it would be all one a hundred years hence. 'It will be all one a hundred years hence.' This is the true art of mystification. It is the very essence of political priestcraft — [*cheers*] — a doctrine by which priests and tyrants have to this day trampled on the world. [*Loud cheering.*] You behold the unfortunate millions of the human family robbed and wounded by the wayside. They have literally fallen among the thieves; the Levites of our day will not help them — [*hear and loud cheering*] — but they were not so bad as their Jewish brethren of old; they will offer up a prayer for a safe landing-place in heaven, and they will console them with the reflection that it will be all one a hundred years hence. [*Hear and cheers.*] Will it be all one a hundred years hence? [*Cheers.*] Will it be all one with those who leagued themselves with the tyrant? [*Cries of 'hear, hear' and loud cheers.*] Will it be all one with us if we will not help to deliver the suffering millions of our fellow-countrymen and of our fellow-men throughout the world, who are now at the mercy of the tyrant? [*Cheers.*] Will it be all one if we will not obey the obligations laid upon us by the God of mercy, who calls upon us to deliver the oppressed, to loose the bonds of wickedness and to undo the heavy burdens, and let the oppressed go free? [*Hear and cheering.*] Will it be all one for our children a hundred years hence, if we meddle not with politics — and would it have been all one with us if our forefathers had not meddled with politics?

At this soiree the unattributed song 'The Hour of Retribution's Nigh' was sung. This song had been sung at Radical occasions in Paisley for some twenty years, as it had also been sung at the celebration in Paisley in 1822 of Orator Hunt's release from jail (see p. 64).

Opinions on Brewster are still divided according to political inclination. For many like John Mitchell, he was a courageous hero. To others he was a nuisance who hopelessly split the chartist movement in the West of Scotland by diverting much energy and argument onto a pledge that was essentially an irrelevance. Historians favourable to Brewster have generally portrayed his opponent in the so-called 'physical force' chartists, Feargus O'Connor, in unfavourable or dismissive terms. A more sympathetic portrait of O'Connor is provided in James Epstein's *The Lion of Freedom: Feargus O'Connor and the Chartist Movement 1832-1842*, Croom Helm, London and Canberra, 1982.

Brewster's own sermons which led to his suspension were published in *Seven Chartist and Military Discourses*.

Anon

Song: The Hour of Retribution's Nigh

TUNE: *Willie Was A Wanton Boy*

The rights of Lords and Kings to reign,
    (Blest mortals who can do no ill!)
Is founded in oppression's claim,
    Regardless of their people's will.
Though void of worth, men's hearts to charm,
    They bind their limbs in hated thrall,
Of soul tho' vile, and nerveless arm,
    Legitimacy's all in all!
Fit cradle, tyrant power to nurse!
    Soft couch of sloth, where despots lie!
Legitimacy, freemen's curse.
    The hour of retribution's nigh!

Thou relic of barbarian times
    Ere freedom tried her infant wings;
When blotted were Earth's fairest climes
    With oracles, and priests, and kings!
The monk and cowl, the priest and gown,
    Like ghosts have fled from reason's ray!
Then, what art thou, with glittering crown!
    Hence to thy native gloom away.
GIANT, when armed with lawless force,
    But *Dwarf*, when reason sits thee by.
Legitimacy, freemen's curse.
    The hour of retribution's nigh!

'Tis folly lights thy temple's fires,
    Thy priests are *havoc, guilt*, and fear!
And human groans, the music dire
    That pleases best thy savage ear!

Upon thy gory altar stain,
    Valour's mistaken millions lie:
Unpitied by one patriotic sigh!
    Stern idol! wa's unfailing source,
Of tyger heart, and vulture eye!
    Legitimacy, freemen's curse!
The hour of retribution's nigh!

Though gorgeous robes, and golden wand,
    And glittering glories fence thee round,
The sceptre shall desert thy hand,
    When Liberty the trump shall sound;
And Liberty two blasts has blown!
    That still in Europe's ears do ring:
And at the third, each tottering throne
    Shall hold a man, or Chosen King.
Then Freedom with a sun-like course,
    Shall o'er the wide creation fly!
Legitimacy! Freemen's curse!
    The hour of retribution's nigh.

John Mitchell

Born Paisley 1786, he was a shoemaker who published books and, in 1823, published a weekly, *The Moral and Literary Observer*. He was prolific, with several volumes of poems and songs, and a number of political or satirical pamphlets including 'Lines on the Celebration of Thomas Paine's Birth-Day' and 'Just Asses of Paisley, or Theatre versus No Theatre'. He died in 1856.

Regarding 'Brewster' referred to in the third poem see pp. 119-21.

*

Cautious Tam

or

HOW TO LOOK A FOE IN THE FACE

Ye wha o'er the foaming bicker
   Throw your precious hours away,
And thro' madness drown in liquor
   What wad cheer some future day.

Listen to the tale I'm telling,
   It is fraught wi' truths I know,
And ye yet may frae your dwelling
   Banish drink, man's direst foe.

Lately on the Scottish border,
   Where men play'd sic pranks of yore,
Lived a youth wha's love of order
   Kept him frae the tavern's roar.

Cautious Tam his neibours ca'd him,
   An' he weel deserved the name,
For to do what prudence bade him
   Was his first — his only aim.

Ne'er a brawl was Tammie found in.
   He despised the boxing crew,
Wha wi' blows were aye expounding
   How a face could be made blue.

Poor his parents were, but never
   Sigh'd they a toom coggie o'er,
Industry they knew wad ever
   Keep grim want far frae their door.

Winter never saw them weary,
   Tho' her nights are drear and lang;
Simmer ever found them cheery
   O'er their wark — green fields amang.

To the school their weans they sent aye,
   Till they could baith read an' write;
And our hero Tam took tent aye
   To keep dux aye in his sight.

Counting he took maist delight in,
   Yet thro' Lindley Murray he
Ran till he the art o' writing
   In its varied forms could see.

Fain his parents to the college
   Wad hae sent their darling son,
But few to that place o' knowledge
   Get wha's meat frae toil is won.

Many wha hae sma' pretensions
   To abilities get there,
If a purse o' big dimensions
   Has fa'en to their parents' share.

But the poor man's son tho' clever,
    Frae his books an' lair maun turn,
An' frae labour's turgid river
    Refuse drag, and learn to mourn.

So our Tam, tho' sair dejected,
    Had to gang an' learn a trade,
An' the ane the youth selected,
    Was to be a cobbler bred.

Eidantly he did whatever
    His employer bade him do;
An' his master said he never
    A mair faithfu' prentice knew.

Five lang years at length roll'd o'er him,
    An' Tam stood unfetter'd free;
While in prospect stretch'd before him
    Charms the slothfu' never see.

For a time he wrought contented
    Wi' his maister; but ae day
Death, wha ne'er sic deeds repented,
    His employer took away.

Tam was sad for he revered him
    As a maister kind an' true,
Wha wi' sage advices cheer'd him,
    To keep honour aye in view.

But stern fate we a' maun bend to,
    Be we cobbler, be we king,
Gold will ne'er an hour append to
    Life, if death is on the wing.

Yet time cures the deepest sorrow
    That afflicts the human mind,
And spreads o'er each coming morrow
    What past griefs throw to the wind.

By his neebours much respected,
    Tam was urged to tak' the trade

His late maister had collected,
  An' which weel his cares had paid.

He to their advice assented —
  Took the shop, the stock and a',
Nor had he cause to repent it,
  For ere twelve months were awa

Greatly had the trade extended,
  Far beyond what it was when
He first shoes baith made and mended,
  To keep dry the soles o' men.

And ere lang the house he dwell'd in
  He wi' ready-money bought,
An' the title deeds he held in
  Hands that for the same had wrought.

An' soon in his cozzie dwellin',
  Morn and e'en was to be seen
Ane wha's every smile was telling
  Tam had married beauty's queen.

Dearly had he lov'd the maiden,
  An' her love to him was true,
Wha's sweet vows to her cam' laden
  Wi' young hope's refreshing dew.

Lang they lived as lovers should do —
  Baith were faithfu', baith were kind,
An' whate'er a husband could do
  For a wife to Tam was join'd.

Round their hearth sat bairnie's smiling,
  Ane on ilka parents' knee,
Ev'ning's weary hours beguiling,
  Till sleep laid them 'neath her key.

And each morning saw them cheerie
  As the lark when frae the sky
Night withdraws her veil, an' pearly
  Dew-drops on our flowerlets lie.

But life's morn may rise unclouded,
  Yet ere noon hope's dreams may be
In the depths o' darkness shrouded,
  Ne'er again joy's light to see.

So it fared wi' Tam — his morning
  Tho' it shone serene an' fair
His wife's hopes wi' flowers adorning,
  Wore ere noon the drunkard's glare.

Customers he had galore o',
  Wha to Tam had ne'er done ill,
Ithers to his Mary's sorrow
  Paid their shoen aye o'er a gill.

Tam, as we hae seen, was cautious,
  But what will not habit do?
Why teach men to drink that nausious
  Stuff that's ken't as '*Mountain Dew*'?

Aften 'neath some dark foreboding
  Wad he in an ale-house sit;
Conscience wi' her arrows goading
  Him frae ruin's haunts to flit.

An' he aften vow'd that never
  Wad he throw his time away
O'er the stuff that's sure to sever
  Peace an' those wha own its sway.

But resolves are sometimes broken,
  As the maist o' men can tell;
And his drouth is ill to sloken
  Wha wi' Bacchus deigns to dwell.

An' so Tam tho' aft resolving
  To avoid drink's banefu' snare,
Saw ilk night the glass revolving
  Round the board, an' had his share.

Gently wad his wife before him
   State what drunkards had to dree,
An' wi' kindly words implore him
   Frae their fetid haunts to flee.

An' Tam saw to his heart's sorrow
   That his trade was in the wane,
And aft wish'd nae coming morrow
   E'er wad see him drunk again.

But Jack Screwcork dealt in spirits,
   In the neeborhood o' Tam,
Wha's companions proved their merits
   Nightly o'er a social dram.

And as soon as they were seated,
   Tam was quickly sent for, wha
When he to a gill was treated,
   Was aye sure to ring for twa.

And ere they wad part the bottle
   They sae aft had fill'd wi' *dew*,
Weel could prove that nae teetotal
   Loon was sitting wi' the crew.

Ev'ning saw them blythe together
   Midnight saw them in a brawl,
Morning tore frae ane anither
   Things that scarcely hame could crawl.

An' their hames, O! ye wha roun' a
   Drunkard's fireside ne'er hae been,
Little dream what sorrows crown a
   Hearth where sic like creatures lean

There a wife may be seen weeping
   Wha wi' smiles should hae been dressed;
There a husband on her heaping
   Oaths, that prudence ne'er express'd.

There sit children wae and weary,
　　Wi' their hearts opprest wi' care,
Wha wad hae been blythe and cheery
　　Had their sire escaped drink's snare.

Misery prevades the dwelling,
　　Love and her delights a' flee,
Whene'er drink the dirge is knelling
　　In it, Industry! of thee.

An' Tam's house ance warm and cheerie
　　Soon became the haunt o' woe,
Which its inmates, wae and eerie,
　　Could nae frae their bosoms throw.

Trade forsook his shop an' gave him
　　To the fiends remorse and shame;
While unhonoured bills maist drave him
　　To seek peace in death's cauld hame.

Need cam', an' his house wi' sorrow
　　He was forc'd 'neath bonds to lay;
Yet wad aft frae neebors borrow
　　What wad his neist reck'ning pay.

Aften wad his wife implore him,
　　While tears trinkled frae her e'e,
Ne'er again to see before him,
　　Drink, man's direst enemy.

An' his bairns ance bien and happy,
　　Wad look volumes in his face,
That tauld weel how deep the drappie
　　Had them cover'd wi' disgrace.

An' his conscience aft wad urge him
　　Ne'er to swallow drink again,
Lest dispair wad some day scourge him
　　On to break life's brittle chain.

But, alas! too soon were broken
    His resolves, for night aye saw
Tam slip out his drouth to sloken
    Wi' whae'er gaed him a ca'.

Hope the bosoms had forsaken
    O' his wife and weans, for they
Fear'd that reason ne'er wad waken
    Him to flee drink's potent sway.

But nane can the future measure,
    Clouds o'er noon may cast a gloom,
Yet ere night we may with pleasure
    See the sun our vales illume.

Oft in youth's gay sunny morning
    We may bend to folly's power.
Yet ere noon may be seen scorning
    What yields age a cheerless dower.

An' Tam stood a famous sample;
    O, how resolution can
Push us boldly on to trample
    On whate'er degradeth man.

Weel, ae night Tam an' some cronies
    Met to drown what they ca'd care.
And a set o' rougher Johnies
    Ne'er assembled onywhere.

Roun' the crack gaed, but the glasses,
    To the brim filled quicker flew,
Till their brains teem'd wi' the gases
    That arise frae 'Mountain Dew'.

Then hame frae ilk mind evanished,
    Madness ruled their wasted hours,
Till dawn frae man's sight had banished
    Moon an' stars, night's fairest flowers.

Still the drouthy loons insisted
    For mair drink, an' Screwcork he
Knowing they were na strait fisted
    Gave what they required wi' glee.

Day wore on, yet still together
    Sat the thoughtless erring crew,
Laith to part wi' ane anither
    While a fu' stoup was in view.

But exhausted nature, spite o'
    A' the whisky man devours,
Must succumb before the might o'
    Sleep an' her resistless powers.

So ere mid-day on the table
    Some o' them had laid their heads.
Ithers tried, tho' quit unable,
    To steer hamewards to their beds.

Ithers inly cursed their folly,
    An' the drink that kept them where
Joy subsides in melancholy,
    And hope in the fiend despair.

Time wi' winged speed swept o'er them
    When they met to test drink's powers,
But neist day time calmly bore them
    Into minutes that seem'd hours.

Yawns, an' faces sair distorted
    In profusion they display'd,
Ere night saw the fools escorted
    To their hames beneath her shade.

Thus time in his course sees changes
    That the stoutest hearts appal,
An' what mair ane's hame deranges
    Than the stuff men whisky call.

Tam's house stood a sad example
  O' what wives and weans maun dree,
If on self respect they trample
  Wha their leading stars should be.

Ance within its wa's presided
  Peace an' plenty, much loved pair,
Wha its happy inmates guided
  Frae the haunts that harbour care.

Ance a mither's smile benignly
  Frae her bairns kept care awa,
While a father's toil wad kindly
  Keep the wee things trig an' braw.

Ance nae morn on the horizon
  Colours mair inchanting threw,
Than Tam hourly cast his eyes on
  When his fireside was in view.

Then his wife an' weans were happy
  As a' wives an' weans maun be,
Wha's protectors shun the drappie,
  An' the haunts o' vice ne'er see.

But Tam's palmy days had vanished
  In a cloud o' mental gloom,
That had frae his wife's face banished
  What he ance lo'ed dear — its bloom.

Words she spake not when he entered.
  Sighs an' tears alone reveal'd
What within her bosom centred,
  As he thro' the dwelling reel'd.

Quickly to his bed he stoited,
  Heedless o' his Mary's tears,
Tho' the blossoms he had blighted
  That adorned her byegane years.

Sleep, ah! precious are the treasures
    Fools an' wise men reap in thee,
For whae'er life's 'bout gait measures
    Find a rich solace in thee.

Toil within thy couch of roses
    Reaps the joys that he ne'er tastes
Wha in sloth's foul arms reposes,
    Or o'er drink a moment wastes.

An' Tam soon in sleep's embraces
    Had his sair-worn carcase laid;
But his haggard face wore traces
    O' what drink o' him had made.

A' night lang foul imprecations
    Frae his lips in torrents fell,
Fruits o' the impure libations
    That he drain'd in Screwcork's cell.

Sleepless lay his wife beside him,
    Tears aft drapping frae her een,
Praying common sense wad guide him
    To be what he ance had been.

Wi' the morn she rose resolving
    In her mind what she would do,
As she had been lang resolving
    To bid Tam for aye adieu.

But her bairns! what wad come o' them
    Were she to forsake their hame?
Want, drink's fruit! she fear'd wad throw them
    In the gulf o' sin and shame.

Morning pass'd while she sat musing
    On the years that were awa,
Ere Tam was by ane seen boozing,
    Or on ale-houses wad ca'.

As she ponder'd, frae his hammock
   Up he gat, the drucken beast,
An' threw frae his nauseous stomach
   A scotch pint o' waste at least.

'O! my head, what will come o' me,'
   Thus he whimper'd to himsel',
'Madness soon I fear will throw me
   If this lasts in horror's hell.

'Curse that drink an' him that made it,
   Ay an' him that tak's it too,
Aften I can say I've pray'd it
   Might be keepit frae my view.

'O! my heart, dear wife forgi'e me,
   I confess I've gane far wrang,
And I hope ye'll live to see me
   Flee my reckless course ere lang.'

'Ay! sic tales ye aft hae tauld me,'
   Mary said, 'but I'm mista'en
If death's arms disna infauld me
   Ere your thirst for drink is gane.

'Thae twa days ye hae been drinking.
   Now your pouches hae run dry,
Or wi' drucken sots I'm thinking
   Ye wad soon to Screwcork's fly.

'Little dream'd I when we married
   Sic a fate wad hae been mine,
Or ye wad to doom's-day tarried
   Ere I'd pledged my troth wi' thine.

'See our weans, ance bien an' happy
   As the lambkins on the lea,
Gaun in rags, because the drappie
   Ye like mair than them or me.

'O! Tam, ance I wad wi' terror
  Think on mankind's final foe,
But, tho' I may be in error,
  I now weary for his blow.

'O! your heart, there's nae heart in you.
  Or wad ye do as ye do?
Troth! ere night I'm sure to fin' you
  In a changehouse roaring fou.'

While she spoke, Tam had got seated
  His disorder'd tools amang,
But their verra sights he hated
  Ever since he had gane wrang.

On his knee his elbow rested,
  On his loof he had his chin,
While remorse frae his heart wrested
  Sighs that told the peace therein.

On the floor his eyes were fixed,
  But it was a vacant stare,
An' within his breast were mixed
  Thoughts that border'd on despair.

Phantoms dark an' grim before him
  Flitted in profusion dire,
Wha wi' deevil's glee waved o'er him
  Fragments o' love's broken lyre.

Starving weans were mingled wi' them,
  Led by ragged weeping wives,
Wha had na a bit to gi'e them,
  Tho' it wad hae saved their lives.

Close beside them stretch'd a river,
  On wha's muddy shores were spread
Germes o' the soul-writhing fever
  That lays drunkards wi' the dead.

And when its dark waves roll o'er them,
   There unpitied they lie,
Not one living to deplore them —
   Not one breathe for them a sigh.

Suddenly as if loud thunder
   On his humble hame had broke,
Tammie, to his Mary's wonder,
   Frae his reveries awoke.

Quickly frae his seat he started,
   Firm resolve stood in each eye.
And his verra gait imparted
   To his wife, a change was nigh.

Frae the door in haste he hurry'd;
   And his wife resolved to see
Tho' wi' dark forbodings flurried,
   Where his resting place wad be.

But to her astonished sense,
   To Screwcork's he bent his way,
And the dreaded consequences
   She fear'd in a bumper lay.

Back wi' heavy heart she trudged,
   To a cauld an' hungry hame,
In which misery was lodged,
   Wi' the woes I needna name.

By her hearth she sat not knowing
   What on earth she next should do,
While tears frae her dark eyes flowing,
   Bath'd her cheeks wi' grief's sad hue.

But she hadna lang been musing,
   When Tam back frae Screwcork's came,
Where instead o' sitting boozing,
   He had brought some whisky hame.

Soon as he the door had steekit,
　　To his wife's astonished view,
A big bottle o' Glenlivet,
　　Frae his apron forth he drew.

This was something new to Mary,
　　Wha had ne'er seen Tam before
Condescend a gill to carry
　　Out o' ony changehouse door.

Down sat Tam, a reaming bottle
　　Firmly corkit on his knee,
While aroun' its sparkling throttle,
　　O' whipcord a yard tied he.

'I'll now to the gibbet send you,'
　　Tam said, 'where ye will remain
Till the cunning rogues wha vend you
　　See me in their shops again.

'Many years ye hae reign'd o'er me,
　　But my bonds are broke, and I
Will for evermore abhor thee,
　　And thy loathsome orgies fly.

'O! my wife, forgi'e, forgi'e me,
　　Lang I ken I hae gane wrang,
But frae this hour ye'll ne'er see me
　　Drucken thoughtless things amang.

'I mysel', an' sair I rue it,
　　Lang hae mixed wi' sic a core,
But should I again e'er do it,
　　May day dawn on me no more.'

'O! Tam, if I could believe you,'
　　Mary said, 'I here declare,
I wha had resolved to leave you
　　Will wi' pride your troubles share.

'Deep in ruin's bog we're lying,
  But we yet, if ye do weel,
May, the pangs o' want defying,
  See love cheer ance mair our biel.

'See our bairns, how weel ye lo'ed them
  Ere to vice ye bent the knee;
An' wi' what delight ye woo'd them
  To be what a' bairns should be.

'Now they may for aught ye're caring
  Headlang into ruin drive,
For while vices' fruits ye're sharing
  Can it be that they will thrive?

'See how braw your frien' Jock Strachan
  Keeps his weans, because ye ken
No a man in a' the clachan
  Can him coax a doit to spen'.

'Then Tam follow his example,
  Keep the vow ye say ye've ta'en,
An' ye yet wi' scorn will trample
  On John Maut and a' his train.'

'Say nae mair,' said Tam, 'nae morrow
  E'er will rise on thee again,
That will for my faults see sorrow
  Thy loved face wi' tear-drops stain.'

Up he gat an' soon suspended
  The bright bottle to a ring;
Tho' his wife scarce comprehended
  What this whim o' his wad bring.

'Ye'll hang there,' he bawl'd, 'untasted,
  While life flutters in my veins,
O! that I saw lang hae wasted
  On sic trash my hard won gains.

'In that dusty neuk I place thee,
   Spiders an' their webs amang,
For its my turn to disgrace thee,
   Wha has me disgraced sae lang.

'Get the breakfast ready, Mary,
   To the kintra I'll repair,
Where till ev'ning I will tarry,
   Nature's balmy breath to share.

'An' while I'm awa', O! dinna
   For a single moment think,
My dear Mary, that I canna
   Keep mysel' apart frae drink.

'In Screwcork's again I never
   Will a moment mair be seen;
O! were I rid o' the fever
   I gat in this house yestreen.'

An' soon Mary on the table
   Had the spoons an' dishes laid,
An' did a' that she was able
   To throw Tam's faults in the shade.

O! thought she I'll yet be happy,
   Tam means to reform his ways,
And if he but flees the drappie
   We will yet see better days.

Breakfast pass'd but Tam ate little,
   His inside was na in tune
To let any kind o' victual
   His sair parched throat get down.

Water was the only craving
   That his stomach had, an' he
On it plenty o't was laving,
   Whisky! to get rid o' thee.

Down the street he gaed despising
   At the door to cast a glance

Where Screwcork wi' words enticeing
    Aft led him a sorry dance.

Frae the town at length he wander'd
    To imbibe the caller air,
Where the silv'ry streams meander'd
    Amang fields an' meadows fair.

O'er him day's bright star was spreading
    Light on mountain and in vale;
Round him flowers an' trees were shedding
    Their sweet odours on the gale.

Birds in ev'ry grove were singing,
    Lambs were bleating on the lea;
Milkmaids frae the faulds were bringing
    What the wisest drink wi' glee.

Tam beheld wi' heart elated
    The rich treasures of each field,
An' rued sair he'd e'er been fated
    To haunt dens that poisons yield.

But his weary frame compell'd him
    To his ain hame to return,
Where his wife wi' joy beheld him
    What was in the bottle spurn.

And soon in his bed he rested,
    Midnight's balmy fruits to reap,
Free o' horrors, unmolested
    By the dreams that murder sleep.

Morning cam', an' Tam resolving
    To redeem his long lost name,
Rose, within his mind resolving
    What wad be his noblest aim.

Soon his kit he had in order,
    Soon a shoe was on his knee,
And nane on the Scottish border
    Had a blyther face than he.

A' that day he wrought, and never
    Was he in a better mood,
To knock soles an' heels together,
    For his ain an' neebors' gude.

At the bottle while he glanced,
    But what it contain'd he ne'er
Thought on, wha was affianced
    The teetotal badge to wear.

Weeks, an' months, an' years roll'd o'er him,
    But his resolutions he
Kept unsullied, an' they bore him
    Far frae vice an' misery.

And, O! what a consolation
    Was it to his weans an' wife
To see what an alteration
    Temperance mak's o' ane's life!

Now 'twas plain his hale ambition
    Was aroun' his hearth to see
Young and auld in the condition
    That a' decent folk should be.

And ere lang the snug bit dwelling
    That years 'neath a bond had lain,
Loud the dirge o' drink was knelling,
    And unfetter'd stood Tam's ain.

Men o' character now sought him,
    For reform in him they saw,
An' the wark they daily brought him
    Kept his house baith bien an' braw.

Years roll'd on, yet still the bottle
    He had fill'd wi' 'Mountain Dew'
Hung suspended by the throttle,
    Just as he had left it — *fou*.

Not a drap had been extracted
    Frae it since the day that he

Frae resolve the vow exacted
    That drink ne'er again he'd *pree*.

'Ay! a coward,' aft said Tammie,
    'Fears to look in a foe's face;
I ne'er had but ane — the dramie —
    And I've brought him to disgrace.

'By the neck he is suspended,
    Where I hourly can him see,
An' when my career is ended
    There I trust the rogue will be.

'Aft when simmer's flowers were shedding,
    Their sweet fragrance on the air,
For his sake hae I been spreading
    In my hame the weeds o' care.

'An' when wintry winds were blawing,
    An' my wife an' weans were cauld,
Hae I for the stuff been ca'ing
    That soon mak's men poor an' auld.

'But I call'd on resolution
    To my aid, an' since that day
I hae been in the condition
    That mak's winter's months seem May.

'Then let man arise an' banish
    Frae his board his direst foe,
An' soon frae his hearth will vanish
    The fell source o' a' his woe.

'O! may ye wha hear my story
    Caution's sacred laws embrace,
An' ye may see before ye
    Without fear a foeman's face.'

Thus spoke Tam, an' may we treasure
    His advices till we know
How drink's banefu' fruits to measure —
    They have yielded man but woe.

The Third Class Train

Ye toil-worn weavers now rejoice,
   Your woes will soon be o'er,
The railway people are resolved,
   You'll walk on foot no more.
Too aft to Glasgow ye hae run,
   On weary feet to see,
Your masters ere the warehouse shut,
   To lift your hard won fee.

But now you may auld *Seestu* leave,
   When clerks their watches draw,
To see how lang time has to run,
   Ere they their locks may thraw;
Yet be in time to lift the pence,
   Your toil deserves sae well,
Which will, ye ken, frae your firesides,
   Want for some days expel.

An' brawly do these worthies ken,
   While you sit on your looms,
Ye aften say that want o' air,
   Your vera health consumes;
So they, in their considerate zeal,
   In studying your good,
Hae made these trains just for *your* sakes,
   As airy as they could.

While they wha every day enjoy
   The benefits o' air,
Are pent up in close carriages,
   Men's fetid breaths to share.
As for the rains and drifting snaw's,
   That on your heads may fa'
Ye're sae weel used to sufferings,
   Ye'll mind them nought ava.

It has been said by thoughtless men,
 That thieves gang there to steal;
But railway owners brawly ken,
 A tradesman does fu' weel,
That can his railway ticket pay,
 Tho' he has nought behin',
An' thieves care little for a pouch,
 In which there's naething in.

An' tradesmen's pouches hae sae lang
 Been curst wi' emptiness,
That thieves ken better than to try
 Their hollowness, I guess,
An' now I think ye'll a' allow,
 A railway is a thing,
Which will to the poor toiling man,
 Sweet consolation bring.

The sky he for a canopy, ·
 Will get wha on them goes;
While on his head most copiously,
 Will fa' baith rains and snows.
Wi' thieves and sic tag-rags he'll mix,
 The drunkard's oaths must face;
Because his purse cannot afford,
 To buy a dearer place.

Ah! sordid gold, why do you still
 Man from his kind divide?
Must fortune's gifts still steel the heart,
 With adamantine pride?
The poor, the toil-worn poor we know,
 The varied wealths supply,
That glitter on the lordly brow,
 Or in his boudoirs lye.

Yet on his wretched, haggard form,
 Falls no consoling smile,
From him who cannot live without
 His unremitting toil.

No! like a felon he is drawn,
    Alang the railway train;
Tho' in his breast may lodge a heart
    That deeply feels the stain.

Farewell my friends, the time may come
    When worth alone will be
The measure of men's consequence,
    Whate'er be their degree.
Till then may all our actions prove,
    That virtue may be found,
Beneath *our* roofs, tho' vice should still
    In lordly ha's abound.

A Braid Glow'r at the Clergy

By Ane *not* o' Themsel's

Preserve us a'! what will come next
    To edify the nation?
Of late we've had a fertile text
    Replete wi' defamation.
Intrusionists ha'e made a din
    That mak's our ears yet tingle,
And Non-Intrusion thinks it sin
    Wi' sic a crew to mingle,
                        By night or day.

Within this lan' I'm verra sure
    Full fifty sects are striving,
To keep the fools frae Satan's power
    That hell-ward straught are driving;
But, as for me, I canna tell
    Which ane o' them's the right ane,

That can the clouds o' sin dispel,
   That's sae apt to benight ane
                In open day.

For, since the learned disagree,
   Can it be thought surprising
Tho' ony plain-bred chiel like me
   Should sometimes be surmising—
That underneath a bigot's cloak
   Should sometimes lurk the notion,
That naething plays sae gude a joke
   On mankind as devotion
                On ony day.

They speak about the poor, as tho'
   O' them they aye were dreaming;
But few o' them their faces show
   Where poortith's tears are streaming.
And O! the poor man's fauts are seen
   Thro' optics telescopic,
While wealth's misdeeds they test wi' e'en
   That's ought but microscopic.
                Alack the day!

Debauchery wi' palsied frame,
   Wi' pious priests may mingle
If they suspect she keeps at hame
   What mak's the pouches jingle.
But Virtue they ne'er recognise
   In rags — so we must grant it,
It is the *coat* the birkies prize —
   The *carcase* they ne'er want it,
                If poor nae day.

He — whom the knaves pretend to preach —
   The poor man's friend was ever,
For which proud priests dared him impeach,
   'For mercy had they never.'
And were he on the earth again,
   The poor man's cause defending,
Our State-paid priests — these 'rogues in grain' —
   Their garments would be rending
                Wi' grief that day.

Had he to tyrants bent the knee,
    And shunn'd the poor man's dwelling,
Ilk priest o' high and low degree
    His train wad ha'e been swelling —
But justice from his lips, like dew,
    On parched flowers descended,
And Truth's unconquerable hue
    He wi' his maxims blended
                In his ain day.

He told the proud ones of the earth
    That wealth ne'er reach'd that Heaven
Where cares and sorrows ne'er had birth,
    Nor souls with anguish riven.
A camel through a needle's e'e,
    Its journey will be wending,
As easily he said, as he
    That's rich will be ascending
                To bliss *yon* day.

'Tis poverty gives priests alarm —
    Wealth is their only study —
Ye seldom see them arm in arm
    Wi' ony ane that's duddy.
And if ane o' their sect should dare
    The poor man's cause be pleading,
Had they the power, he soon wad share —
    What a' men hate — beheading,
                That verra day.

And nane will doubt what I ha'e said
    Wha kens ought o' the story,
How Brewster bared Truth's sacred blade,
    In spite o' Whig or Tory;
And told the toil-worn man that he
    Nor ony i' the nation,
Should for a single moment be
    Subjected to starvation,
                No, not one day.

He preached unto the poor, and they
   Were with his words delighted;
But tyrants quail'd beneath his sway,
   And from him fled affrighted;
Even armed men the church forsook!
   Where he plain truths delivered,
Nor dared within its wa's to look,
   Whar wi' sic pain they quiver'd
                 Ae Sabbath day.

He urged on men the rights to guard
   That ane and a' should cherish,
And fame, at least, would them reward,
   Who in Truth's cause dared perish;
While those who would oppressors prop
   Would find, whate'er their station,
Their names, without ae ray of hope,
   Consigned to execration
                 Thro' endless day.

His foes — man's foes — beheld with fear
   The progress he was making,
And inly vow'd they for a year
   Would ha'e nae cause for quaking;
They'd stop his mouth, they'd put him down,
   They'd o'er him hang 'suspension;'
And doubtless if they durst, wad stown
   Frae him his place and pension,
                 As sure's its day.

Then pious Presbyteries met
   The subject to consither,
And try if persecution's net
   They could get roun' a brither.
They told him Major So-and-so
   Wi' him was much offended,
For daring to the poor to show
   What his class ne'er intended
                 They'd see nae day.

'Nay more, in Glasgow, we're aware,'
  They said, 'ye preach'd last season
To Chartists, words, that we declare
  Smell'd horribly o' treason;
The verra soldiers shun the kirk
  On days that ye are preaching;
And had their major had a dirk,
  Your hin' en' he'd been reaching —
                    Yon awfu' day.

'Wi' Dan O'Connell, too, ye dined,
  A man that's lang been working
To get our kirk and state disjoin'd,
  Tho' it should be by Burking.
·An' weel ye ken that rascal rude
  Is doing a' he can, sir,
To prove a Catholic's as good
  As ony ither man, sir —
                    O! dool this day.

'Ye speak about the rich as tho'
  They were the greatest sinners —
But had ye common sense, ye'd know
  Frae them we aft get dinners;
An' that should steek your gab, we think,
  If onything can steek it,
An' mak you on their failings wink,
  Wha's aye sae bienly theekit,
                    Baith night an' day.

'They may get drunk, or tak' a lass —
  But then, they can afford it —
An' that man surely is an ass
  Wha wad try to record it.
Be ruled by us then, if ye're wise,
  An' shun a' Chartist Meetings,
Or ye may aiblins fin' the price
  Worth mair than their loud greetings —
                    Be warned this day.

'Lay down the sermons, we command,
    Before us on that table,
Ye preached in Glasgow to a band
    Wha think our creed's a fable —
Or, in your pulpit for a year
    Ye winna set a foot in,
To fill our soldiers' hearts wi' fear,
    Tho' we a stirk should put in
                Your place ilk day.'

Reader, ye possibly ha'e seen
    Some ill-bred curs molesting
A noble dog, whose gallant mein
    Seem'd as he thought them jesting;
At length, tired o' their yelping din,
    The noble beast leuks roun' him,
Syne lifts his leg, and frae his linn,
    Wi' squashes near-haun drowns 'em,
                In scorn that day.

Alarmed, the creatures steek their gabs,
    And hurry helter-skelter
Right belly flaught owre dykes an' stabs
    To whar they might fin' shelter;
While he whom they suppose their foe
    Scarce notices their terror,
But calmly walks about as tho'
    He pitied the error
                They made that day.

So Brewster look'd, when in his ear
    The priest-like dogmas enter'd —
But naething in the shape o' fear
    Within his bosom centr'd;
He told them that the poor man's cause
    He ever would be pleading,
As lang's within the Abbey's wa's
    The service he was leading
                In face o' day.

As for the sermons that they sought,
   He hoped they wad buy them,
And read them duly as they ought,
   And properly apply them;
Then would they learn to feel for those
   Whose toil alone produces
What furnishes baith food and clothes
   For them that for nae use is
                    On earth this day.

Amid the storm o' tongues he stood
   Serene's the sky in July,
And smiled to see the holy brood
   Behaving sae unruly;
He knew right weel the days had been
   When he would have been treated
As Calvin treated ance a frien',
   For which his name is hated,
                    Ev'n to this day.

Poor Michael Serverus, had he
   Been rather mair complying,
And to John Calvin bent the knee,
   He wadna died by frying.
But Michael thought he had a right
   To cherish his opinion
As weel as ony ither wight
   That gied the Pope's dominion
                    The gunk that day.

And he learned, sweetly to his cost —
   Calvin and his adherents,
Whene'er they had the power, could roast,
   As weel's the Pope's vicegerents.
For flaming faggots quickly turned
   His body to a cinder;
And few folk like to be inurn'd
   When in the form o' tinder,
                    Like him that day.

But what can Truth hersel' expect,
 When pious Priests assemble,
An individual to eject
 Wha's facts aft made them tremble?
Why naething; truth hersel' might ken
 That mercy's ne'er presiding
Where priests get noosed within their den
 Those wha daur spurn their guiding,
                    No not one day.

And Brewster lang may bliss the hour
 When common sense rejected
The law that gave to priests a power
 That hangmen but respected.
Our fathers bled beneath their ire,
 And he too would have tasted
The sweets of persecution's fire,
 Tho' fuel they had wasted
                    On him that day.

The dungeon and the stake, 'tis true,
 The law from them has taken,
As weel's the dreaded thumbiscrew,
 That mony a frame has shaken.
But weel we ken had they the power
 They had when Knox was preaching,
Some folk wad fin', this verra hour,
 A rack their bodies stretching.
                    Lang, lang this day.

Our Presbyterians declaim
 Against the bloody Mary —
Wha doubtless was a heartless dame
 As e'er a crown did carry;
But 'Bess' could persecution's rod
 Apply, as weel as ony,
That e'er the paths o' vengeance trode,
 Wi' Satan for a crony,
                    We ken this day.

And where was Knox's clemency
   When he proclaimed that never
Wad ane in Scotland bend the knee
   To Rome's far-famed law-giver;
Or he, within a prison's wa's
   Wad hae been thrust, for daring
To own a creed sae fu' o' flaws,
   And quite beyond repairing —
                As 'twas that day.

And while men to fanatics yield
   The destinies o' nations,
Truth's sacred fount must lie conceal'd
   Within mystifications.
And every creed we ken can boast
   Its advocates and martyrs —
Not ane o' which wad, for a roast,
   To ither creeds cry quarters,
                I'll proved this day.

'Tis Conscience tells a catholic
   That his creed is the best ane,
To circumvent the rascal Nick,
   That e'er humbug was drest in;
But conscience aye should wear a veil,
   When priests ha'e the ascendant,
Or act like ony sliding scale,
   That rogues make a dependant,
                On them ilk day.

A Catholic yet hates to hear,
   About the Reformation;
And Protestants wad wi' a cheer,
   Send papists to damnation.
In Turkey, Mahomet's the chiel
   That points the way to Heaven,
While China's sons to Fo appeal,
   When they wad be forgiven,
                Their sins this day.

Of Zoroaster Persians sing —
   A sage renown'd in story —
And Crishna, Vishnu, Bramah, bring
   All India's sons to glory;
While Afric's sons content themsel's,
   Wi' praying to their Makers,
Thro' apes and cats, wha's frightfu' yells,
   Aye gi'es their deil the shakers,
               Be't night or day.

America, again, combines
   Within it a' persuasions,
And every ane o' them opines
   The rest are mere evasions,
That ne'er will lift a single soul
   Frae out o' Satan's clutches,
Beneath wha's sway in anguish howl,
   Baith reprobates and witches,
               Far frae Hope's day.

O! when will Science ope her stores
   That ignorance may view them,
And learn, while she their depth explores,
   With prudence to pursue them.
O! when will man rise in his might,
   And rend the veil asunder,
That hides from his bewildered sight,
   The cunning rogues that plunder,
               Him every day.

Go view the teeming earth, and then
   Believe, if you are able,
The creeds that will, if they remain,
   Keep it an endless Babel.
'I'm right,' each cries, — 'the rest are wrang,
   That ha'e frae me dissented,
Wha will fin' out, ere it be lang,
   Their bodies weel fermented,
               In hell, some day.'

The hills, exulting in their might,
  Proclaim the power infinite
Who gave to being glorious light,
  And all that is seen in it.
The lightning's glance, the balmy breeze,
  His wonders are declaring;
The waveless and the stormy seas
  Alike his smiles are sharing,
                  Day after day.

You orbs that beautify the sky
  To common sense is teaching;
The truths that will not, cannot die,
  Despite their over-reaching.
Who in their pulpits tell that he
  Who made them has to grapple,
Wi' an old rebel Saint that he
  Allow'd to gie an apple
                  To Eve a'e day.

Believe them not — the veil is torn;
  See — science is progressing,
And men now look with innate scorn
  On mystery, I'm guessing.
Plain facts are stubborn things we're tauld,
  By ane* wha kent a trifle,
And now since mystery's turn'd auld,
  Her breath we soon will stifle,
                  Wi' them some day.

Let reason guide the helm, and soon
  The haven we'll arrive at
Where peace, frae 'neath her olive crown
  Nae faction will connive at.
Let ane and a' the maxim keep —
  Be sure we do to others,
What we from them expect to reap —
  And mankind will be brothers,
                  Is't sae this day?

* Burns

Anon ('Candidus')

Tee-Total Song

AIR: Willie Wabster

My wife and I, when we were wed,
　Had routh o' every thing we needit;
Our meat an' claes we duly paid,
　An' landlords visits never dreaded.
Morn cam', an' wi' the lark we raise,
　An' eidently we toiled thegither,
While blyth Content learned in our hame,
　That Industry was Plenty's mither.

Night cam', and ere we gaed to rest,
　We sat and talked o' prospects cheering;
Syne, fand in slumber's silken faulds,
　The joys to labour sae endearing.
To keep the weans baith clean and braw,
　Was aye my thrifty wifie's pleasure;
And on their buiks she'd 'targe them tight,'
　Whene'er she had a moment's leisure.

Respect did aye our steps attend,
　Our weel won gear was aye increasing:
Nae morning raise without its joys;
　Ilk e'ening brought with it a blessing.
But waes my heart that I should tell't,
　A neighbour lad set up a change house;
And O! it had been weel for me,
　If I had made it, still, a strange house.

But I, wi' mony mae gaed there,
　To hear and tell some clishmaclavers;
An cracks ye ken, without a gill,
　Are fushonless lang-winded havers.

157

And things just a beginning need,
   And sae it fared wi' our carousing,
For soon it turned frae ance a-week,
   To a hail week o' dounright bousing.

Night cam', and at the club we met,
   We aye grew fonder o' each ither;
Ilk gill fresh disputation brought,
   To settle which we ca'd anither:
Morn cam', and found us in our beds,
   Wi' parched tongues and three-fourths crazy,
Wi' bluid-red-eyes and aching heads,
   An' spirits sair depressed and hazy.

Our feeble knees, our shrunken frames,
   Our state to neighbours was revealing,
And sober men would shun our path,
   As if we had been ken't for stealing.
Wark gaed ahin'; our hard won gear
   Took wings, an' we had nought to live on,
Our credit dwindled wi' our claes,
   An' left us emptiness to grieve on.

Our bairns frae being trig and braw,
   Turned ragged, lean, an' heedless creatures;
Our vexed wives laid by their smiles,
   An' discontent possessed their features.
I saw the wreck that I had made,
   An' often cursed my reckless folly,
An' aften swore I'd be reformed,
   An' give up drinking spirits wholly.

Yet still at night I'd to the club,
   To hear what news my frien's had gathered;
Where ae glass o' the ruin *'blue'*,
   Me in the magic circle tethered.
At length remorse cam' to my aid,
   An' mildly sketched my late condition,
An' urged me to forsake the ways,
   Which lead directly to perdition.

A retrospective glance displayed,
  My wife an' weans ance bien an' happy,
Now to the brink o' ruin brought,
  Because I wadna want the drappie.
Conviction flashed upon my mind,
  A sense of shame stole slowly o'er me,
A film dropt from my eyes; I saw
  The loathsome way which stretched before me.

I fled — I sought my ruined hame,
  I called on stern resolve to aid me;
An' from that hour I ne'er touched drink,
  Nor will again till judgment fade me.

My house, again, is clean an' trig,
  My wifie has resumed her smiling,
My weans are every thing I wish,
  An' I ne'er tire o' honest toiling.
Then learn frae me, ye thoughtless fools,
  Wha think ye're happiness pursuing,
To seek it at your ain firesides,
  And strive to do as I am doing.

Edward Polin

Born in New Street, Paisley, in 1816. He worked as a weaver and a pattern-setter in Paisley. He was an active Radical in the town before he moved to Edinburgh to work for the *Edinburgh Weekly Chronicle*. In 1843 he assumed editorship of the *Newcastle Courant*, but he decided to move on to London after a few months in Newcastle. He was drowned when swimming off the Newcastle-London ship while it was at anchor.

As a Radical in Paisley, Polin was at odds with Patrick Brewster, Provost John Henderson and other 'moral force' chartists. Polin maintained that the people needed to be able to use arms if need be, not to attack the government, but to defend themselves from armed government law-enforcers. (See the *True Scotsman* for March 7th 1840 in Paisley Central Library.)

'In the Days when We Were Radicals' and 'John Henderson, My Jo' are from a spoof play *Councillors in their Cups* wherein councillors — drunk — tell all.

*

Married the Morn

AIR: *Woo'd an' Married, an' a'*

O Freedom! you're muckle deservin'
    A' the sangs that are sung in your praise,
An' me ye've been servin' an' servin'
    A' the blythest an' best o' my days;
But we ne'er prize our pleasures eneuch
    Till we see that frae us they are torn
Sae I'm singin' o' freedom the nicht,
    For I'm to be married the morn.

Married at last the morn,
    Buckled sae fast the morn;
Sae I'm singing o' freedom the nicht,
    For I'm to be married the morn.

But I trow ye, I wadna be buckled
    Gin I saw it could otherwise be,
For I ken that when twa folk are coupled
    Nor ane nor the ither is free;
But that deil o' a lassie has wiled me—
    She's witched me, as sure as I'm born;
Wi' the glamour o' love she's beguiled me,
    Sae I'm to be married the morn.

Married at last the morn,
    Buckled sae fast the morn;
Wi' the glamour o' love she's beguiled me,
    Sae I'm to be married the morn.

Already the lassie can guide me
    To gae or to come at her ca',
Then whit may I guess to betide me
    When she rules wi' baith love an' the law!
But gudesake! it canna be helpit,
    To mak' her my ain I ha'e sworn—
At the kirk a' the parish was telt it,
    Sae I'm to be married the morn.

Married at last the morn,
    Buckled sae fast the morn;
At the kirk a' the parish was telt it,
    Sae I'm to be married the morn.

An' noo, sin' it canna be better,
　　We'll e'en mak' the best o't we can;
An' sin' for a wife I maun get her,
　　She just maun get me for a man.
We dinna ken what was intended,
　　We maybe for this o't were born;
An' noo, folk, my sang maun be ended,
　　For I'm to be married the morn.

　　　Married at last the morn,
　　　　Buckled sae fast the morn;
　　　An' noo, folk, my sang maun be ended,
　　　　For I'm to be married the morn.

In The Days When We Were Radicals

TUNE: *In the Days When We Went Gipsying*

In the days when we were Radicals
　　A short time ago,
We spouted much of labour's wrongs,
　　And of the people's woe;
We held that Whigs, and Tories both,
　　Had always tyrants been,
And bawled the people's rights were lost
　　Those robbers vile between;
　　　　　And thus we ranted to the crowd
　　　　　　With pleasant wordy show,
　　　　　In the days when we were Radicals,
　　　　　　A short time ago.

With speeches bright about their right,
　　We fill'd the people's ear,
And swore their welfare still to us
　　Would be the one thing dear;

And from all selfish feeling free
   We vowed that we should stand
Unflinching thus, till we should right
   Our injured native land.
         And thus, etc.

Glass after glass we'd often pass,
   And make the rafters ring,
With roaring toasts for Radicals,
   And songs that traitors sing.
We gave the Queen, but drank the toast
   That laughed that she might be,
And pray'd that she might ne'er have peace
   Till Britons all were free.
         And thus etc.

And when we find that we shall need
   The people's aid again,
We'll soon forget that Whigs we've turn'd
   Although 'tis now so plain;
Our voices shall be raised once more
   As loud as e'er they've been,
To spout and sing our treason songs,
   And laugh at Prince and Queen.
         And thus again we'll gull the crowd
            With pleasant wordy show,
          As we did when we were Radicals
            A short time ago.

John Henderson My Jo, John

John Henderson, my jo, John,
  When first that we were frien's,
Auld time was licht upon your broo,
  You werena out your teens;
But many changin' years, John,
  Hae past sin' you were so,
An' muckle ye hae changed yoursel',
  John Henderson, my jo.

John Henderson, my jo, John,
  When we were first acquaint,
Ye werena verra meek o' min',
  Nor sic a Quaker saunt
As ye hae turned tae noo, John,
  At least in outward show;
The bible then ye caredna for,
  John Henderson, my jo.

John Henderson, my jo, John,
  I won'er what you mean,
Ye talk sae loud o' moral force,
  O' traitors, an' the Queen;
Hae ye forgot the time, John,
  Some twenty years or so
When ye made pikes at aughtpence each?
  John Henderson, my jo.

John Henderson, my jo, John,
  I think the step was wrang
That led ye 'mang the Chartist crood,
  Or sic a graceless gang;
For they, the fules, were serious,
  An' onward meant to go,
An' ye ken it wasna sae wi' you,
  John Henderson, my jo.

John Henderson, my jo, John,
    Ye turned in time tae see
That neither cash nor provostships
    The Chartists had tae gie;
You're now a Whigling Provost, John,
    But mair a Whig you'll grow,
An' you'll maybe be our member yet,
    John Henderson, my jo.

John Henderson, my jo, John,
    I'm proud indeed tae tell,
That aye whate'er the public did,
    Ye minded weel yersel';
Your nest you've snugly feather'd John,
    In spite o' frien' or foe,
An' that was a' ye bargained for,
    John Henderson, my jo.

Alex McGilvray

Born 1800 in Paisley, he lived in the town as a baker and was a member of the town council. He removed to Glasgow before 1850, where he died in 1871. The preface to his 1850 collection reads:

> Should the Reader consider the publication of the following Pieces an imposition on a discerning Public, and that it ought at least to be apologised for, he is most respectfully informed, that such is not the opinion of his very humble and obedient servant,
>
> THE AUTHOR

*

Song: Of Whig and Tory

TUNE: *Nae Luck Aboot the Hoose*

CHORUS
Of Whig and Tory we can see
Nae difference but in name;
Although their creeds may disagree,
Their drifts are a' the same.

When Whigs got in, we dream'd at last
Corruption's doom was sealed,
The wicked laws the Tories pass'd
Would soon be a' repealed:
But Whigs grow Tories when in place,
And Tories out grow Whigs;
And I can tell them to their face,
They're a' the same sow's pigs.

Nae war on sinecures they wage,
   The Debt they never heed;
Extension of the suffrage
   And vote by ballot's dead.
Of shorter Parliaments, nae mair
   We hear a single word;
And many a thing they now ca' fair
   They used to ca' absurd.

And though we Chartists they despise,
   Yet soon the day will come,
When we'll o'er selfish factions rise,
   And gar them a' sing dumb.
We hope to gi'e posterity
   The pleasant tale to tell,
We sent the Whigs to purgat'ry,
   The Tories down to hell.

Song: When I wi' the Laird did Enlist

TUNE: *Tak' it man, tak' it*

When I wi' the laird did enlist,
   A volunteer loyal and clever,
I swore fair or foul to resist
   The claims of the people for ever;
And with my sword, pistol, and horse,
   I'm still ready, willing, and able
To scatter by physical force
   The low lousy radical rabble.
      Sing fal de dal lal de lal lay, &c.

Awa' ye tax-haters frae me,
   Ye starving mechanics and artists,
Reformers of every degree,
   Whigs, corn-law repealers and chartists;
And may every curs'd reprobate
   Be soon with the devil his father,
Wha the kirk would divide frae the state,
   So usefully buckled together.
      Sing fal de dal lal, &c.

O! hing up the speech making loons,
   An' riddle them through with your bullets,
Infesting, like rattons, the towns,
   And ready to pounce on our wallets;
And try if the cat-and-nine-tails
   Can keep them content wi' their drummock,
Wha basely the corn-law assails,
   For pinching their back and their stomach.
      Sing fal de dal lal, &c.

What were the land-owners to do,
   Wha now in their carriages caper,
And live a' so het and so fu'
   Were victual and land to be cheaper;

Nae doubt it would better the poor,
   And mak' them more happy and healthy;
But wha' such a change would endure,
   When made at the cost of the wealthy?
      Sing fal de dal lal, &c.

Success to our yeomanry band,
   The bold volunteers o' our country,
Prepared at the word o' command,
   To die in defence o' the gentry:
With Wellington, Lyndhurst, and Peel,
   And a' the conservatives noble,
The whole, who by powder and steel,
   Are willing to keep down the rabble.
      Sing fal de dal lal, &c.

An Address

DELIVERED BY A CERTAIN GALLANT GENTLEMAN
TO THE CONSERVATIVE ELECTORS OF PAISLEY

CRAVING THEIR SUFFRAGES TO ENABLE HIM TO REPRESENT
THEM IN PARLIAMENT.—1835

> In all he said or did, he therefore
> Could always give the why and wherefore.
> Ghost of Butler, *Author of Hudibras*

Ye Tory electors of Paisley, give ear,
And my declaration attentively hear!
Before you I now as a candidate stand,
With the greatest *submission* your votes to *demand:*
For, if true to your principles, where can you find
A candidate better cut out to your mind?
Return me your Member, and I'll do my best
To have some of you plac'd on the sinecure list;
At least, I assure you I'll do my endeavour,
By voting aright, to obtain such a favour.
For well are our rulers aware of the fact,
That those whom they pension remain at their back;
And whether their conduct deserves praise or blame,
'Tis puff'd to the skies, and defended by them.

I own I'm attach'd to the great Duke and Peel,
Who would govern the nation by bullet and steel;
I'm a strong measure man, and I ever will be—
Abuses, and so forth, I never could see.
I'm true to my Order, King, country, and God;
A lover of war — if conducted abroad; —
For, believe me, a war tends to check the increase
Of all the disturbers of order and peace;
And likewise affords to our junior gentry,
Commissions and posts at the cost of the country.

With regard to the Church, now, I know it is said,
That profession is faith, and that preaching's a trade.
Perhaps it is so; but I'm sure you will grant
The Church, as established, we cannot well want.
Our priesthood, provided by Government pay,
Teach passive submission to Government sway,
And manage the rabble, whom none else can lead,
To bow to their measures, and toil for our bread;
And hence the last drop in my veins I will drain,
The union of Church and of State to maintain.

I never have heard a good argument yet
Against the amount of our national debt!
'Twas contracted to put down the rabblement's reign,
And the rights of crown'd heads to defend and maintain.
Besides, it secures to our interests a host,
Who succumb to our rule without pension or post.

The duties on coffee, tea, sugar, and snuff,
Tobacco, *et cetera*, can ne'er be enough,
For these can be wanted. I'd also maintain
The duties on cattle, cheese, butter, and grain.
We should all mind the landlords and farmers at hand,
And keep up the rents of our own native land;
Nor depend upon self-seeking strangers to serve us,
Who, just as it suits them, may feed us or starve us.

Besides this, the wages which labour commands,
Depends on the outcome obtained from our lands;
Hence farmers, and lab'rers, and tradesmen, all should
Unite to maintain our high prices for food.
'Tis said that our armies at home and abroad,
While at peace with the world, are a mere useless load;
But I ask, with submission, would peace long exist,
Would the laws be obeyed, were the army dismiss'd?
The Chartists at home, and our old foes abroad,
Soon would ride o'er our old institutions rough shod!
God help this poor country, with all her resources,
When once we adopt such Republican courses.

Attach'd to the army, since I was a strippling,
Of course, I contend for the strictest discipline;
I know that civilians object to the Cat,
As a relic of barbarous ages, and that.
But, gentlemen, this mode of army correction
Is solely applied to those born to subjection;
Forbid it, just heaven, it should e'er be applied,
In the slightest degree, to a gentleman's hide!
Ah, no! and I'd henceforth have these sympathisers
Leave matters of this kind to better advisers.

With regard to the navy, our famed wooden walls,
If we dare to curtail it, Britannia falls;
Let it guard our blest shores with our banners unfurl'd,
The wonder of nations, and dread of the world.
Low Democrats say, that for this our taxation,
Drives yearly some thousands to die of starvation;
If true, we deplore it; but surely the knaves
Would prefer to die freemen, than live to be slaves?
Hence — better for all — keep our fleets in repair,
Than die the vile serfs of the great Russian Bear.

With regard to Septennial Parliaments; why,
I believe that just now there's a mighty outcry;
Some wish them abridged to one year, some to three;
But the slightest reflection should lead us to see,
That the very best men we could possibly get,
Ere he learn'd half his work might be hurl'd from his seat.
Depend on't, the business of mere legislation
Requires long experience, and vast application.
The man is not born who could half understand
In three, or in six years, the laws of the land; —
The thousands repeal'd and again re-enacted,
With new portions added, and portions subtracted;
And learn how to lay on a plausible tax,
So adapted as only to fall on the backs
Of the labouring millions — a delicate job
To cozen and pillage the great grumbling mob—
No gentleman, either, would choose to appear
On the hustings, soliciting votes, every year;
And, as a reward for his service and trouble,
Get nothing — excepting the howls of the rabble;

As once I found out, when, besides hoots and groans,
They pelted my body with brickbats and stones;
And, what was yet worse to a man in his senses,
I lost the election — my time — and expenses!

With respect to the franchise, I think it too low;
But now being law, we had best let it go;
But to lower it further, is quite to abuse it,
And take it away from the class that can use it;
Or render its usefulness not worth a groat,
For the rabble will swamp every gentleman's vote.
What nonsense to give to the class who can't thole us,
A legal and permanent power to control us?
A class, too, the scum and refuse of the state,
Who from poverty's depths curse the rich and the great;
A class only meant, by our King and our God,
To fight for our int'rests at home and abroad.
Give them the franchise! why, 'tis tempting our ruin
And paving the way to our utter undoin'.

I'm a friend to the negro; but, tutor'd to serve,
Were he cast on the world, he would doubtlessly starve;
The trials of life are to him all unknown;
In the name of *humanity*, let him alone!

Of late we have heard, without any just cause,
A mighty outcry rais'd against the game laws;
It must be apparent, to him who reflects,
That a man owns the beasts that he feeds and protects.
Should we cancel this law, then they next would demand
To have all things in common, our cattle and land.

To reply to all questions this meeting demands
I am here, and I put myself in your hands.
By voting for me, you will show your just sense,
Which is of itself a complete recompense;
Not to talk of the here-before hinted intention,
Of greasing a few of your palms with a pension.
To conclude, dear electors; I hope from my soul
You may all have your health to appear at the poll.
Till the canvas is over, be active and fervent,
And I'll soon have the honour of being your *servant*.

Song

TUNE: *Laird of Cockpen*

What diel has gane wrang with the true holy kirk,
Which th' Clergy themselves are prepar'd now to *burke*;
'Tis only of late that the priesthood we saw
Defending the kirk as establish'd by law.

A short time ago they were loud in their call
To get kirks, where no kirks were wanted at all;
But wrangling and fighting, more power to acquire,
They've leap'd from the frying pan into the fire.

The law now appears too indulgent for them,
And like other gamblers they're playing a game:
The power of the patron they wish to put down,
A popular shop to set up of their own.

The march of improvement they cannot withstand,
Unless they can use by the law of the land,
The faggot, tar barrel, the gallows, and sword,
And burn, hang, and butcher in name of the Lord.

Oppressive as monarchs and statesmen may be,
Yet to live under them is to live and be free,
Compar'd to the freedom the priests would alloo,
If history, or even the bible, be true.

For lucre and power, in all ages and climes,
The clergy have stoop'd to the basest of crimes;
Allow them the power that they wielded of yore,
And error and terror they yet would restore.

Red-hot persecution they yet would renew,
Resort to the torturing boot and the screw;
A trait in their character cannot be seen,
To differ a shade now from that it has been.

They say they appear as the servants of peace,
And such they may be while their flocks they can fleece;
But if ye resist their imperious will,
The *soul* they would d-mn, and the body they'd kill.

Opposing the laws of both reason and man,
B—g, Ch-lm-rs, and C-ndl-sh appear in the van;
Wee Johnny, whose *bell* put him wrang in the skull,
With all the old women they've manag'd to gull.

'Bout leaving the kirk tho' they made a great roose,
To bully the Government into their views,
Yet plenty are left, in the midst of the stour,
To pocket their stipends and stick to the Wh-re.

To mankind the bones of contention they throw,
The seeds of disunion, of hatred and woe;
Their cool-blooded, inhuman, monstrous deeds,
Are just of a piece with their humbugging creeds.

If rid of the Clergy, the whole human race,
With th' image of Deity stamp'd on their face,
Would soon be united in harmony sweet,
And lovingly meet, as all brothers should meet.

Peter Notman

Born in Paisley in 1818. Brown's *Paisley's Poets* does not supply information on Notman's life other than that the poet's father was a cowfeeder in the town remembered by many as someone who in the summer took holidaymakers down to Largs, Saltcoats and other resorts in his caravan. The father died when Peter was fifteen. The poet's sons settled in Canada.

When 'Lines on Mechanism' appeared in 1840 there was in fact great unemployment and poverty in Paisley. The third last line of the poem was therefore inappropriate, and a footnote to that line read 'At present trade is dull'.

*

Lines on Mechanism

Tremendous wheels at work, robust in form,
Their mighty motion awes, vast labour's done.
The care of Engineman is aye employed
About the engine of the noisy house,
Where he doth watch the wheels from morn till night;
Aye cleansing parts and oiling them, and e'en
Augmenting fire against the constant waste.
The steam's begun, as now the Engineman
With slumbers sweet refresh'd has timeously
Up got to work, prepar'd for careful toil,
And endeth not until the stopping work
Has warn'd each one to leave the dinful place.
Then he retires his vigilant eyes to rest,
And so enjoys through night most calm repose
From toil and noisiest occupation.

And more than this, each morn he riseth up,
In early time resuming pointed work.
Bright metal works, all shining and all smooth,
In movement regular, (bathed in streams of oil)
Impressive to the eye and ear, working
In Artists' varied form of motion.
Renumeration this for mental toil,
And more, still more enlarg'd is the reward:
Vast quantities forth come of weaving thread,
Of snowy hue and every size, well twin'd
With work both great and wonderful, with which
Our looms are fill'd, our lays are made to move,
By which our bodily wants are all supplied.
Is not love due and wond'ring praise to bright
Mechanic genius, for such display of ART?

James Fisher

Born Glasgow, 1818, he worked as a foreman in a calico printers in Barrhead, then after working some time in Manchester, he returned to Scotland and settled in Kilmarnock, 'where he acted as schoolmaster for sixteen years, under Lord Ashley's Act relative to the education of under-age workers in printfields'. He bought *The Soulis Tavern* in Kilmarnock, and after Fisher had some success with a play, *Tam Raeburn, or the Ayrshire Hermit*, his place became the haunt of local theatre people.

While at Barrhead he edited *The Barrhead Minstrel* and produced his *Poems and Songs* of 1842. The Pollokshaws racecourse of Fisher's poem was on the estate of Sir John Maxwell of Pollok.

*

The Queer Folk in the 'Shaws

I thocht untae mysel' ae day, I'd like tae see a 'Race',
For mony other lads like me had been tae sic a place;
Sae up I gat, an' wash't mysel', put on my Sunday braws,
And wi' a stick intae my han' I started for the 'Shaws.

My mither tichtly counsell'd me, before that I gaed oot,
Tae tak' good care, an' min' my e'e wi' what I was aboot.
Said she, 'Ye may be trod to death beneath the horse's paws;
An' min' ye, lad, the saying's true — "There's queer folk in the
    'Shaws".'

The 'Races' pleas'd me unco weel — gosh, they were gran' to see;
The horses ran sae awfu' swift, I thocht they 'maist did flee.
When they cam' near the winning-post — haith, siccan lood huzzas;
Ye wad ha'e thocht they'd a' gaen daft — the queer folk in the
    'Shaws.

A bonnie lass cam' up to me, an' ask'd me for a gill;
Quo' I, 'If that's the fashion here, I maunna tak' it ill.'
She wiled me owre intil a tent, and half-a-mutchkin ca's;
Thinks I, my lass, I see it's true — There's queer folk in the 'Shaws.

The whisky made my love to bleeze, I fan' in perfect bliss,
So I gripp'd the lassie roun' the neck to tak' a wee bit kiss;
When in a crack she lifts her nieve, an' bangs it in my jaws —
Says I, 'My dear, what means a' this?' — There's queer folk in the
    'Shaws.

A strappin' chiel cam' forrit then, an' took awa' my lass;
Misca'd me for a kintra loon, a stupid silly ass.
Says I, 'If I've done ony ill, just let me ken the cause' —
When he made his fit spin aff my hip — There's queer folk in the
    'Shaws.

Arous'd at last, I drew my fist an' gied him on the lug,
Though sairly I was worried for't by his big collie dug;
It bate my legs, it bate my arms, an' tore my Sunday braws —
And in the row I lost my watch — wi' the queer folk in the 'Shaws.

The police then cam' up to me, and haul'd me aff to quod —
They put their twines aboot my wrists, an' thump'd me on the road,
An' gart me pay a guid pound-note e'er I got oot their claws —
Catch me again when I'm ta'en in wi' the queer folk in the 'Shaws.

W. C. Cameron

Brown (Vol. 1, p. 436) states that he 'cannot supply much information' about the poet. He records that the copy of Cameron's *Mall Jamieson's Ghost* that he owns has in pencil on the first page: 'A curious poem — queer ideas — written by a fireman in Backhall Factory — a coarse fellow is the author.'

*

Epitaph

Here lies wee Jamie Bruckleb---ks,
   Wi' naething on but the shirt;
Ae day when drinkin' a capfu' o' yill,
   Death knocket him down i' the dirt.

Sair did he spurtle an' battle for breath,
   For he wasna prepared for his doom;
He ettled to pray, but auld grim death
   On his wun-pipe clappet his thum'.

Through life he gaed wi' coals an' stanes,
   Now the cuddy's extinct and the graith is selt;
The grave and the worms got his skin an' banes
   And Pate got his tackety shoon and *felt*.

Anon

Memento Mori

INSCRIBED ON A TOMB STONE

When you look on my grave,
And behold how they wave —
The Cypress, the Yew, and the Willow —
You think 'tis the breeze
That gives motion to these —
'Tis the laughter that's shaking my pillow!

I must laugh when I see
A poor insect like thee
Dare to pity the fate thou must own;
Let a few moments slide,
We shall lie side by side,
And crumble to dust, bone for bone!

Go weep thine own doom!
Thou wert born for the tomb,
Thou hast lived like myself but to die;
Whilst thou pity'st my lot,
Secure fool thou's forgot
Thou art no more immortal than I!

Robert Clark

Born in Castle Street, Paisley, in 1811. After a brief schooling he became a weaver's drawboy when he was six, teaching himself to read and write at night school. In 1836 after his wife died he emigrated to America for five years. Returning to Paisley he worked as a weaver again until economic depression made him decide to return to America. The ship on which he sailed in 1847 was wrecked in crossing, all passengers being drowned. Clark was then 36 years of age.

*

Song

AIR: *Cam ye by Athol*

O come, dearest lass, let us stray through the glen alane,
    Though the sun's sinkin' doun, dinna be eerie;
See yon mild moon rising, sweet to enrich the scene,
    Nature seems blyther when, Jeanie, thou'rt near me.

Come by yon birken shaw, come, lassie, come awa,
    Wild flowers are blooming, and warblers sing cheerie,
Peace and contentment reigns over our hills and plains,
    Wars now are fled, ever dismal and dreary.

O Jeanie, the flow o' thy saft waving yellow locks,
    Peace frae my bosom hath ta'en awa, fairly;
But, would ye, smiling, gie that lillie han' to me,
    O then how happy I'd be late and early.

In yon rural cot by the side o' yon mossy rill,
    There we might live, and enjoy life serenely;
For, in the morning, wi' collie I'd tak the hill,
    And at the gloamin return to my Jeanie.

O sweet are the heathery hills o' Caledonia,
    Dear are the deeds o' her sons sae victorious;
But, a' the laurels bright won on the field o' fight,
    Dear lovely Jeanie to me is more glorious.

Tho' wealth or grandeur, should aye frae our dwelling be,
    Joyfu' contentment would keep us aye cheerie;
For, while I'm blest wi' health, poortith wi' doolfu' e'e,
    Dear lovely Jeanie, would never come near me.

H

David Brown

Born in High Street, Paisley, 1826. Was a weaver, then keeper of the West End Reading Room. He died in the burgh poorhouse in 1886.

*

When Johnnie was gi'en to the Weeting his Mou'.

AIR: *Toddlin hame*

When Johnnie was gi'en to the weeting his mou',
Our dwalling was scantily plenish'd enow:
A slave to the whisky, for *it* but he wrought,
And how to get mair o't was a' that he thought;
As he staucher'd but, and he staucher'd ben,
And what he was doing did scarce ever ken.

The laird wad aft grumble and gloom for his rent;
The young anes be girning and greeting for want;
Their backs were ill clad, and their bellies were toom;
But Johnnie gat fou', and 'twas a' ane to him:
For he staucher'd but, and he staucher'd ben,
Regardless o' landlord, o' wife, or o' wean.

O mony a lang night, wi' a tear in my e'e,
Nae fire in the grate, and the bairn on my knee,
I've waited on Johnnie when out at the dram;
For ne'er could I rest till I saw him come hame:
Then he'd staucher but, and he'd staucher ben,
Or sleep but to wake and cry, 'whisky' again.

My heart was sae broken, sae dreary my life,
It seem'd as a' Nature and I were at strife;
The vera day-light that gave a' besides glee,
Dawn'd only to darken creation to me;
As he staucher'd but, and he staucher'd ben,
I aften maist wish'd my existence wad en'.

But Gude bless the Temp'rance, for ay since he join'd,
My life is sae alter'd — my Johnnie's sae kind;
Our bien house and bairns are his pleasure and pride,
Contented he sits at his ain ingle side.
Now I'm happy but, and I'm happy ben,
And think but to smile on the days that are gane.

O wae upon liquors, the strong and the sma',
An' wae upon whisky — the warst o' them a';
They ca' it a *spirit* — weel sae they may do;
And mony ha'e found it an *evil* ane too;
But we'll banish the fiend to his ain wicked den,
Syne plenty and peace o'er the warld shall reign!

William Kennedy

Born 1799 'a native of the North of Ireland' (Brown, Vol. 1, p. 327), he became editor of the *Paisley Advertiser* from 1826 until 1828, when he moved to London. He became British Consul at Galveston, Texas, publishing in 1841 *The Rise, Progress and Prospects of the Republic of Texas*. He retired to Britain in 1847, settling in London where he died two years later in 1849.

*

Och! While I Live, I'll Ne'er Forget

Och! while I live, I'll ne'er forget
   The troubles of that day,
When bound unto this distant land,
   Our ship got under weigh.
My friends I left at Belfast town,
   My love at Carrick shore,
And I gave to poor old Ireland
   My blessing o'er and o'er.

Och! well I knew, as off we sailed,
   What my hard fate would be;
For, gazing on my country's hills,
   They seemed to fly from me.
I watched them, as they wore away,
   Until my eyes grew sore,
And I felt that I was doomed to walk,
   The shamrock sod no more!

WILLIAM KENNEDY

They say I'm now in Freedom's land,
    Where all men masters be;
But were I in my winding-sheet,
    There's none to care for me!
I must, to eat the stranger's bread,
    Abide the stranger's scorn,
Who taunts me with thy dear-loved name,
    Sweet isle, where I was born!

Och! where — och! where's the careless heart
    I once could call my own?
It bade a long farewell to me,
    That day I left Tyrone.
Not all the wealth, by hardship, won
    Beyond the western main,
Thy pleasures, my own absent home!
    Can bring to me again!

Joanna Picken

Joanna Picken was born in Edinburgh in 1798. She was the daughter of one of Paisley's then best-known though later forgotten poets, Ebenezer Picken. Unlike her father or her brother David, who also became highly regarded, Joanna's work was never collected. She contributed to the *Glasgow Courier* in 1828, and after emigrating to Canada in 1842, in Montreal she contributed under the pen-name 'Alpha' to the *Literary Garland and Transcript*. She worked as a music teacher until her death in Montreal in 1859.

*

The Death-Watch

Tic, tic, tic!—
I've a quarrel to pick
With thee, thou little elf—
For my heart beats quick
As thy tic, tic, tic,
Resounds from the old green shelf.

When I cease to weep,
When I strive to sleep,
Thou art there with thy tiny voice;
And thoughts of the past
Come rushing fast,
E'en with that still, small voice.

'Tis said thou hast power,
At the midnight hour,
Of death and of doom to tell;
Of rest in the grave,
That the world ne'er gave,
And I love on this theme to dwell.

Dost thou call *me* home?—
Oh! I come, I come;
For never did lone heart pine
For a quiet berth
In its mother earth,
With a deeper throb than mine.

Then tic, tic, tic—
Let thy work be quick;
I ask for no lengthen'd day—
'Tis enough, kind one,
If thy work be done
In the merry month of May.

For birds in the bowers,
And the blooming flowers,
Then gladden the teeming earth;
And methinks that I
Would like to die
In the month that gave me birth.

An Auld Friend wi' a New Face

A queer kind o' lott'ry is marriage—
Ye never ken what ye may draw,
Ye may get a braw hoose an' a carriage,
Or maybe get nae hoose ava.

I say na 'tis *best* to be single,
But ae thing's to me unco clear:
Far better sit *lane* by the ingle
Than thole what some wives hae to bear.
    It's braw to be dancin' and gaffin'
    As lang as nae trouble befa'—
    But hech! she is sune ower wi' daffin'
    That's woo'd, an' married, an a'.

She maun labour frae sunrise till dark,
An' aft tho' her means be but sma',
She gets little thanks for her wark—
Or as aften gets nae thanks ava.
She maun tak just whatever may come,
An' say nocht o' her fear or her hope;
There's nae use o' lievin' in Rome,
An' tryin' to fecht wi' the Pope.
    Hectored an' lectured an a',
    Snubbed for whate'er may befa',
    Than *this*, she is far better aff—
    That never gets married ava.

Oh, then come the bairns without number,
An' there's naething but kisses an' licks—
Adieu then to sleep an' to slumber,
An' the Pa is as cross as twa sticks.
A' the week she is makin' their parritch,
An' turnin' auld frocks into new;
An' on Sunday she learns them their carritch,
Puir wife! there's nae rest-day for you.
    Warkin' an' fechtin awa,
    Saturday, Sunday, an' a';
    In troth she is no that ill aff
    That never gets married ava.

In nae time the cauld an' the wheesles
Get into your family sae sma',
An' the chincough, the croup, or the measles
Is sure to tak' aff ane or twa.
An' wi' them gang the puir mither's joys,
Nae comfort seems left her ava—
As she pits by the claes an' the toys
That belanged to the wee things awa'.

Doctors an' drugs an' a',
Bills an' buryin's an' a',
Oh surely her heart may be lichter
That never was married ava.

The married maun aft bear man's scornin',
An' humour his capers an' fykes;
But the single can rise in the mornin',
An' gang to her bed when she likes;
An' when ye're in sickness and trouble,
Just tell me at wha's door ye ca';
It's no whar ten bairns mak' a hubble,
But at *hers* that has nae bairns ava.
    Usefu', an' peacefu', an' cantie,
    Quiet, an' canny, an' a',
    It's gude to ha'e sister or auntie
    That never was married ava.

A wife maun be humble an' hamely,
Aye ready to rise, or to rin;
An' oh! when she's brocht up a family,
It's then her warst sorrows begin;
For the son, he maun e'en ha'e a wife;
An' the dochter a hoose o' her ain;
An' then, thro' the battle o' life,
They ne'er may forgather again.
    Cantie, an' quiet, an' a',
    Altho' her bit mailin be sma',
    In truth she is no that ill aff
    That never gets married ava.

It's far better still to keep single
Than sit wi' yer face at the wa',
An' greet ower the sons and the dochters
Ye've buried and married awa'.
I fain wad deny, but I cannae,
Altho' to confess it I grieve,
Folks seldom care muckle for grannie,
Unless she has something to leave.
    It's nae that I seek to prevent ye,
    For that wad be rhyme thrown awa';
    But, lassies, I pray, just content ye,
    Altho' ye're ne'er married ava.

William Graham

Born in County Down in 1816, he came with his parents to Paisley when he was about six. He worked as a drawboy then as a weaver until 1835, when he joined the British Legion and sailed to Spain. After a year there he was jailed for five months on a convict island, he and eighty-five others having laid down their arms 'because their pay was in arrear and they were not furnished with their full rations of beef, bread, and wine etc.'. Sent back to England, Graham worked 'at coal work' for four months in Newcastle before returning to Paisley and resuming work as a weaver.

*

My Ain Toun

TUNE: *Johnny's Grey Breeks*

It has been my fate to roam of late,
    And many a gate I've tried my skill;
In search of trade I journeyed,
    Observing man and manners still.
And this I say, from Tweed to Tay,
    Or all the way that I did roam,
I never found a place or town
    Could match the one I started from.
        I'll lo'e thee, yet, my ain toun,
            Though fortune's sun blinks seldom there;
        I'll no forget my ain toun—
            Its merry lads and lasses fair.

In Glasgow town I first sat down,
  And said I there would make my home;
Mid noisy glee and jollity
  I'd live content, no more to roam.
To work I fell, and, to dispel
  My sombre thoughts, I humm'd a song;
My mind in verse I did rehearse,
  And thus the chorus still went on:
    I'll lo'e thee, yet, &c.

Auld Reekie's fame, like meteor gleam,
  Goes through the world far and wide;
The Modern Athens is a name
  Of which its sons may boast with pride.
Yet take the mass, the populace,
  The toiling class, 'tis them I'd test,
And, to my mind, they're yet behind
  The thinking men that's farther west.
    I'll lo'e thee yet, &c.

To pleasant Ayr I did repair,
  And mang its fairest scenes did dwell;
Great Rabby Burns, his home was there,
  Whom few could equal, none excel.
I roam'd at will, by bank and rill,
  Yet Fancy still behind would lag,
Where Tannahill his song did thrill,
  Where 'Watty' he reformed his 'Meg'.
    I'll lo'e thee yet, &c.

To Dumfries next I took my way,
  I paced its streets in mournful mood—
I view'd its buildings and its quay,
  Where Nith doth pour its limpid flood;
But oh, my heart was in the part
  Where winding Cart does gently glide,
Or, dashing, spin o'er rocky linn,
  Wi' honest worth on ilka side.
    I'll lo'e thee yet, &c.

Was't Paisley's Cart which caused the smart?
   Perhaps in part it was the cause;
Or was't her sense? intelligence
   Should still be prized, and still it was.
Or was't the thrill which Tannahill
   Or Wilson gave, which caused regret?
I blush to say, that fair Jeannie
   To me had more attractions yet.
     For her I lo'ed my ain toun,
       And every street where she had been,
     I welcome noo my ain toun,
       Since I am welcomed by my Jean.

Alexander Borland

Born in Bridge Street, Paisley, in 1793. He was a weaver and a pattern-designer before becoming a shawl manufacturer. His partner in this having absconded to America with all the money and stock, Borland was jailed for six weeks for thereafter intercepting and opening his partner's letters from America to relatives in Scotland. Borland became an agent for the Clydesdale Bank in 1844 before setting up in business as an accountant. He died in 1858.

*

The Brown Cleuk On

Some chaps are ne'er at rest
But in crouds o' lasses prest,
A' drest up in their best,
    Wi' their kirk claes on;
But I pleasure greater find,
And a mair contented mind,
Wi' a lassie true and kind
    Wi' a brown cleuck on.

My father, honest carle,
Cries, 'Oh! this weary warl','
My verra heart does harl,
    For joys he gets nane;
Yet weary though it be,
It never fashes me,
When my comforter I see
    Wi' her brown cleuk on.

Our gentry that are great,
And who ride in pompous state,
May thank their lucky fate
    For the dress they ha'e on;
Yet though in state they move,
But cauldrife is their love
Compair'd wi' my sweet dove
    When her brown cleuk's on.

My mother she cries, 'Son,
Thou art lucky soon begun
Wi' lasses for to run—
    It's ruin's road ye're on;'
Though I halflins think she's right,
Yet hersel', when young, at night
She could hide a lad frae sight,
    Wi' her brown cleuk on.

There's some, nae doubt, do cry,
'Tis her dress that takes my eye,
When me she passes by,
    Wi' her silks and satins on;
Sic clavering tongues may cease,
For what's the silk pelisse
To a gloaming walk in peace
    Wi' her brown cleuk on.

Even my grannie cries, 'Beware!'
Maist afraid her ringlets fair
Will my youthfu' heart ensnare,
    When her gala dress is on.
But has my grannie seen
The smiling charms o' Jean,
When she gaes out at e'en
    Wi' her brown cleuk on?

I heard my uncle tell,
When wi' a lass himsel',
When he heard the *ten-hours'-bell*,
    He for hame hied on;
A' sic whims I've laid aside,
For till morning I can bide,
When my lassie's at my side
    Wi' her brown cleuk on.

Anon — 1853

The Honest Farmer's Declaration — printed as back page, p. 24, of the *New Paisley Repository*, No. 3, Saturday January 1st 1853. Printed by A. Barry, 25 High Street, published by Wm. Anderson, 60 High Street, Paisley, 'of whom may be had the Philosopher's Stone of Business Figures'. This latter publication was advertised in the magazine as 'a new system of arithmetic' for working out business calculations: 'We confess ourselves astonished at the cleverness, simplicity, completeness and perfection of the plan.' The advertisement for the business calculator states that 'The author may be consulted on curious, difficult and quirty questions, addressed to him care of the publisher.' Perhaps this author, a Paisley weaver called David Stirrat, had a hand in the composition of the lettrist typographical poem overleaf.

The sentence that spirals from the centre of the top field 'We canna want the rot' and its answer from the bottom field 'It pays the rent' (the tit to the ewe) refers to articles in prior issues of the magazine which claimed that local farmers were able to make more money from compensation on their blighted potato-fields than from the sale of the potatoes if they remained healthy.

*

The Honest Farmer's Declaration

PRINTED VERBATIM FROM HIS OWN MOUTH

```
t o R e h T T t n a n t T h e R o t
o R e h T T t n a W a n t T h e R o
R e h T T t n a W a W a n t T h e R
e h T T t n a W a n a W a n t T h e
h T T t n a W a n n n a W a n t T h
T t n a W a n n a n n a W a n t T
t n a W a n n a C a n n a W a n t
n a W a n n a C e C a n n a W a n
a W a n n a C e W c C a n n a W a
n a W a n n a C e C a n n a W a n
t n a W a n n a C a n n a W a n t
T t n a W a n n a n n a W a n t T
h T T t n a W a n n n a W a n t T h
e h T t n a W a n a W a n t T h e
R e h T T t n a W a W a n t T h e R
o R e h T T t n a W a n t T h e R o
t o R e h T T t n a n t T h e R o t
```

```
t n e R e h T h e R e n t
n e R e h T s T h e R e n
e R e h T s y s T h e R e
R e h T s y a y s T h e R
e h T s y a P a y s T h e
h T s y a P t P a y s T h
T s y a P t I t P a y s T
h T s y a P t P a y s T h
e h T s y a P a y s T h e
R e h T s y a y s T h e R
e R e h T s y s T h e R e
n e R e h T s T h e R e n
t n e R e h T h e R e n t
```

Charles Marshall

Born Millarston, Paisley, in 1795. Educated at the universities of Glasgow and Edinburgh, he became a minister at Dunfermline in 1840. He left the Established Church with the Disruption, founding a new church in his parish with most of his congregation. He retired from the ministry in 1866, and was killed in a road accident in his eighty-seventh year, being knocked down by a cab in 1882.

*

A Poor Victim

O wae betide the yill-house,
   The curse o' Scottish lan',
The wreck o' social fellows,
   And mony an honest man.

A wooer had I, trig and braw,
   The pride o' a' the toun;
But wae's me, he's fa'n sair awa',
   A duddy, dyvour loon.
      O wae betide, &c.

His good auld mither's heart he'll break;
   He's daily breaking mine.
A gallant lad! what now? — a wreck
   O' what he was short syne.
      O wae betide, &c.

O' a' thing gude regardless grown,
   He rins in ruin's road;
That weary drink his wits has stown,
   And driven him frae God.
         O wae betide, &c.

My curse upon that barley broo,
   The source o' ev'ry ill;
I'd banish makers, sellers too,
   Had I my way and will.
         O wae betide, &c.

Stick To Your Last

What think ye o' chiels wha's conceit
   Would mend the affairs o' our nation,
Without either gumption or wit
   To govern themsel's wi' discretion?

Wha think that a' knowledge and sense
   Are wrapt up in flimsy newspapers;
And grudge neither time nor expense
   To fill their vain noddles wi' vapours?

Wha grumble — and envy the great,
   Reviling a' statesmen as jobbers;
Wha envy their betters, and hate
   A' rulers, and curse them as robbers?

Wha mak the warkshop, wi' their din,
   A perfect political hot-house;
And flee, when a saxpence they win,
   To wrangle and roar i' the pot-house?

I think they should stick to their wark,
    And haud them within their ain tethers;
Nor rin, like lowse nowt in a park,
    Rowtin' a' kinds o' nonsense and blethers.

Scotland's Curse

O weary fa' the drinkin' o't,
    The gill stoup, and the clinkin' o't;
And weary fa' the drunkards a',
    Wha canna rest for thinkin' o't.

Some twa three happy, happy years,
    My John and me hae seen.
They fled — now sorrow's scaddin' tears
    For ever blear my een.
        O weary fa, &c.

The wee short mornin' blink o' life
    Flew by in pleasure's bowers;
But drink and want, and endless strife,
    Soon wither'd fancy's flowers.
        O weary fa, &c.

Our cozie house, kail-yard and a',
    Bless'd fruit o' thrift and care,
Soon melted; — now through winter's snaw,
    We wander cauld and bare.
        O weary fa, &c.

Borne headlong to destruction's flood,
    On ruin's ragged wings,
Our bairns are fleein' — scarce a dud
    To hap the naked things.

I've clouted, darned, and stitch'd the dears,
　　Till I can clout nae mair:
Sad patches I sew on wi' tears,
　　Vile tatters wi' despair.

O mony a dreary day and night
　　I've silent borne my load;
I needna look to man for light,
　　Help, help me, gracious God.

John Wilson

Born Paisley 1785, of a wealthy merchant family. He was early taught Latin and Greek before education at Glasgow University then at Oxford. He was first an advocate, then was appointed Professor of Moral Philosophy at Glasgow University on grounds that were political, not academic. His main reputation was based on his contributions as 'Christopher North' to the Tory *Blackwood's Magazine*.

He was regarded as a major literary figure, the poet Hugh MacDonald (q.v.) writing after having obtained a meeting with Wilson, 'I came away with a heart rinin' ower wi' gratitude, pride, and love to the greatest mind I have ever met, or in all likelihood ever may meet in this world' (Brown, Vol. 2, p. 98). Wilson died in Edinburgh in 1854, and in 1865 a statue was erected in Princes Street Gardens. Wilson's poetry, including his once best-regarded narrative 'The Isle of Palms' and the sonnet 'The Evening Cloud', is cast in a moralising 'antiqued' poetic diction that makes it indistinguishable from that produced by many others of his class. The song 'Turn Ye To Me' will be familiar to some readers, and for this reason it is included.

*

Turn Ye To Me

The stars are shining cheerily, cheerily,
Horo Mhairi dhu, turn ye to me:
The sea-mew is moaning, drearily, drearily,
Horo Mhairi dhu, turn ye to me.

Cold is the storm-wind that ruffles his breast,
But warm are the downy plumes lining his nest;
Cold blows the tempest there,
Soft falls the snow there,
Horo Mhairi dhu, turn ye to me.

The waves are dancing, merrily, merrily,
Horo Mhairi dhu, turn ye to me:
The sea-birds are wailing wearily, wearily,
Horo Mhairi dhu, turn ye to me.

Hush'd be thy moaning, lone bird of the sea,
Thy home on the rocks is a shelter to thee;
Thine is the angry wave,
Mine but the lonely grave,
Horo Mhairi dhu, turn ye to me.

Anon ('B.O.P.')

The Renfrew Volunteers

TUNE: *Burns's Farewell*

While Curlers show their wonted skill,
  And Skaters swiftly glide along,
I take my pen with all good will,
  To write some verses of a song,
In praises of an heroic band,
  Whose loyalty so bright appears
That they're esteemed throughout the land
  I mean the Renfrew Volunteers.

The fifth December was the day,
  On which their loyalty was seen,
And more efficient service they
  Desired to give our gracious Queen;
In foreign lands 'midst war's alarms,
  Mars' sons will find them true compeers
With valiant hearts and willing arms
  The gallant Renfrew Volunteers.

And should they to the Crimea go,
  A-hunting of the grizzly Bear,
Those heroes will attack the foe
  And him pursue from lair to lair;
And side by side with brave allies
  Whose martial spirit never veers
Unflinchingly they'll death despise
  The daring Renfrew Volunteers.

But Oh! the parting caused much pain,
  The word Farewell made many mourn
For tender hearts could scarce refrain
  From dreading they might ne'er return.

The Father sat in grief profound,
   The Mother sought relief in tears
And wailing made the air resound
   At parting of the Volunteers.

Of lovely lasses not a few
   Appear dejected and forlorn,
And since they bade the last adieu,
   You'd think their hearts in twain were torn.
Their lovers absence they deplore
   And audibly express their fears
That perils great are yet in store
   For the brave Renfrew Volunteers.

Then let us hope that Fortune kind
   Courageously their path may tread,
And should they ever hardships find,
   That honours they may gain instead.
When Freedom shall aloud proclaim
   That Peace her vessel safely steers,
Let Justice then award due fame
   Unto the Renfrew Volunteers.

Alexander Smith

Born Kilmarnock, December 31st 1829. By 1832 his parents had moved with him to Paisley, then when he was twelve he was sent to learn his father's trade of pattern-designing in a warehouse in Glasgow. His poetry appeared in the 'Poet's Corner' of the *Glasgow Citizen* and he was favourably noticed by George Gilfillan in the *Critic* after Smith had sent Gilfillan some of his work. The play in verse, *A Life-Drama*, published in 1852 in London, attracted much critical attention, and soon went through several editions. In 1853 Smith obtained the position of Secretary to Edinburgh University, which position he held until his death from typhoid and diphtheria in 1886.

*

Glasgow

Sing, Poet, 'tis a merry world;
That cottage smoke is rolled and curled
    In sport; that every moss
Is happy, every inch of soil:—
Before me runs a road of toil
    With my grave cut across.
Sing trailing showers and breezy downs—
I know the tragic heart of towns.

City! I am true son of thine:
Ne'er dwelt I where great mornings shine
    Around the bleating pens:
Ne'er by the rivulets I strayed,
And ne'er upon my childhood weighed
    The silence of the glens.
Instead of shores where ocean beats
I hear the ebb and flow of streets.

Black Labour draws his weary waves
Into their secret-moaning caves;
  But with the morning light
That sea again will overflow
With a long, weary sound of woe,
  Again to faint in night.
Wave am I in that sea of woes,
Which night and morning ebbs and flows.

I dwelt within a gloomy court
Wherein did never sunbeam sport;
  Yet there my heart was stirred—
My very blood did dance and thrill
When on my narrow window sill
  Spring lighted like a bird.
Poor flowers! I watched them pine for weeks
With leaves as pale as human cheeks.

Afar, one summer, I was borne;
Through golden vapours of the morn
  I heard the hills of sheep:
I trod with a wild ecstasy
The bright fringe of the living sea,
  And on a ruined keep
I sat and watched an endless plain
Blacken beneath the gloom of rain.

O fair the lightly sprinkled waste
O'er which a laughing shower has raced
  O fair the April shoots!
O fair the woods on summer days,
While a blue hyacinthine haze
  Is dreaming round the roots!
In thee, O City, I discern
Another beauty sad and stern.

Draw thy fierce streams of blinding ore,
Smite on a thousand anvils, roar
  Down to the harbour bars;
Smoulder in smoky sunsets, flare
On rainy nights, with street and square
  Lie empty to the stars.
From terrace proud to alley base
I know thee as my mother's face.

When sunset bathes thee in his gold
In wreaths of bronze thy sides are rolled,
    Thy smoke is dusky fire;
And, from the glory round thee poured,
A sunbeam, like an angel's sword,
    Shivers upon a spire.
Thus have I watched thee, Terror! Dream!
While the blue Night crept up the stream.

The wild train plunges in the hills,
He shrieks across the midnight rills;
    Streams through the shifting glare
The roar and flap of foundry fires,
That shake with light the sleeping shires
    And on the moorlands bare
He sees afar a crown of light
Hung o'er thee in the hollow night.

At midnight, when thy suburbs lie
As silent as a noonday sky,
    When larks with heat are mute,
I love to linger on thy bridge,
All lonely as a mountain ridge,
    Disturbed but by my foot;
While the black, lazy stream beneath
Steals from its far-off wilds of heath.

And through thy heart, as through a dream,
Flows on that black, disdainful stream;
    All scornfully it flows,
Between the huddled gloom of masts,
Silent as pines unvexed by blasts—
    'Tween lamps in streaming rows.
O wondrous sight! O stream of dread!
O long, dark river of the dead!

Afar, the banner of the year
Unfurls; but dimly prisoned here,
    'Tis only when I greet
A dropt rose lying in my way,
A butterfly that flutters gay
    Athwart the noisy street,
I know the happy summer smiles
Around thy suburbs, miles on miles.

'Twere neither pæan now, nor dirge,
The flash and thunder of the surge
    On flat sands wide and bare;
No haunting joy or anguish dwells
In the green light of sunny dells
    Or in the starry air.
Alike to me the desert flower,
The rainbow laughing o'er the shower.

While o'er thy walls the darkness sails,
I lean against the churchyard rails;
    Up in the midnight towers
The belfried spire; the street is dead;
I hear in silence overhead
    The clang of iron hours.
It moves me not — I know her tomb
Is yonder in the shapeless gloom.

All raptures of this mortal breath,
Solemnities of life and death,
    Dwell in thy noise alone;
Of me thou hast become a part—
Some kindred with my human heart
    Lives in thy streets of stone;
For we have been familiar more
Than galley-slave and weary oar.

The beech is dipped in wine; the shower
Is burnished; on the swinging flower
    The latest bee doth sit.
The low sun stares through dust of gold,
And o'er the darkening heath and wold
    The large ghost-moth doth flit.
In every orchard autumn stands
With apples in his golden hands.

But all these sights and sounds are strange,
Then wherefore from thee should I range?
    Thou hast my kith and kin,
My childhood, youth, and manhood brave—
Thou hast that unforgotten grave
    Within thy central din.
A sacredness of love and death
Dwells in thy noise and smoky breath.

from A Boy's Poem — Part Two

The morn rose blue and glorious o'er the world;
The steamer left the black and oozy wharves,
And floated down between dark ranks of masts.
We heard the swarming streets, the noisy mills;
Saw sooty foundries full of glare and gloom,
Great bellied chimneys tipped by tongues of flame,
Quiver in smoky heat.   We slowly passed
Loud building-yards, where every slip contained
A mighty vessel with a hundred men
Battering its iron sides. A cheer! a ship
In a gay flutter of innumerous flags
Slid gaily to her home.   At length the stream
Broadened 'tween banks of daisies, and afar
The shadows flew upon the sunny hills;
And down the river, 'gainst the pale blue sky,
A town sat in its smoke.   Look backward now!
Distance has stilled three hundred thousand hearts,
Drowned the loud roar of commerce, changed the proud
Metropolis which turns all things to gold,
To a thick vapour o'er which stands a staff
With smoky pennon streaming on the air.
Blotting the azure too, we floated on,
Leaving a long and weltering wake behind.
And now the grand and solitary hills
That never knew the toil and stress of man,
Dappled with sun and cloud, rose far away.
My heart stood up to greet the distant land
Within the hollows of whose mountains lochs
Moan in their restless sleep; around whose peaks,
And scraggy islands ever dim with rain,
The lonely eagle flies.   The ample stream
Widened into a sea.   The boundless day
Was full of sunshine and divinest light,
And far above the region of the wind
The barred and rippled cirrus slept serene,
With combed and winnowed streaks of faintest cloud
Melting into the blue.   A sudden veil
Of rain dimmed all; and when the shade drew off,
Before us, out toward the mighty sun,
The firth was throbbing with glad flakes of light.

The mountains from their solitary pines
Ran down in bleating pastures to the sea;
And round and round the yellow coasts I saw
Each curve and bend of the delightful shore
Hemmed with a line of villas white as foam.
Far off, the village smiled amid the light;
And on the level sands, the merriest troops
Of children sported with the laughing waves,
The sunshine glancing on their naked limbs.
White cottages, half smothered in rose blooms,
Peeped at us as we passed.   We reached the pier,
Whence girls in fluttering dresses, shady hats,
Smiled rosy welcome.   An impatient roar
Of hasty steam; from the broad paddles rushed
A flood of pale green foam, that hissed and freathed
Ere it subsided in the quiet sea.
With a glad foot I leapt upon the shore,
And, as I went, the frank and lavish winds
Told me about the lilac's mass of bloom,
The slim laburnum showering golden tears,
The roses of the gardens where they played.

Blaavin

O wonderful mountain of Blaavin,
How oft since our parting hour
You have roared with the wintry torrents,
You have gloomed through the thunder-shower!
But by this time the lichens are creeping
Grey-green o'er your rocks and your stones,
And each hot afternoon is steeping
Your bulk in its sultriest bronze.
O sweet is the spring wind, Blaavin,
When it loosens your torrents' flow,
When with one little touch of a sunny hand
It unclasps your cloak of snow.

O sweet is the spring wind, Blaavin,
And sweet it was to me—
For before the bell of the dewdrop
Or the pink of the apple tree—
Long before your first spring torrent
Came down with a flash and a whirl,
In the breast of its happy mother
There nestled my little girl.
O Blaavin, rocky Blaavin,
It was with the strangest start
That I felt, at the little querulous cry,
The new pulse awake in my heart,
A pulse that will live and beat, Blaavin,
Till, standing around my bed,
While the chirrup of birds is heard out in the dawn,
The watchers whisper, He's dead!
O another heart is mine, Blaavin,
Sin' this time seven year,
For Life is brighter by a charm,
Death darker by a fear.
O Blaavin, rocky Blaavin,
How I long to be with you again,
To see lashed gulf and gully
Smoke white in the windy rain—
To see in the scarlet sunrise
The mist wreaths perish with heat,
The wet rock slide with a trickling gleam
Right down to the cataracts' feet;
While towards the crimson islands,
Where the sea-birds flutter and skirl,
A cormorant flaps o'er a sleek ocean floor
Of tremulous mother-of-pearl.

II

Ah me! as wearily I tread
The winding hill-road mute and slow,
Each rock and rill are to my heart
So conscious of the long-ago.
My passion with its fulness ached,
I filled this region with my love,
Ye listened to me, barrier crags,
Thou heard'st me singing, blue above.

O never can I know again
The sweetness of that happy dream,
But thou remember'st, iron crag!
And thou remember'st, falling stream!
O look not so on me, ye rocks,
The past is past, and let it be;
Thy music, ever-falling stream,
Brings more of pain than joy to me.
O cloud, high dozing on the peak,
O tarn, that gleams so far below,
O distant ocean, blue and sleek,
On which the white sails come and go,
Ye look the same; thou sound'st the same,
Thou ever-falling, falling stream—
Ye are the changeless dial-face,
And I the passing beam.

III

As adown the long glen I hurried,
With the torrent from fall to fall,
The invisible spirit of Blaavin
Seemed ever on me to call.
As I passed the red lake fringed with rushes
A duck burst away from its heart,
And before the bright circles and wrinkles
Had subsided again into rest,
At a clear open turn of the roadway
My passion went up in a cry,
For the wonderful mountain of Blaavin
Was bearing his huge bulk on high,
Each precipice keen and purple
Against the yellow sky.

Hugh MacDonald

Born Bridgeton, Glasgow, in 1817, he worked for four years as a printer in Paisley. His poetry contributions to the *Glasgow Citizen* led to his appointment to the literary staff there. Afterwards he joined the *Glasgow Sentinel*, was between 1855 and 1858 editor of the *Glasgow Times*, and for two years until his death in 1860, was literary editor of the *Morning Journal*. In addition to his poetry, his highly popular *Rambles Round Glasgow* (1854) and *Days at the Coast* (1857) remain very readable descriptions of what the area covered by this anthology looked like in the mid-nineteenth century.

*

The Trysted Hour

The moon is in the lift, love,
   The stars are twinkling pale;
The blackbird's song has ceased to wake
   The echoes of the vale.
The bat is on the wing, love,
   The dew is on the flower;
Then haste, and meet me here, love,
   It is the trysted hour.

The lily hangs her head, love,
   The daisy's closed her e'e;
The modest violet folds her leaves
   Out ower the dewy lea:
The cushat's in her nest, love,
   The nightbird leaves the tower,
Then haste and meet me here, love,
   It is the trysted hour.

Life were a starless night, love,
 A barren flow'rless lea,
A vale of grief and care, love,
 Apart from hope and thee;
Then come, thou star of life, love—
 O! leave, O! leave thy bower,
And haste to meet me here, love,
 It is the trysted hour.

For Gudesake Let's Agree

AIR: *Miller o' Dee*

Some auchteen hunder years ago,
 Man's noblest Teacher said:—
'A house divided 'gainst itsel'
 Maun sune be prostrate laid.'
Now on this text, to puir folk a'
 A sermon I wad gie;
Join hands, fling discord to the winds,
 And, Gudesake, a' agree.

The with'ring thrall of priest and king,
 We a' ower lang hae borne;
The meed of a' our care and toil—
 Insult and bitter scorn.
But had my text been borne in mind,
 Sic wrangs we wadna dree;
Their power on our discord is built,
 Then, Gudesake, let's agree.

We sow, and ithers reap the fruit;
    We weave, and ithers wear;
We're scrimpet baith in caup and cog,
    That knaves may hae guid cheer.
But were puir folk true to themsels,
    Sic wrangs we wadna dree;
'Tis discord breeds us a' our wae,
    Then, Gudesake, let's agree.

Save in a bated beggar voice,
    Our richts we scarce daur name;
Bluid-hounds they hae wiled frae our ranks,
    Ilk wae-wild heart to tame.
But were we to oursels a' true,
    Sic tools nae king wad see;
'Tis discord breeds us a' our wae,
    Then, Gudesake, let's agree.

The priest wrapt in his misty creed,
    The chainless mind may ban;
Lordlings and kings bar Freedom's path,
    And mar the weal of man.
But gi'es your hand, the day draws near,
    These nicht-birds sune maun flee;
The puir man yet shall hae his ain,
    We're learning fast to 'gree.

HUGH MacDONALD

Young Spring

Thou'rt welcome, thrice welcome, again young spring,
Wi' the bud and the bloom in your train, young spring;
　　　Wi' your streams gushing free,
　　　Like wee bairnies in glee,
Singin' blithe as they jink to the main, young spring.

Weel I mind in the dead of the year, young spring,
When Nature lay dowie and drear, young spring;
　　　When the snell norlan' breeze
　　　Gar'd us creep round the bleeze,
How our hearts langed to see you appear, young spring.

Now your firstling, the snawdrap, 's in bloom, young spring,
A wee morning star in the gloom, young spring;
　　　'Midst cauld wintry climes,
　　　Lone pointing to times
Of sunshine, of sang, and perfume, young spring.

Sune the celandine stars will unfold, young spring,
And the coltsfoot wee circlets of gold, young spring;
　　　Sune the violet's blue e'e
　　　'Neath the hedgerows we'll see,
And the gowans thick spangling the wold, young spring.

The mavis lilts blithe in the glen, young spring,
And the lark soars in sang 'yont our ken, young spring;
　　　While the wudmouse fu' fain,
　　　'Neath the grey lichened stane,
Keeks in joy frae its dark winter den, young spring.

Thou hast buskit the lone hazel shaw, young spring;
Wi' catkins it's tasselled fu' braw, young spring;
　　　And the saughen-bush gay,
　　　In its siller array,
Sheds a gleam o'er the dark waterfa', young spring.

Duncan McFarlane McNeil

Born Renfrew 1830. Worked as a weaver's drawboy in Paisley before being apprenticed to a baker, at which he became a foreman in Richmond & Sons, Moss Street, Paisley. The 'drawboy' was a weaver's assistant. The Rev. Alexander Wallace, writing of Paisley shawls and plaids and the drawboys' part in their manufacture, wrote:

> Great skill and ingenuity were required in the production of these. The drawboy had his part, which he performed with great nimbleness, by drawing down (hence his name) a certain number of slender cords, which raised the threads of warp, under which perhaps no fewer than ten shuttles were driven with various coloured wefts, to form the lovely floral design. Drawboys were frequently so much in demand that the town-crier went round ringing his bell at certain stages, and giving notice to all and sundry of the urgent need . . . There were drawgirls as well as boys, but they all went by the same name. . . . By the application of the Jacquand machine to shawl weaving, and to the harness loom in general, the 'drawboys' occupation was brought to an end.
>
> (Wallace, Rev. A.; *The Last of the Drawboys*, Scottish Temperance League, Glasgow; National Temperance League and Houlston & Sons, London; John Menzies & Co., Edinburgh, 1883).

*

When I was a Drawboy

In the village o' Charleston, near Paisley toun,
I there was brocht up mony years noo gane roun',
When plides were in vogue, an' the weavin' was thrang,
And the swing o' the 'lay' was aye heard wi' a bang.

The click o' the shuttle, an' whirr o' the wheel,
The tramp o' the treadles, an' swish o' the 'deil',
The shout tae 'draw't up' or the notes o' a sang,
Were heard a' aroun' as ye steppit alang—
   When I was a drawboy.

Some guid folk were in it, an' that is quite true;
Some bien folk were in it, but o' them mighty few;
But they a' had the knack baith to speak an' discuss—
'Bout religion an' politics they made a big fuss.
At Union Street corner, what disputes took place!
Till some wid turn red an' some white in the face.
I've thocht aft sin' syne, an' it isna a joke,
That they were funny bodies, the Charleston folk—
   When I was a drawboy.

On Mondays in thae days the looms made nae din,
For the 'lay' was at rest wi' the hard 'pookin' pin';
They were a' their ain masters — they hadna a boss—
Some played at the bullets, some played pitch-and-toss.
Nae police tae fash them or roar in their lugs,
Some had great cock-battles, an' some foucht their dogs;
And whiles at the en' o't, the truth for tae tell,
The principals aft had a battle themsel—
   When I was a drawboy.

What noise an' rinnin', and O! what dispute,
When a meetin' was ca'd, and the drum was sent oot!
When a Causeyside magnate wid prices reduce,
There was rinnin', an' stumpin', an' muckle abuse;
An' his effigy hung up 'tween twa mid-room lums,
Wi' his belly filled fu' o' tar'd ravelins an' thrums—
What shots they fir'd intil't till late in the nicht,
An' then it illumed the hale street wi' its licht—
   When I was a drawboy.

But that has a' gane noo for mony a year,
And the click o' the shuttle you'll scarcely noo hear;
The 'tail' and the 'simple', the 'lashes', and a',
Wi the 'deil' and the drawboy, hae pass'd clean awa',

And the place noo looks better than what it did then;
And may it be better in women and men,
And healthier, and cleaner, and happier too,
Than when the first 'lash' and first 'simple' I drew—
   When I was a drawboy.

The Three Elders

It fell upon a winter nicht, three elders of the free
They met into a tavern to ha'e a wee bit spree,
So first they fill'd ae gill, and syne they fill'd anither,
About the matters o' the kirk they a' discuss'd thegither.

Chorus
 So they fill'd the glass—anither glass—
  And aye they coup'd it aff,
 And at the ane wha us'd them best
  The made a geer and laugh.

Quoth John unto the ither twa, the last ane I was at,
I'll lay my life, my brethren, ye'll no guess what I gat:
I made a prayer sweet and big, wi' a face sae lang and sma',
They gied me wine, and ham and eggs, before I gaed awa.
   So they fill'd the glass, &c.

O aye, quoth Will, it's very true, I was sent for the ither
            nicht,
And when I rapt they op't the door, losh me, I got a fricht;
There were beef, brandy, rum, and wine, a' raw'd upon the
            table,
And they made me pray and eat as hard as I was able.
   So they fill'd the glass, &c.

A bairn they wanted christen'd, they would leave it a' to me,
For nane o' them were members, nor didna want to be;
When the meal was done, and grace weel said, I on the floor
did staun,
When the guidwife fu' slyly slipped five shillings in my haun.
So they fill'd the glass, &c.

But Watty sat and naething said, for he was auld i' the horn,
But mony a thing like that he's seen sin' for elder he got on,
But aye he cried, my brethren, the stoup again is toum—
That's only three gills the piece, we've no got richt begun.
So they fill'd the glass, &c.

So the stoup was fill'd anither time — aye owre and owre
again—
The word was never mention'd yet about them steppin'
hame;
So they sat, and sat till morning, until it sounded twa,
And then they stagger'd up and said, I think we'll gang awa.

But they fill'd the glass — anither glass—
And they did pray to God,
He would be kind, and mercy show,
And help them on their road.

Auld Watty

Auld Watty cam' owre the brae yestreen,
I wonner'd ava what the body could mean;
I saw him aye glint, and speak o' my een,
When tittlin' wi' my mither.
They speer'd at my father, my father was snell,
He slipped awa, and I heard him tell,
I'se let the lassie please her sell,
Gin she may like anither.

He rubbed his cheeks till like the rose,
His specks he tane frae aff his nose,
I'm sure a bowle o' peasmeal brose
     Would answer'd the body better.
He glinted, and squinted, for blin' was he;
He smirked, and smacked, and glower'd at me;
He stammer'd, and speer'd gin his bride I would be—
     Wi' silks and braws I would glitter.

Poor body, he seemed to be in a fix,
His shanks they rattled just like twa sticks,
I could ha'e gi'en the body his licks—
     He micht my granfather been.
He said he had siller and lawn fu' plenty,
A guid house and hauding, and ilka thing denty,
And when 'twas my pleasure I could gang and jaut aye
     To places I never had seen.

I said, rin awa, ye're a silly auld man,
I winna tak ye wi' yer gear an' your lawn—
Nae, haud aff, gae wa', dinna grip at my haun—
     Wi' yer a' I winna tak' thee.
My mither she flate, and sadly misca'd me,
The body he pray'd, and tried to uphaud me;
He said I was bonnie, and loud did aplaud me,
     But I cried, gae wa' frae me.

The poor auld bit body, he downward did bow,
And poud out a ring, and purse shining fu',
Saying, this as a present I've brocht unto you,
     Consent noo, and gi'e me your haun.
I said tak' your ring, your purse, and your a',
To a bonnie blithe laddie my heart's gi'en awa',
And I'll happier be in his cot than in your ha',
     Wi' a' your gear and your lawn.

John Barr

Born Paisley 1822. A partner in an engineering firm, the first to make iron steamships in Paisley. After some years of success the firm got into difficulties, and Barr emigrated to Otago, New Zealand in 1852. There he became in time a successful farmer, his poetry in later years taking on the platitudes of the professional expatriate as 'Poet to the Caledonian Society of Otago'. He died in 1892.

*

A Twa-Handit Crack

MRS SCANDAL AND MRS ENVY

S.— Sae Robin at last has got buckled—
      It's been a sair strussel wi' Rab;
Some say he has gotten a leddy,
      An' some say a puir silly drab.
Some threep that she washes wi' gloves on,
      An' bakes wi' a veil owre her face!
Did ye ever hear tell o' the like o't?
      Losh me! It's a pitifu' case!

E.—Ay! but ithers mainteen she's nae leddy,
      But has owermuckle pride in her skin—
That her faither was just an auld carter,
      An' he was the best o' his kin.
But Robin, the sumph, is enchanted,
      For love mak's a puir bodie blin';
He'll ken something better aboot it
      At the en' o' the daft hinnymuin.

224

S.— Weel, I'se tell ye ae thing that they claiver'd,
      But didna believ't for a blink—
Some hint that she cocks her wee crannie,
      In short, that she's gi'en to the drink.
But ye maunna lat on that I tauld ye,
      For clashin' I never could bide,
An' I never speak ill o' my neebors—
      That's kent thro' the haill kintra-side.

E.— They blaw 'twas an' unco fine waddin',
      Wi' ilka thing graun' an' genteel,
For they borrow'd Miss Skirlin's piano,
      An' syne rumbl'd thro' a quadreel.
They had siller forks set at the supper—
      They micht ha'e been daein' wi' less;
But they werena their ain, I can tell ye—
      Whaur they cam' frae ye brawly can guess.

S.— Did ye hear hoo puir Rab was affrontit?
      At carvin' a turkey he'd strive,
But he flang doon the knife in a passion,
      An' yokit to rug an' to rive.
The stuffin' cam' oot like plum-parritch
      When Robin the legs o't wad thraw;
An' he roar'd — 'Gude be here! yer fine turkey
      Has never been guttit ava!'

E.— Do ye ken gin it's true she's pock-markit?
      Yet what aboot that tho' she be?
They say that her mither cried 'Herrin','
      But that maun be surely a lee.
Hoots! I never could bear to hear clashin',
      An' never was gi'en till't mysel'—
Ye'll be gaun to the kirk, Mrs Scandal—
      Weel, there's the first clink o' the bell!

Rise Oot Your Bed

Rise oot your bed, ye worthless wretch,
　　The sun's far in the lift,
I never kent a drunken man
　　That e'er cam muckle thrift;
See, I've been up since morning grey
　　Amang the dirt and weet,
It taks it a', I weel I wat,
　　To gar the twa ends meet.

O, woman, will ye haud your tongue,
　　My throat is like to crack,
Fling here my breeks, they're at the fire,
　　Hung ower the auld chair back.
What time did I come hame yestreen?
　　It was a fearfu' nicht;
For Guidsake gie's a nobbler,
　　'Twill maybe put me richt.

O weary on your nobblers,
　　Your drinking, and your splores,
And weary on your toun exploits,
　　Amang your drunken cores.
Ye'll sure be in the newspapers,
　　And that ye'll see ere lang,
They needna say Tam Maut is dead
　　As lang's ye're fit to gang.

Noo steek your gab, ye've said eneugh,
　　And what ye've said's no true,
A pretty pickle ye'd be in
　　But for mysel' and pleugh.
Let's see a glass, or haud your tongue,
　　I want nane o' your strife,
'Tis pity ye've got sic a man,
　　And I've got sic a wife.

And wha's the warst ane o' the twa,
　　Ye'll maybe tell me that?
It sets ye weel to lie up there,
　　And see me dreepin' wat,

Wi' fechting 'mang the sharney kye,
    'Mang glaur up to the kuits,
Wi' scarce a sark upon my back,
    My taes clean oot my buits.

O swear awa, just swear awa,
    Ye canna bear the truth;
Ye'll what? ye'll rise and tak your nieve
    And gie me ower the mouth:
But, Guidsake, here comes Craigielee,
    Let's a' oor fauts conceal;—
'O come awa, ye're welcome here,
    Our Johnnie's no that weel.'

Tam Maut

Drunken Tam Maut's gane awa' to the toon,
His sense and his siller in liquor to droon,
And he winna come back till he's in the blue deils,
Seein' cats and red monkeys wi' spurs on their heels:
When drunken Tam Maut gets ance on the spree,
He'll fecht wi' the wind, or he'll fecht wi' a flee,
He'll roar, curse, and swear, without sense or shame,
And he caresna a feg for his wife or his hame.
Then he'll roar out for drink to slocken his drouth,
Wi' his teeth set on edge, and the foam at his mouth,
Then he'll dance roun' the room wi' a whoop and a yell,
But that's reckoned naething when Tam's on the gell.
His breakfast is whisky, his dinner's the same,
And he taks it for supper, to smother his shame;
Then he lies in his bed like a lump o' deid clay,
And he roars out for drink by the first screigh o' day.
As his senses gang oot, then the deevil comes in,
And ye'll ken its Tam Maut by his roarin' and din;
There's a croud at the door for they're turnin' him oot,
And he lands in the dirt as he's wheelin' aboot.

Noo drunken Tam Maut has gane hame to his wife,
He has broken her heart and embittered her life;
But what cares Tam Maut for man, wife, or wean,
He has noo dune his warst, and his judgment is gane.
Noo he'll rage through the house like a bull in a ring,
Then he'll sit down and greet, then he'll jump up and sing;
Then he'll gang to his bed, but he'll no sleep a wink,
For his brain is on fire wi' the fumes o' the drink.
Noo he'll jump oot o' bed, swear the deil's in the house,
Tho' its naething ava but the squeak o' a mouse;
But there's deil eneugh there when Tam's in it himsel',
For he's noo in confab wi' the demons o' hell.
Cauld sweat noo in torrents pour down his pale face,
And 'tis plain to be seen he has finished his race;
He pants noo for breath, and he clutches his hair,
Death closes the scene, and he dies in despair.
Puir drunken Tam Maut's noo laid in his grave,
He wisna a thief, nor was he a knave;
And yet he was waur, for wi' drinkin' and strife,
He cheated himsel', and he shortened his life.

There's Nae Place Like Otago Yet

There's nae place like Otago yet,
  There's nae wee beggar weans,
Or auld men shivering at our doors,
  To beg for scraps or banes.
We never see puir working folk
  Wi' bauchles on their feet,
Like perfect icicles wi' cauld,
  Gaun starving through the street.

We never hear o' breaking stanes
  A shilling by the yard;
Or poor folk roupit to the door
  To pay the needu' laird;
Nae purse-proud, upstart, mushroom lord
  To scowl at honest toil,
Or break it down that he, the wretch,
  May feast on roast and boil.

My curse upon them, root and branch,
  A tyrant I abhor;
May despotism's iron foot
  Ne'er mark Otago's shore:
May wealth and labour hand in hand
  Work out our glorious plan,
But never let it be allowed
  That money makes the man.

When To Otago First I Came

When to Otago first I came,
    The truth I'm bound to tell,
I thocht I never would get on,
    And maist gaed by mysel'.
The season was baith cauld and wat,
    The like had ne'er been seen;
For at the end o' harvest time,
    The stooks were growing green.

Awhile I grumbled nicht and day,
    Misca'd Otago weel;
I didna blame kind Providence,
    But faith I blamed the Deil,
For bringing me sae grey a gate
    To ruin wife and wean;
I wad hae gien my very sark,
    To be at hame again.

I thocht upon my native land,
    And on the crystal streams;
And often I returned again,
    While slumbering in my dreams.
My wife, puir body, wasna weel,
    And whiles she took a greet;
The bairns were runnin' thro' the toun,
    Wi' bare and bluidy feet.

At last I plucket up my heart,
    And tackled to the wark;
I rose up wi' the mornin' sun,
    And knocket aff at dark.
Wi' toiling at the grubbin' hoe,
    I got a pickle wheat;
I'll ne'er forget as lang's I live,
    How sweet the bread did eat.

At lang and length I got a cow,
    She is yet to the fore;
I got another by and by,
    And now I've twa three score.
Ten acres was my little farm,
    That's no the way o't noo;
I wark nae mare wi' grubbin' hoe,
    But whistle at the pleugh.

So come along, my jolly boys,
    You're welcome ane and a';
Ne'er fash your thumb tho' ye be poor,
    You'll soon be bien and braw.
We a' were poor as weel as you,
    And thocht it nae disgrace;
So dinna ye doun-hearted be,
    Or rashly judge the place.

But put your shoulder to the wheel,
    You'll see how it will row;
A British heart must never yield,
    So draw a gallant bow.
Depend upon't you will succeed,
    If you'll but persevere;
When ye will bless the happy day,
    That ever ye cam here.

Daniel Richmond

Born Paisley 1812. He practised as a doctor in the town, was on the board of Paisley Infirmary for forty years, and was appointed official Medical Officer to Paisley. He was known as a Temperance advocate. He died in 1885.

*

Subject Matter of the Books of the Bible

In *Genesis* the world was made by God's creative hand.
In *Exodus* the Hebrews marched to gain the promised land.
Leviticus contains the Law — holy, and just, and good.
Numbers records the tribes enrolled, all sons of Abraham's blood.
Moses in *Deuteronomy* recounts God's mighty deeds.
Brave *Joshua* into Canaan's land the host of Israel leads.
In *Judges* their rebellion oft provokes the Lord to smite.
But *Ruth* records the faith of one well-pleasing in His sight.
In *First* and *Second Samuel* of Jesse's son we read.
Ten tribes in *First* and *Second Kings* revolted from his seed.
In *First* and *Second Chronicles* see Judah captive made.
But *Ezra* leads a remnant back by princely Cyrus' aid.
The city walls of Zion *Nehemiah* builds again.
While *Esther* saves her people from plots of wicked men.
In *Job* we read how faith will live beneath affliction's rod.
And David's *Psalms* are precious songs to every child of God.
The *Proverbs* like a goodly string of choicest pearls appear.
Ecclesiastes teaches man how vain are all things here.
The mystic *Song of Solomon* exalts sweet Sharon's Rose.
While Christ the Saviour and the King the rapt *Isaiah* shows.
The warning *Jeremiah* apostate Israel scorns.
His plaintive *Lamentations* their awful downfall mourns.

Ezekiel tells in wondrous words of dazzling mysteries.
Whilst kings and empires yet to come *Daniel* in vision sees.
Of judgment and of mercy *Hosea* loves to tell.
Joel describes the blessed days when God with man shall dwell.
Among Teloa's herdsmen *Amos* received his call.
While *Obadiah* prophesies of Edom's final fall.
Jonah enshrines a wondrous type of Christ our risen Lord.
Micah pronounces Judah lost — lost, but again restored.
Nahum declares on Nineveh just judgment shall be poured.
A view of Chaldea's coming doom *Habakkuk*'s visions give.
Next *Zephaniah* warns the Jews to turn, repent, and live.
Haggai wrote to those who saw the temple built again.
And *Zachariah* prophesied of Christ's triumphant reign.
Malachi was the last who touched the high prophetic chord;
Its final notes sublimely show the coming of the Lord.
Matthew, and *Mark*, and *Luke*, and *John*, the holy Gospel wrote,
Describing how the Saviour died, His life, and all He taught.
Acts prove how God the Apostles owned with signs in every place.
St Paul in *Romans* teaches us how man is saved by grace.
The Apostle in *Corinthians* instructs, exhorts, reproves.
Galatians shows that faith in Christ alone the Father loves.
Ephesians and *Philippians* tell what Christians ought to be.
Colossians bids us live to God and for eternity.
In *Thessalonians* we are taught the Lord will come from Heaven.
In *Timothy* and *Titus* a bishop's rule is given.
Philemon marks a Christian's love, which only Christians know.
Hebrews reveals the Gospel well prefigured by the law.
James teaches without holiness faith is but vain and dead.
St Peter points the narrow way in which the saints are led.
John in his three epistles still on love delights to dwell.
St Jude gives awful warnings of judgment, wrath, and hell.
The *Revelations* prophesy of that tremendous day
When Christ, and Christ alone, shall be the trembling sinners' stay.

Anon ('Isabel')

Jenny — A Love Lay

I knew a child, so sweet, so fair,
  You must have known her too,
With floating waves of sunny hair
  Above her eyes of blue.
Of household born, alike unknown
  To fortune and to fame—
Fair as the daughter of a throne,
  Sweet Jenny was her name.

I knew her when a child she played
  Beneath yon aged tree;
I knew her when to school she strayed
  Across the verdant lea.
The day was dark, the lessons long—
  All cheerless was the play;
There was no music in our song
  When Jenny was away.

I knew her as my schoolmate then,
  My glad companion now;
When care first writes, with iron pen,
  His name upon my brow.
Her very smile my heart could move
  To strange wild throbs of joy;
With Jenny I'd have fallen in love,
  If I had been a boy.

Her voice may lose its witching tone,
  Her step its girlish glee:
Dear Jenny still can lose not one
  Of all her charms for me!
As did she once, she doth to-day,
  The same sweet strength impart:
Let none my jewel steal away,
  My Jenny from my heart!

234

Robert Burns Thomson

Born in Pollokshaws in 1817, he was a grandson of Robert Burns and Ann Park. Ann Park died shortly after R. B. Thomson's mother's birth. The baby girl was taken to Dumfries and grew up with the Burns family and Jean Armour as mother.

Robert Burns Thomson began his working life as a weaver, became a mill manager, then set up his own business as a mill furnisher.

The poem here was 'from what he calls "The Flae Affair", in a letter with a packet of sweeties to his sister in Australia'. A description of R. B. Thomson at home is given by Hugh McDonald (q.v.) in chapter seven of his *Rambles Round Glasgow*.

*

The Flae Affair

Whan oor faither sat readin', an' mother men't claes,
Or deep doon 'mang the blankets she howkit for flaes;
An' a better auld hunter ne'er pat on her specs
Than oor mother; ye'll mind hoo she nippit their necks,
An' hoo when she saw ane her een kin'lt up,
An' her haun grew as soople's the crack o' a whup,
An' her spittle-wat finger gaed doon like a dert,
Then a rub an' a squeeze, and in twa gaed its hert.
O' were they a leevin' that mother has slain,
Proud Russia's battalions shou'd taunt us in vain;
For twa bagfu' sent o' them, I vow by the law,
Thro' the rest o' their lives they'd dae naething but claw.

Alexander McLachlan

Born in Johnstone, 1818. Worked in a cotton factory, then was apprenticed to a tailor. McLachlan's father emigrated to Canada but died before his family could join him. Alexander then emigrated in 1840, taking possession of his father's farm. He was not successful as a farmer, relying more on tailoring, writing and lecturing before his sons were able to work the farm for him. McLachlan became a Canadian government lecturer and emigration agent for emigration from Scotland to Canada. He died in Orangeville in 1896.

*

The Log Cabin

The little log cabin is far in the woods,
    And the foot of the wayfarer seldom comes there.
Around it are stretching the great solitudes,
    Where the deer loves to roam, and the wolf makes his lair,
And the Red Man crawls on the surly bear,
    And the dead tree falls with a heavy crash;
And the jagged hemlock and pine are there,
    And the dismal swamp and the dreary ash,
    And the eagle sits waiting the moment to dash.

And the roving son of the wilderness,
    While tracking the steps of the gentle deer,
The little log cabin will seldom miss,
    For the ringing sound of the ax he'll hear.

As he comes to taste of the welcome cheer,
  The children, who first had gazed in affright
When they saw his shaggy wolf-dog appear,
  Now run out to meet him with wild delight—
  And the heart of the savage is tamed at the sight.

The little log cabin is all alone;
  Its windows are rude, and its walls are bare,
And the wind without has a weary moan.
  Yet Peace, like an angel, is nestling there;
And hope, with her rapt, uplifted air,
  Beholds in the distance the eglantine,
And the corn with its silver tassel, where
  The hemlock is anchor'd beside the tall pine,
  And the creeping weed hangs with its long fringing vine.

And close by the cabin, tho' hid in the wood,
  Ontario lies, like a mirror of blue,
Where the children hunt the wild-duck's brood,
  And scare the tall crane and the lonely mew.
The eldest has fashion'd a light canoe,
  And with noisy glee they paddle along,
Or dash for the cliff where the eagle flew,
  Or sing in their gladness the fisherman's song,
  Till they waken the echoes the green woods among.

Young Canada

Or, Jack's as Good's his Master

I love this land of forest grand,
  The land where labor's free;
Let others roam away from home,
  Be this the land for me!
Where no one moils and strains and toils
  That snobs may thrive the faster,
But all are free as men should be,
  And Jack's as good's his master!

Where none are slaves that lordly knaves
  May idle all the year;
For rank and caste are of the past—
  They'll never flourish here!
And Jew or Turk, if he'll but work,
  Need never fear disaster;
He reaps the crop he sowed in hope,
  For Jack's as good's his master.

Our aristocracy of toil
  Have made us what you see,
The nobles of the forge and soil,
  With ne'er a pedigree.
It makes one feel himself a man,
  His very blood leaps faster,
Where wit or worth's preferr'd to birth
  And Jack's as good's his master.

Here's to the land of forests grand,
  The land where labor's free;
Let others roam away from home,
  Be this the land for me!
For here 'tis plain the heart and brain,
  The very soul, grow vaster,
Where men are free as they should be,
  And Jack's as good's his master.

Margaret Thomson Laird

Born Paisley, contributed articles and poetry to the local press, married Rev. John MacLeod of the West Free Church, Alloa. She died of cancer in 1869. 'Her remains were brought to Paisley Cemetery, and interred beside those of her only son.'

*

Anniversary Lines on the Death of My Only Son, Removed in Early Childhood

Again the green leaves bud, the daisies bloom,
   Again I hail the summer's gladsome hours,
But ah! he comes not from the silent tomb;
   Life-giving Spring, that wakes from earth the flowers,
And clothes with verdure fresh the forest tree,
Will ne'er bring back my darling boy to me.

Ten times the primrose pale its leaves hath spread
   Since from my fond embrace I mourned him torn;
Ah! many a cherished hope for ever fled
   When to the cold dark earth I saw him borne,
And turned to feel the bitterness of one
Who weepeth for a first — an only son.

No sympathy had Nature with my grief,
   But threw her sunbeams on the little grave,
While on her brow the opening flower and leaf
   Glad promise of her coming glory gave;
Alas for me! nipped in its early bloom,
I hid my flowret in the cheerless tomb.

Sad silent was our home, for that fair face
   Of radiant beauty evermore was gone,
And still I mused on every winning grace,
   The beaming smile, the artless loving tone,
Until, o'ercome by sense and unbelief,
My wayward heart clung to its selfish grief.

But comfort came; Faith o'er my sorrow threw
   The beams effulgent of eternal day,
Spanned the tomb's portal with Hope's rainbow hue,
   And life immortal claimed the mouldering clay,
While seraph voices seemed around to sing—
Where Grave thy triumph? where, O Death, thy sting?

David Wingate

Born Cowglen, 1828. His father died when he was five, and David went down the mines when he was nine. By 1850 some of his poems aroused the attention of Hugh MacDonald (q.v.) at the *Glasgow Citizen*, whose encouragement eventually led to the publication of Wingate's *Poems and Songs* in 1862. With the profits from this Wingate went to the School of Mining at night and studied chemistry. He became subsequently employed as colliery manager at Garscadden and at Cambuslang. He died in his home at Mount Cottage, Tollcross, Glasgow.

'The Collier's Ragged Wean' was deliberately titled with reference to the popular 'The Drunkard's Ragged Wean' written by David Crawford a few years earlier.

*

A Miner's Morning Song

Awake, brother miner! The stars have grown dim,
'Tis time to be stirring the sleep-strengthened limb;
The lark is saluting the regions of love,
And soon will the sun flash the grey mists above:
Prepare thee to sink, though the fancy should soar;
We must to the dark scenes of labour once more.

Come! rise, brother, rise! and from grumbling refrain;
He who murmurs in idleness, murmurs in vain:
A sweet slumber hangs on thy little one's brows,
A love-hallowed prayer's in the heart of thy spouse:

She pleads where thou knowst she has pled well before,
That angels may guard thee to safety once more.

Arise! brother miner! 'Twas only a dream,
That hum of green woodlands, that stroll by the stream;
Some joy-loving fairy, in portraiture gay,
Hath shown thee by night what thou seest not by day.
Yet, brother, despair not; the hours will pass o'er:
We'll rise, as the day wanes, to gladness once more.

Suppress those deep sighs, brother, though it may be
The fate of thy kinsman is waiting for thee:
O'er sorrows untasted 'tis folly to brood;
We must, like that kinsman, brave danger for food.
Then up and be stirring; like serf-men of yore,
We'll rest when we've plodded our portion once more.

Be cheerful, poor brother! I've heard of a land
Where no over-labour e'er blisters the hand—
A land where no fetters of slavery are seen,
Where the grindstone of tyranny never hath been.
Perhaps we'll go there when our ploddings are o'er,
And then we'll be weary-boned miners no more.

A Day Amang the Haws

When the beech-nuts fast are drappin',
    And the days are creepin' in,
When ilk carefu' mither's thinkin'
    O' the winter's hose and shoon;
When the mornin' bells loud ringin'
    To the Fast-day worship ca's,
Out comes the city callan'
    For his day amang the haws.

O' the dangers that await him
   Ne'er a troublous thought has he,
Nought cares he for the tearin'
   He his claes is sure to gie;
But the light o' comin' pleasure
   On his heart like sunshine fa's,
For dear as stolen waters
   Is a day amang the haws.

Frae the mill where stourie 'jennies'
   Round him aye are whirrin' thrang;
Or the forge where ponderous 'Condies'
   Dunt and dirl the hale day lang;
Or the press-room's inky regions,
   And the gaffer's cuff and ire;
Or the needle, or the lingle,
   On he plods through mud and mire.
Frae the lane where Vice holds revel,
   Where beneath fair Virtue's shield,
Like birds escaped the snarer,
   Aye a gratefu' few find bield;
Frae the stench that kens nae sweetenin',
   And the din that has nae pause,
To the freshness and the freedom
   O' a day amang the haws.

Think ye thus? — 'The graceless callan'
   To the kirk should rather gang;
Does his mither never warn him
   That sic Fast-day traikin's wrang?
If her heart is for him pleadin',
   Kennin' weel how sair he's wrought,
For the customs o' her faithers
   Has she ne'er a reverend thought?'
Oh, rather thus excuse her:
   'She was born amang the hills,
And she minds the autumn grandeur
   O' the thorns beside the rills;
There are memories fresh frae girlhood
   Crowdin' fast to plead his cause,
And she canna keep the callan'
   Frae his day amang the haws.

Like a flood the rain's been pourin',
  But the sun beams through at last,
As amang a host o' ithers
  Frae the town he hastens fast;
On the whinny slopes o' Cathkin,
  Or on Pollock's woody knowes,
He already roams in fancy
  Where he kens the haw-tree grows.
On the bitter blast that's brewin'
  He looks west wi' hopefu' ee,
For he kens the woods frae keepers
  In sic weather will be free.
If the bells around him ringin'
  Whisper whiles o' broken laws,
'Oh!' he thinks, 'there's surely pardon
  For ae day amang the haws.'

Fu' boldly has he ventured,
  And in darin' weel has thriven,
He the ripest, richest branches
  Frae the sweetest trees has riven.
See his jacket hangs in tatters,
  Owre his hands the bluid-draps steal;
But his mither mends fu' neatly,
  And his scarts again will heal.
Frae his hair the rain is dreepin',
  But he never thinks o' harm,
For Pleasure, wanderin' wi' him,
  Wi' her mantle keeps him warm.
How his heart wi' pride is swellin',
  As he near the city draws,
For he kens he comes joy-laden
  Frae his day amang the haws.

Wha thinks he frae his ramble
  Winna better come, but worse,
Wi' its memory hangin' owre him
  Like an angry father's curse?
In Nature's face what is there
  That a city bairn should fear?
In the woodland's autumn whisper
  Is there ought he shouldna hear?

Wha kens what heavenly music
  May be stirred his breast within,
As the sapless leaf's faint rustlin'
  Turns the sparklin' ee aboon,
While his fancy paints the Painter
  O' the million-tinted shaws,
And the poet-spark is kindled
  In his soul, amang the haws?

Oh! keepers, spare the callan'—
  And sweet dreams ye shall not lack—
For the wee things' sake that weary
  Wait the wanderer's coming back;
They hae shared the city's hardships,
  And o' plenty little ken—
Let them taste in rich abundance
  O' the spoils o' hill and glen.
Owre the priceless feast they'll linger,
  Till their lips and teeth grow brown;
Or wi' the ruddy treasure
  In their bosoms cuddle down.
Oh, there's nane the joy can measure,
  That a boon sae sma' may cause!
Tears are dried and sorrows's lightened
  Wi' a day amang the haws.

And ye whase lot is coosten
  Aye amang the caller air,
Wha on a gift sae common
  May a thought but seldom wair,
Oh! think if Heaven had placed ye
  Far frae glen and mountain stream,
Where the woods are things o' fancy,
  And the yorlin's sang a dream—
Oh! think how ye would weary
  But to hear ae laverock sing,
And to watch the matron peesweep
  Chase the hawk wi' daring wing—
How wild would be your longin'
  For the breeze on hills that blaws!
How muckle would ye venture
  For ae day amang the haws!

The Collier's Ragged Wean

He's up at early morning, howe'er the win' may blaw,
Lang before the sun comes roun' to chase the stars awa';
And 'mang a thoosand dangers, unkent in sweet daylight,
He'll toil until the stars again keek through the chilly night.
See the puir wee callan', 'neath the cauld clear moon!
His knees oot through his troosers and his taes oot through his
shoon;
Wading through the freezing snaw, thinking owre again.
How happy every wean maun be that's no a collier's wean.

His cheeks are blae wi' cauld, and the chittering winna cease,
To gie the hungry callan' time to eat his mornin' piece;
His lamp is burning on his head wi' feeble flickering ray,
And in his heart the lamp o' Hope is burning feebly tae.
Nae wonner that the callan's sweert to face his daily toil,
Nae wonner he sae seldom greets the morning wi' a smile;
For weel he kens he's growing up to face the cauld disdain
That lang the world has measured oot to every collier's wean.

The puir wee hirpling laddie! how mournfully he's gaun,
Aye dichting aff the ither tear wi's wee hard hackit haun'!
Sair, sair he's tempit 'mang the snaw to toom his flask o' oil,
But ah! — ae flash o' faither's ire were waur than weeks o' toil.
In vain the stars look on the youth wi' merry twinkling een,
Through clouds o' care sae dense as his their glory is nae seen;
He thinks 'twad been a better plan if coal had boon-most lain,
And wonners why his faither made a collier o' his wean.

Oh! ye that row in Fortune's lap, his waefu' story hear;
Aft sorrows no sae deep as his hae won a pitying tear;
And lichter wrangs than he endures your sympathy hae won—
Although he is a collier's, mind he's still a Briton's son.
And ye wha mak' and mend oor laws, tak' pity on the bairn;
Oh! bring him sooner frae the pit, and gie him time to learn:
Sae shall ye lift him frae the mire 'mang which he lang has lain,
And win a blessing frae the heart o' every collier's wean.

from Annie Weir

'Owre bye, near yonder bank,
　　Where the coltsfoot's growing rank,
And the binweed thrives where the bere should be;
　　Where the rigs are hower yet,
　　Langsyne there was a pit,
And auld anes owre ayont it were twa or three.

''Twere owre lang a tale to tell,
　　How, in thae times, aft it fell
That sic pits, wi' bounds unmarked, and of water brimming fou,
　　Were but traps for maids and men;
　　The pent flood now and then,
Wi' ruin in its roar, bursting through.

'In the pit near yonder bank,
　　Where the coltsfoot grows sae rank,
And the binweed thrives sae weel, 'twas mine to toil;
　　And there earth's dearest maid,
　　Like a glow-worm in the shade,
Made an Eden o' the gloom wi' her smile.

'Oh! she was fairer far
　　Than the gowan or the star,
In the green glades o' earth or the blue o' heaven,
　　And gentler than the dove;
　　And her heart's first love,
In its freshness and its faith, to me was given.

'She wasnae seventeen,
　　But at work she lang had been,
And up the weary stairs wi' her coal-creel laden,
　　Day by day, wi' trembling limb,
　　In the twilight dim,
For her frail old father's sake, clamb the peerless maiden.

'That her silken auburn hair,
　　Snawy hauns, and face so fair,
Should be daily soiled sae sair I aye was mourning;

But my Annie at her wark,
Aye as lichtsome as the lark,
Gaed singing to the stair, and sang returning.

'Oh! sweet's the laverock's trill
In the cloud that crowns the hill,
And the hidden blackbird's sang in the hazel bush at e'en;
But ne'er sae sweet nor dear
As the sang o' Annie Weir,
In the darkness o' the pit heard — hersel' unseen.

'Ae morn — ae summer morn—
When white was every thorn—
When the barley braird was silvered wi' the dew,
Sweet was every scene and soun',
And but few I mind gaed doun,
But I and Annie Weir were o' the few.

'Frae the ithers far awa'
We toiled our ainsels twa—
Strange fears that day came owre me now and then;
Aften down my pick I flang,
Listening eerie for her sang,
And thinking she was lang o' coming ben.

'Tak' yoursels in fancy doun,
And frae the waste aroun'
Let this sudden cry o' terror strike the ear—
"Oh! the water's broken in!
To the stair for safety rin!"
And fancy a' the fears o' Annie Weir.

'She heard the awesome din,
And she saw the others rin—
She saw them to the stair for safety flee;
She heard the distant rush
O' the water's coming gush,
Looked upward, and the sunshine filled her e'e.
Her foot was on the stair,
But, oh! I wasnae there;
Sae, flinging aff her creel, she flew for me.

'In the shearing I was thrang
Crooning Annie's fav'rite sang
(A lay of humble love and its reward),
When from the silent waste
Cam' the voice o' ane in haste,
And "Reuben, Reuben, rin!" I wondering heard.

' "Oh, Reuben, Reuben, rin!
For the water's broken in—
They a' cam' to the bottom but yoursel'.
Oh! Reuben, haste ye fast,
For it's coming like a blast,
And how we're to win oot I canna tell."

'Though I trusted she was wrang,
Yet I didna tarry lang,
But hurried out my frichted burd to meet,
And we ran to win the stair,
Oh! but lang ere we were there,
The black and stoury flood was at our feet.

'Turning roun' wi' frantic speed
O' nae danger taking heed,
Through the waste for safety's path we sought in vain,
Then eerie, bruised and sair,
Haun' in haun' and in despair,
To the road that best we kent we came again.

'We didna tear our hair,
But it surely was despair,
That made us ither's hauns sae wildly tak';
For our heavy hearts aye sunk,
As wi' hollow, dismal, clunk,
The water slowly rose and drove us back.

'For hope there was nae room,
There we saw and kent our doom,
Nae skill, nor faith, nor prayer could scaur't awa,
It would creep up pace by pace,
And to reach the farthest face
It could but tak' a day, or maybe twa.

'"Come, Annie, let's gae ben,
   A' our sorrows soon will en',
For us nae earthly morn can hae a breakin',
   We'll our watch in patience keep—
   Oh! that we could but sleep,
Ere owre us creeps the flood, and never waken.'

'"Oh! Reuben, Reuben Shaw,
   I' the' nae way out ava?
Wi' this ae feeble light on our white faces streaming,
   Maun we our hopes resign
   And our dear lives tyne?
Oh! waefu' waefu' end o' a' our gouden dreaming!"

'Sae in the first wild hour
   Did we our wailing pour,
Nor thought how e'en the feeble light would fail us;
   Nor that the flood might stay,
   Far frae us on the brae,
And yet a sterner foe ere lang assail us.

'Let your fancy, if it can,
   Paint us sitting worn and wan,
Watching owre our last bit candle as it flared its dying flare;
   Fled our guardian Angel seemed,
   And till then we had not dreamed,
That ony darker shade could fa' on our despair.

'Like parents owre a child,
   That its hindmost smile hath smiled,
Owre the glowing loweless wick low we leaned wi' fondling care,
   And gently blowing strave
   The lowe alive to save,
And chase away the gloom for ae brief moment mair.

'But we gently blew in vain,
   So we raised our een again
At ance, I kenna why nor what we wished to see;
   But I saw—and see it noo—
   Beaming memory's mazes through,
The old sweet look o' love and trust in Annie's ee.

'But the wick a faint dull red
In its ain white ase half hid,
Lang glowed and seemed a soul that the Fates were loath to sever;
Then it dwindled to a spark,
That a star seemed in the dark—
A star that sudden set to rise no more for ever.

'And then no more was seen,
Save as we strained our een,
To bless our longing hearts wi' anither look o' ither,
Ae flash we thought we saw,
But it could be nocht ava',
Save the ee o' frenzied Hope as she left us a'thegither.

'Oh! ne'er before since Light
Half his kingdom won frae Night,
Had the darkness of the pit haen a dreariness sae drear;
For the shadow seemed to clasp
With a stifling, chilling grasp,
While uncannie feet we heard on the water drawing near.

'How the laneness grew mair lane,
When a' note o' time was gane;
How our hearts sank now and then, and to die we laid us doun;
How the hours crept into days;
How we prayed and warbled praise,
That wakened in the waste a sadly solemn soun';

'How the hunger pang we bare
When the water was our fare;
How we tried to be contented with our cheer;
How the flood rose to our feet;
How it stood, and durstnae weet
The garments o' the Angel, Annie Weir;

'How we heard sweet music swell,
If asleep we briefly fell,
And, waking, heard what seemed the hum o' bees;
How we closer crept in awe
When the phosphor-light we saw,
That seemed a spirit sitting 'mong the trees;

'How the old folks were our thought—
How to want they might be brought;
How the God aboon would surely guide them through;
What we would hae done ava,
Had our number no been twa,
And how a solace aye from that we drew;

'How the fearfu' thought that death
Mightnae come at ance to baith,
Made the sore-tried reason reel, and the blood with horror chill,—
A' this, and mickle mair,
Ye the telling o' maun spare,
For the memory o't awakens horror still.

'But the end at last drew near:
At my side lay Annie Weir,
And murmured lowly, "Reuben, part maun we.
Oh! how wearied I hae grown,
Like a hunted bird that's flown,
Despairing, lang, across a biel'less lea.

'"Oh! sweet it was to dream
We at ance should cross the stream
Whase shores are Earth and Heaven, but 'twinna be;
A' my dreaming's been in vain;
I the stream maun cross alane,
And ye your weary doom alane maun dree."

'Then she seemed asleep to fa',
And I thought she was awa',
When, hark! 'twas surely voices in the waste
(It sae like a fancy seemed,
That I thought I had but dreamed),—
'Twas the searchers coming cautious in their haste.

'Frae another, ebber pit—
I can tell ye where it's yet—
Three weary days they, hour aboot, had redd;
Like giants had they toiled,
And success had on them smiled,
For safely to the sunshine were we led.

*

'Annie Weir and I were wed,
But her bloom for aye was fled;
Ae year she lived, and ere she was a mither,
She was laid in yon kirkyaird,
'Neath the greenest o' its swaird,
And oh, that we were ance again thegither.'

The Birdie

I met a wee birdie in the early dawn,
    When the morning star was shining,
That hovering aboon me said, 'Whaur are ye gaun,
    Your morning slumber tyneing?'

'I'm gaun to yon cliff wi' the broomy brow,
    With the linn beyond it leaping,
To sit and gaze on the pool below,
    With peace in its bosom sleeping.

'I'm gaun to gaze on the tranquil pool,
    While the star-decked east is brightening,
To dream of the ending of sorrow's rule,
    And labour's burden lightening.'

'What sorrows hae ye?' said the little bird,
    Its dark e'e kindly beaming,
'And what is the labour that leans so hard,
    And tints wi' grief your dreaming?

'Why come ye on tempting cliffs to mope,
    In the dark pool's peace believing?
I fear you've been listening to flattering Hope,
    And bear like a bairn her deceiving.'

'Oh! little ye ken, bonnie bird,' I said,
  'The strength of a human longing,
When sleep-reiving cares on a ruthless raid
  Are round his pillow thronging;

'And little ye ken how he longs for peace,
  When the future gives no token
That the bark of life will from heaving cease
  Till the anchor-chain is broken.

'Ye hae nae been fretting 'neath sorrow's rule,
  Nor vigils with care been keeping,
And ken nae how sweet is the tranquil pool,
  Wi' peace in its bosom sleeping.'

'Gang hame to your bairns,' said the little bird,
  'And the wife that waits and wearies,
And blush if nae sweeter thoughts are stirred
  By the glee o' your lisping dearies.

'Gang hame to your bairns,' said the scornful bird,
  'And as you're hameward faring,
Observe the poor in yon rows that herd,
  Your lot with theirs comparing.

'There children in squalid rags you'll meet,
  The breath of Boreas scorning,
While leaving the print of their naked feet
  In the snow of the winter morning;

'And Hope with their fathers and mothers has been,
  With tales of bliss deceiving;
But none on yon tempting cliff are seen,
  In the dark pool's peace believing.'

'And what are their troubles, O bird! to me,
  But danger-beacons burning?
I fear them as landsmen fear at sea
  The weathered gale's returning.

'I saw in the starlight a shadow gaunt,
　　And as the day grows clearer,
I fear 'tis the form of the giant Want
　　That's slowly drawing nearer:

I knew him of old, and I fear his rule—
　　How grandly the linn is leaping!—
Sweet bird, let me pass to the tranquil pool,
　　With peace in its bosom sleeping.'

So on to the cliff with the brow of broom,
　　The tortuous path I wended,
And me far up in the 'scattering gloom'
　　The little bird attended.

But the linn now fell with a sullen roar,
　　That seemed of the angry ocean,
And the once still pool was trembling o'er
　　With an eerily-glimmering motion.

There Peace, no more like a spirit bright,
　　Me down to her breast seemed wooing;
But a writing in fire was the ripple-light,
　　And the written word was 'Ruin.'

Wha'll Buy My Linties?

SCENE: *The Marketplace — a Boy singing*

Wha'll buy my linties? grey linties and green,
And laverocks and gooldies, the brawest e'er seen;
They come from the woodlands, from meadow and muir,
And wha wadna buy them that heard them sing there?
　　And wha wadna buy them, &c.

I searched 'mang the bushes ere spring made them green,
In woods and on meadow ere blue-bell was seen;
I kenned the nests biggin', and ere my birds flew,
I ta'en them and fed them, and wha'll buy them noo?
    I ta'en them and fed them, &c.

I saved my wee laverocks frae starling and craw,
The hawk frae my linties I frichtit awa';
And if the fell gowk could their nests hae won near,
I trow my braw gooldies wad ne'er hae been here.
    I trow my braw gooldies, &c.

At mornin' and e'enin' their sang ye will hear;
They'll sing in the daytime your labour to cheer;
You'll think, when ye hear them, o' meadow and muir,
Whare first my birds nestled, and wish ye were there,
    Whare first my birds nestled, &c.

Nae peeries nor bools with their price will I buy;
If hame I maun take them, my mither will sigh,
And tears o'er her cheeks, while she clasps me, will steal;
But buy them, and mither will pray for your weal;
Oh, buy them, and mither will pray for your weal!

The Sin o' Sang

I've come, sweet Jean, while owre the hills
    The evening shadows steal—
I've come to give thee back thy love,
    And say for aye, fareweel:
It is nae that my love's grown cauld—
    For that can never be;
But I hae sinned the sin o' sang,
    And daurnae wed with thee.

I thought my dreams were 'beams frae heaven,'
    And hailed them aye wi' glee;
For aft they showed a happy home,
    Whare thou the queen should be.
And Hope was ever at my side,
    New pleasures to reveal;
And so I sinned the sin o' sang,
    And I maun say fareweel.

Oh! dinna look sae waefu', Jean;
    Nae heartless loon am I,
To win a bonny lassie's love,
    Then careless bid good-bye.
Oh! fondly, fondly I hae wished
    To win thee for my ain;
But I hae sinned the sin o' sang,
    And now maun wed wi' nane.

To him who sins that deadly sin,
    And canna frae't refrain,
Thrift's sure to be the rainbow's base,
    Pursued for aye in vain.
Oh! seldom will they drink o' joy,
    Who life's cup wi' him pree,
And, Jeannie, I hae sinned that sin,
    And daurnae wed wi' thee.

Oh! had I but in secret sung,
    And won nae praise but thine,
A lot that angels might hae grudged,
    Dear Jeannie, would been mine.
But, far and near, the're some that ken,
    And my reward is sure—
A loveless and a lonely home,
    And eke a life o' care.

Oh! if there had been but one hope
    To shimmer in the van
Of labour's battle, I for thee
    Would fouchten like a man;

And like a man I'll fight, although
Success will smile nae mair;
For I hae sinned the sin o' sang,
And maun for aye be puir.

Thou kens that in the hive o' life
No idler I hae been,
But aye wi' glowing hands amang
The toilers hae been seen;
But 'This is he that murdered Time'
Is written on my brow,
And wha in a' the busy world
Will dare to trust me now?

from The Better Land

Will and Geordie

'Come ben and tak' the muckle chair, the wife's at Wishaw toun;
Fu' blithe she'll be to see ye, and the 'bus will bring her doun.
Sit doun and warm your feet, and thowe the cranreugh frae your
                                                    hair;
I fear ye shouldnae venture out in sic a frosty air.

'The bottle's toom; but, Geordie, Jean has ta'en the jar awa',
And, to gi'e you the hans'ling o't, the cork she'll blithely draw;
I seldom fash wi't noo — indeed, I swore I ne'er wad pree,
But Jeanie whiles insists, and draps a cinder in my tea.

'And so, till she comes hame, we'll fill our pipes and tak' our smoke,
And crack o' times awa', when we bore lichtly labour's yoke—
When hearts were light and bluid was warm, and short the blithe-
                                                    some year—
When mist and frost, and rain and win', were faced without a fear.'

'Ay, Willie, we are turnin' auld and frail; for me, I'm done,
My picks beneath the bed ha'e lain unused sin' sixty-ane;
My auld pit-breeks this mornin' wi' the ragman gaed on tramp,
And Peggy for a scourin' thing's hung up my auld pit-lamp.

'I'm sure I neednae keep my picks nae mair than keep my claes—
An auld and weel-worn collier, Will, I maun be a' my days;
Sweert's, sweert's my breath to come and gang, and whiles it seems
                                              to swither,
And wonder if it were nae best to leave me a'thegither.

'Whiles, Will, I dover in my chair, and muse on days awa',
When Peg and me were young, and had nae backs to cleed but twa—
How hard I wrocht, what sprees I had (for I was foolish then),
And thocht (if e'er I thocht) the aim o' life was 'won and spen'.'

'My Peggy hain't as weel's she could, and wrocht when'er she micht,
And muckle flate, and weel advised, and strave to keep me richt.
I ne'er would own't, but weel I kent 'twas wrang—and unco wrang:
But what's the guid o' frettin' owre a thing that's by sae lang?

'When roun' me whiles I look and see the plenishin' we hae—
A meal for every mornin', and a hap for every day—
And think 'Whase guidin's this?' man, Will, a mist comes owre my
                                              e'e;
There never was a better wife, sin' wives began to be.

'She minds it yet. Teth! ay, she minds't, and mentions't noo and then,
When neebor wives come in to bann their idle, drunken men.
But even then wi' kindly clasp she tak's my pithless haun',
And whispers, 'Gude be thankit, ye were ne'er a lazy man.'

'It's perfit true! I likit wark, and blithely at it sang,
My verra pick was proud o' me, and while I wrocht it rang;
There's joy in drinkin'! even in stauns (if short) there's wealth o'
                                              mirth,
But nocht's sae sweet as weel-paid wark amang the joys o' earth.

'Ah, Will! when stauns tak' place, we sit amang the chiefs nae mair;
Ye never hear them cryin' noo, 'Put Geordie in the chair!'
But ance I was an oracle, and crowds o' men could charm;
I needed but to lift my voice and wave abreed my arm.

'Ah, man! It was a triumph aye to see in print my name,
And ken that 'Geordie's' words were read a thousand miles from
hame;
And hear the fules o' editors denounce me for a rogue,
A stirrer-up o' strife — a pest — a wanderin' demagogue.

'I likit it! but, Will, thae days are frae us ever gane;
The wark we had to do is done, and a' our say is sain;
We noo maun turn our een to things that ance were reckoned nocht,
And mair about 'the Better Land' maun think than ance we thocht.

'Our Missioner, an honest man, wha jokes a harmless joke,
And has a humble heart, and likes a hamely crack and smoke,
And has a hope for a', and has nae fearsome tale to tell
O' weepin, and o' wailin' in the lampless pit o' hell—

'He says that in 'the Better Land' there's food and raiment aye,
And noble drink that rins in burns, and naething for't to pay;
Nor rent, nor stent, nor heavy darg, to cross its borders dare,
And collier, master, lord, and laird, are equal-aqual there.

'Nae asthma's there, wi' weary wheeze, to wear the life awa',
Nor rheumatism, Will, for there there are nae banes to gnaw;
Bereavement comes nae there to clip Affection's cord in twain,
And Discord's voice is never heard in a' the wide domain.

'We'll soom about on wings, like doos, and blithesome hymns will
chant,
Wi' which compared, earth's sweetest airs are yill-house roar and
rant,
And join wi' fau'tless skill, untaught, some 'Hallelujah baun','
Or dreamin' sit, on gouden harps to thrum wi' tireless haun';

'Or wanderin' owre the sunny hills, 'mang flowers that never dee,
We'll crack, and wonder at our lair o' a' we hear and see;
And surely, Will, if hearts we hae, they'll warm wi' gratefu' glow,
When we the life in heaven compare wi' collier-life below.

'And, Will, we hae nae lang to wait— Death soon will draw the
screen,
And prove the land we dream o' has nae human fancy been;
And what we'll dae, or what we'll say, a wonder needna be—
That there's a Better Land ava's enough for you and me.'

Robert Mutrie

Born King Street, Paisley, 1832. He worked as a weaver, and died in 1880.

*

The Shilling in the Puir Man's Pouch

I hear fock talk o' guid kind frien's,
    I own I've felt the same;
I've felt a guid turn done abroad,
    I've felt the like at hame.
But this I saw, where'er I went,
    In every place I've been,
That a shilling in a puir man's pouch
    Turned aye out his best frien'.

I've travelled east, I've travelled west,
    O'er many a weary mile,
And I hae seen ten times o' gloom
    For ae kind frien'ly smile.
But this I felt where'er I went,
    In every place I've been,
That a shilling in a puir man's pouch
    Turned aye out his best frien'.

I've ta'en some cash at times mysel',
    Then frien's aroun' me cam',
They deaved me with flattering tongues
    While circled roun' the dram.
But when misfortune turned the wheel,
    I saw, wi' weel cleared een,
That a shilling in a puir man's pouch
    Turned aye out his best frien'.

Anon ('A Working Man')

Queen Victoria granted royal assent to the marriage of Princess Louise and the Marquis of Lorne in October 1870. The marriage took place in March 1871.

*

Lorne and Louise

A Republican Rhyme
Dedicated to our Scottish Representatives in Parliament

In this free land, in high command,
Enshrined as wonderfully grand,
    There's something we term Royalty,
Which all the good, it's understood,
Uphold for purity of blood,
    Against all vile disloyalty.

'God save the King' — or Queen, doth ring
Throughout the land, so people sing
    To those charmed with regality;
For what? The bliss, the happiness
That through their wisdom we possess
    Despite of all rascality?

Approach the throne of that bright one,
Who for the people's good hath done—
    How much? the good VICTORIA;
And honour her, and every heir
Whom she has reared with matron care,
    To lead us on to glory aye!

Lorne and Louise are going to wed
    The people say;
By flunkeyism we are led
    To hail the day
That is to give the LORD OF LORNE a wife,
And raise his clan a higher stage in life,
And pass a friendly bond across the Tweed,
And change the tune from German unto Highland greed.

In honour of the happy pair,
    'Gentility'
Proclaims in accents strong, from everywhere,
    Servility
The nation owes to this high-destined chief,
And by that feeling strengthens the belief
In our deep loyalty to England's throne—
That power whose interests are the people's own.

Happy that nation, happy too that king,
    Where unity
Of purpose, mutual gain doth bring.
    Humanity
Directing to that glorious goal
Where peace and progress point as needle to the pole,
Where Justice holds the scales as stern as fate,
Unflinching 'twixt the lowly and the great.

In language such as this folk speak of you,
    Britannia.
Is it in every leading feature true,
    Or mania
Of people, led like cattle by the nose?
In leading strings adroitly pulled by those
Whose interest it is the mass to rule,
And sway as they were children in a school.

We had a very mighty fuss about
    The PRINCE OF WALES
When he got married, and people did loudly shout
    At his coat tails;
But has he yet done anything to win his coat
Of honour, if, by merit, such a thing was got;
His highest merit is he is his mother's son,
For of himself *what* has the fellow done.

The stripling got married. What of that
  To any one
If he would keep his wife and family right,
  Himself alone;
Do something useful for himself and them,
And not, like lazy pauper, make a claim
On Parliament, that it may raise relief
For Prince and Princess, husband, children, wife.

A dowry and a pension to Louise
  We now must grant,
Because before the nation ye did fleece;
  What silly cant,
Of members sent from home to Parliament;
Because they did *profess* Reform and Retrenchment,
So that we might be governed cheap and well;
But now it seems another tale they tell.

Ye Scottish members, what a lame excuse
  Ye lately gave,
Who could not muster courage to refuse
  The grant, ye brave!
Because that precedent had given grants before
To German paupers, haply, by the score,
Ye now appeal to every greedy Scot
That our own clan may now receive its groat.

Is this what ye call principle, ye Squires
  With Scottish pride,
That can appeal to selfish mean desires
  Thus to decide?
Instead of testing this, and every case,
On its own merits, now you try to trace,
In precedent, a reason and a guide
To settle questions that good sense denied.

Will this alliance with the Royal blood
  A blessing bring,
Or make the nation happier than it would,
  Should no such thing
Occur; entailing great expenses,
That people grant as they were out their senses,
Supplying money to the undeserving,
While those who labour in our native land are starving.

Are Royal influences so often used
    For public weal,
That this tomfoolery should be excused;
    This stupid zeal,
Of which the people yet may well repent,
When this young family's tried on whom its spent;
For, hark ye, what are emperors or kings
As such, at best, but vicious, vulgar things.

To raise a set of common mortals high
    Above the mass,
Is simply creating tyranny;
    The rule of class.
It is contemptible to say the nation
Should place a person in the highest station,
Because his father did the same inherit;
Without there being in either special merit.

Is this the nineteenth century that men vaunt
    So much about,
And still for monarchy the banner flaunt,
    And raise the shout!
Away with such grim nonsense — a disgrace
To those who follow reason — look it in the face;
And act in every instance on the plan
That to his fitting place sends every man.

Mary Pyper

Born in Greenock in 1795, she lived a life of poverty in Edinburgh working as a lacemaker then as a seamstress. After her mother's death she peddled buttons and fringes from a basket, and was described in 1860 as 'an old woman, scarcely able to do needlework, very poor, very industrious, and very independent and respectable'. She wrote mainly religious verse much of her life, and this was collected and published in Edinburgh in 1865. She died in 1870, and a memorial cross was erected to her in Greyfriars Churchyard.

*

Epitaph — A Life

I came at Morn — 'twas Spring, I smiled,
    The fields with green were clad;
I walked abroad at Noon — and lo!
    'Twas Summer — I was glad.
I sate me down — 'twas Autumn eve,
    And I with sadness wept;
I laid me down at Night, and then
    'Twas Winter — and I slept!

John Andrew

Born in Ochiltree, Ayrshire, 1826. He studied theology at the Evangelical Union Theological Academy, the Andersonian University, and Latin, Greek and Hebrew at Glasgow University. He became Evangelical Union pastor in churches in Glasgow, Tillicoultry, Barrhead and Dundee. While in Barrhead he published the prophetic *The Ages and the Purpose of God*. He eventually left for the millenialist Catholic Apostolic Church, becoming 'angel' of congregations in Dundee then Belfast. He also published 'The Pendulograph' (1881) and 'Thoughts on the Evolution Theory of Creation'. He was elected President of the Dundee Microscopical Society 1868-69.

The diatoms and desmidiaceae referred to in the poem are aqueous single-cell algae visible only under high magnification.

*

from
Address to the Dundee Microscopical Society

> Fain would my willing pen have spoken
> Of tiny microscopic token
> That life's great chain is nowhere broken;
>   But on does run
> Adown the silence all unwoken
>   Of sight outdone.

These green Desmidiaceae
And Diatoms of pearly grey,
The small dust of Life's balance they,
     Which turn the scale
So gently that we scarce can say
     Where that does fail;
And where this other life gives way
     To that's curtail.

Fain had I shown that farther still
Adown the far invisible
There is a life whose pulses fill
     All nature's veins,
And cause a quickening sense to thrill
     Even death's domains.

Than Diatoms minuter yet
Are Atoms in each substance set;
Hidden away from gaze or get
     Of man's keen eye,
Which microscopes even fail to whet
     Sufficiently.

When atoms still are living free,
And feeling their affinity,
To come together two or three
     In combination;

And with minute Atomic glee
     And palpitation;
Do seek each other out to the
     Affiliation.

Then as with Chemic forces driven,
A kind of atom life is liven
Until each to the other's given
     In chemic love;
But when this wooing strife is striven,
     They cease to move.

'They are dynamically dead,'
Once and again hath Tyndall said,
'Their force hath ceased, their part is played,
      And they at rest' —
This doctrine should be fully weighed,
      Ere it be pressed.

'Tis true the motive-force hath ceased
When in Atomic love embraced,
One Atom with its mate is placed
      In still repose.
But does the force now go to waste,
      And nature lose?

Does it not need the force to hold
The Atoms thus together rolled,
As much as when with movement bold
      And strange commotion,
They sought each other in the wold
      Or in the ocean?

What is it makes a beam, or bar,
Or carriage thill or mainsail spar
So strong for use in peace or war,
      Save force at rest?
In wooden less, in iron more,
      All for the best!

All for the best? for Nature measures
The force to hold in all our treasures,
As best will suit our use and pleasures;
      This to do duty,
And bear utilitarian pressures;
      While that for beauty.

Some things, as beams, in strains as strong;
Some things a twist will not put wrong;
Some pillars, you may crush as long
      As generations;
To some strength in a pull belong
      Strength for all stations!

Fain had I proved that life is there
Sublimely silent; holding where,
In strength to pull, or strength to bear,
   Or strength at all,
You find cohesion everywhere,
   In great and small.

John Hamilton

Born Paisley, 1827. He became a calenderer by trade, then after leaving Paisley he took up business as a photographer in Greenock and in Port Glasgow. Around 1880 he emigrated to New Zealand.

The Bogle Stone was a large rock on the hill above Port Glasgow which at one time had a reputation for being haunted. Tired of people using it as a meeting place though, a Reverend Parker, on whose land it was, had it blown up, but it was later rebuilt and is now set in a stone wall. Its history is discussed in the chapter on Port Glasgow in the 1857 *Days at the Coast* of Hugh MacDonald (q.v.). A photograph of its present appearance is included in the manuscript biography by Norman McKim, *B.V. and His Visitants* (Glasgow University MS Gen 1092) in which biography McKim sees the Bogle Stone as the subconscious source of the figure of Melencolia in the final section of 'The City of Dreadful Night' by James Thomson (q.v.). This interpretation McKim also published in an article in the *Greenock Telegraph* of July 15th 1952; the article was the fourth of four called 'The Port Born Poet and the Boglestone'.

*

from The Lay of the Bogle Stone

When, Christians say, the graves shall open wide
And vomit forth, in myriads, all the dead
That ever lived — at least of human shape,

271

Why they exclude the horse, the ass, the ape,
In this great final grand resuscitation,
Is quite beyond my mental computation:
Nor have I any way of proving, whether
This resurrection story is a *blether*
Or old wife's fable. Sure, I cannot tell;
Did I speak slang, I'd say it was a *sell*,
Contrived for those who don't know fact from fiction,
Who nothing know of good but by prescription;
And who believe in kingdoms still to come,
And yet go on in sin *ad libitum*;
Live all their earthly days in social crime;
At the last moment, they are quite in time
To lay hold on the Cross, and be forgiven,
Washed white as snow, made subjects fit for heaven;
Who reckon manly virtue and restraint
As naught — the sinner vile, is the great saint,
If he but howl and whine enough, and give
His ill-got wealth to kirks and priests, he'll live
In bliss eternal, from the resurrection,
With other scamps made just unto perfection.
Just let a scoundrel breathe a late repentance,
'Twill cause more joy than ninety-nine just persons.
The white-washed rogue thus finds more grace in heaven
Than hundred men who no offence have given:
A life of crime, closed with brief regret,
Transforms the villain to an angel's pet!
Oh! should I ever enter life anew,
God keep me out of such a blackguard crew;
For, if allowed to choose between two evils,
I'd rather consort with plain honest Devils.
I'll ever shun the whole black brotherhood;
Mysterious mummers, taught to whine and prate
One hour a-week about a future state;
While they, themselves, no more believe in Hell
Than I in Heaven, or all the lies they tell.
Oh! may the Fates, that govern all, decree
That priest again may ne'er have power o'er me:
And, if I might advise, it would be this—
Avoid the Clergy and their mysteries;
For while they act the saint, and pray for you,
'Tis to hoodwink and prey upon you too.

JOHN HAMILTON

Then seek for Truth at God's stream, undiluted,
And drink above that part they have polluted;
Be free, be true unto yourselves, and just
To every one; then in God put your trust;
For, if you put more faith in cleric prater,
There is a great gulf 'twixt you and your Maker;
Shake off the bonds of ignorance and vice,
Of ill-formed habits, and of prejudice;
Have faith in God, abandon every doubt,
And give the canting quacks the right-about.

*

Oh, Church! with what assumed authority
You keep in thrall a purblind laity,
Who, for the greater part, are never able
To note the differences 'twixt truth and fable.
Your teaching only keeps them ignorant,
Vain, cunning, selfish, and intolerant
Of every form of worship but their own:
One only can be right — and theirs alone.
Don't think, kind reader, I am Atheist,
I only try to clear away the mist
That hangs between us and the fount of knowledge,
And certainly that fount is not the College;
And I will also say it's not the Bible,
Even at the risk of being charged with libel;
For I have found the man most orthodox,
As something 'twixt a donkey and the fox;
And never see him with his solemn face
But I'm reminded of the long-eared race;
I think the clerics try, with all their strength,
Who best can draw his ears the greatest length.
You must not argue with him, but for granted
Take all his Creed, although the proof is wanted.

He says, he feels his shibboleth is true,
Damns all to Hell, if they don't feel it too;
He's bigoted, conceited, and straitlaced;
He's stubborn, stupid, and is multifaced:
A Papist, Presbyter, and Covenanter,
High Church, Low Church, Methodist, Ranter,
Macmillanarian, Lutheran, and Calvinian,
Anabaptist, Quaker, and Arminian.
Mormon, Plymouth Brother, and Evangelist,
And many another name is on the list.
I almost had forgot the Trinitarians,
And, most absurd of all, the Unitarians:
The first asserts — there's only One in Three,
The latter holds, that One is Unity;
And yet contrives to keep the name of Christian,
Though he is but an Infidel in fustian.
Jumpers, Shakers, and more queer fanatics;
Fill up the Bedlam of these strange lunatics;
And all this sanctified and childish crew
Presume that they make up God's chosen few;
All travelling, they say, toward one God,
And each asserts he's found the nearest road.
Their ceremonies and their vain pretences
Are but an outrage to our common senses;
Their virgin Mothers, and their mock Redeemers,
But fancies all of visionary dreamers;
A motely group of silly fools and knaves,
The latter rules and all the rest are slaves.

John Lorimer

Born 1812, Paisley, son of a teacher at Paisley Grammar. He worked as a clothier then as an agent for the shipping company MacBrayne and MacIntosh. He was elected Town Chamberlain of Paisley, which job he held until he was offered a staff position with J. & P. Coats. He died in 1878.

Lorimer was known more as a musician than a poet. He played the violin and conducted for many years the orchestra of the Paisley Philharmonic Society, which he had helped to found. He wrote orchestral pieces for the orchestra, and also conducted them in airs from his own and others' songs. He was also a member of the Aeolian Society and the Paisley Musical Association. 'It was a common thing for Mr Lorimer and some other friends to go to Glasgow when there was a good concert, and walk home when it was over.'

The poem here perhaps suggests a more disputative character than his friends found him: 'Public questions had not much charm for him . . . if a question did arise which involved much conflict of opinion, he generally became a quiet listener.'

*

Instructions for the Police

Bobbies! pull up the boys
Who play with dangerous toys,
Pocket their tops, but let alone
The slides that fracture many a bone.

Bobbies! seize all the brood
Who beg their daily food,
But don't refuse when Mary Jane
Proffers a plate of cold again.

Bobbies! seize all who play
Leap-frog, and make them pay,
But, when you smell a murderous fight,
Cut your stick, get out of sight.

Bobbies! creep near the schools,
Confiscate all the bools,
But never venture, on your life,
To seize the brute who whips his wife.

Bobbies! come show your birr,
And capture every girr,
But don't molest the man of straw
Who kicks his horse upon the raw.

Bobbies! arrest the gals
Whene'er they play pallalls,
But smoke the pipe of peace with all
The nymphs when shades of evening fall.

Bobbies! seize all who beat
Their carpets after eight,
But let the precious glaur alone
That plasters every pavement stone.

Bobbies! disperse the gang
Near furnace doors that hang,
But don't forget your patent spats,
Your top-coat, mitts, and warm cravats.

Bobbies! look sharp and shrewd
Whene'er a poor man's screw'd,
But close your peepers when you scan
An elevated gentleman.

Bobbies! drive from the street
The poor who sing so sweet,
But let the drums and trumpets blare
As loud's they like at County Square.

Bobbies! don't light the lanes
Where great darkness reigns,
But when the moon shines clear and bright
Then every lamp be sure to light.

William Elder

Born in the parish of St Andrews, Fife, in 1829. He worked as an apprentice gardener in the Duke of Atholl's gardens, Dunkeld, and in 1867 was appointed to be superintendent of the Fountain Gardens, Paisley — formerly known as Hope Temple Gardens — that were officially donated to the public by Thomas Coats in 1868. Elder published a series of pamphlet 'bouquets': *A Shakespeare Bouquet* (1872) (P/ELD PC95); *A Milton Bouquet* (1874) (P/MIL PC622); *A Burns Bouquet* (1875) (080-REN-1 PC6862); *A Tannahill Bouquet* (1877) (P/TAN PC623). In these pamphlets the common and the botanical names of flora were arranged in sequence with quotes from the authors' works that mentioned them.

*

To the Defenders of Things As They Are

Why speak of peace, of order, and of law?
Teach mute subserviency to those who draw
The water, hew the wood, and dig the soil,
Whose piteous fate is hard incessant toil?
On land and sea, to work from day to day,
To heap up wealth, but which they may
Ne'er hope to share with those who rule
Their fate, and who in church and school
Teach obedience passive, doctrine fit for slaves
To make men bow to tyrants, priests, and knaves,
Oh! when will mankind cease to heed such teachers?
Send to the 'right about' the glib and oily preachers
Of such a gospel, who, in the past as now,
Have taught the people 'twas their fate to bow

And be content and happy in that station,
Where 'God has placed them' to enrich the nation,
To work for kings, aristocrats, and priests so vile,
Who live at ease upon the 'holy' spoil
They wring from labour, and who feed and gorge
Revel in pomp, while others toil in mine and forge.
Oh! let the people's teachers now proclaim
An end to such vile laws, and nobly aim
To legislate for human nature, and to sweep
From off the path of progress, those who'd keep
Mankind still sunk in misery and want,
Repress our aspirations by vile cant,
Teach us to bear the ills we suffer here
For promised blessings in some other sphere,
Where, freed from what the priests call 'bodies vile',
We'll neither need for clothes nor food to toil.
They'll kindly ease us there from digging, spinning,
And promise we shall have a glorious 'inning'.
And so to enter on this world of bliss,
They point to, we patiently must bear in this
Our life of care, of want, of work, and woe —
See misery stamp'd upon our children's brow,
See them condemn'd in early youth to toil
For food and clothes, above, below the soil;
In crowded lanes and courts condemn'd to herd,
Fresh air, sweet flowers, nor song of bird
May they ere hope to know, their life to cheer.
Work, work, is their sad fate from year to year,
And this, Oh God! Thy robber priests proclaim
To be thy law, and in Thy name
Teach men to cherish feelings worthy slaves,
That they with kings, and lords, and such like knaves,
May still continue to divide the spoil
They fleece from us, and from our children's toil.
That they in broadcloth, and in linnen fine,
May be deck'd out, and 'daily wine and dine',
On sumptuous dishes, heedless of the tale they tell:—
That those who fare thus will go down to 'Hell'.
Oh! could I think 'twere any use to pray,
How I would 'wrestle with high Heaven' night and day;

Call God, to purge the world of saintly preachers,
And send people other, truer teachers,
Who'd aid and teach them how to raise the life
We know; show them how to put down social strife;
Make class distinctions cease, and end the cruel
Divisions raised, and blessed by priestly rule.
Teach Labour's sons to cease to bow
To those who rule them, and, by 'law' allow
To them the 'pauper's dole', when want and age
Unfits them longer in the world to wage
Life's battle, to sow the seed, the grain to rear,
To weave the fabrics which their 'masters' wear,
All which they take, and cast a sullen frown
On those who dare to claim their own.
Such is alas! the workman's lot in life,
And when kind death comes to end the strife,
Cruel laws, and custom has for him endowed,
He gets a pauper's grave, a Bastile shroud!

James Thomson

Born Port Glasgow, 1834. His father, a merchant ship's officer, was disabled by a stroke and the family moved to East London in 1840, supported by Mrs Thomson's work as a dressmaker. Thomson's mother, 'mystically inclined' with the millenialist Edward Irving, died two years later, having given birth to a baby boy who was then sent to be reared by an aunt in Scotland. The eight-year-old James on the other hand, his father unable to support him, was placed in the Royal Caledonian Asylum in Islington. On leaving this he moved to the Royal Military Asylum in Chelsea, where he trained to be a schoolmaster in the British Army. He subsequently taught in barracks in Ireland, England and Guernsey before leaving the army in 1862.

He then lodged in London with Charles Bradlaugh, atheist orator and editor of the National Secular Society's weekly newspaper, the *National Reformer*. Bradlaugh had met and befriended Thomson eight years before in barracks near Cork, and he now used his influence as a barrister and financier to find office work for Thomson. But the poet's most consistent source of income for the remaining twenty years of his life from 1862 was literary criticism, essays and poetry, mostly published — until the mid-1870s — in the *National Reformer* itself. It was in the *National Reformer* in 1874 that Thomson's masterpiece, 'The City of Dreadful Night' appeared, in four instalments.

In the mid-seventies Thomson became estranged — bitterly — from Bradlaugh, and sought his living from other journals such as *The Secularist* and a literary-cum-tobacco manufacturer's monthly, *Cope's Tobacco Plant*. He was hard working all his life, teaching himself German, French and Italian, and his reviews over the years included works by such writers as Flaubert, Balzac, Gautier, and Baudelaire, before their translation to English. He published the earliest translations of Leopardi (to whose memory he dedicated his first collection, *The City of Dreadful Night* in 1880) and his translations of Heine were highly praised by, among others, Karl Marx. What Thomson saw as the insularity of British contemporary literature, its prudishness and remoteness from issues tackled by European writers, was a frequent theme of his criticism and essays.

But such views were not likely to make him popular, and his increasing inability to control unexpected drinking bouts also left him guilty, suicidal and, near the end, homeless and in jail. He died on June 3rd 1882, having had a haemorrhage while visiting his friend the blind poet Philip Bourke Marston.

A summary of 'The City of Dreadful Night' might put the following excerpts from the poem in context. 'The City of Dreadful Night' is in twenty-one numbered sections after the opening Proem (pp. 284-5). The odd-numbered sections are in the present tense, describing the city and its inhabitants: its situation, its people, their insomnia; its darkness and strange sounds; that people don't know how they got there, but once there they are fated to keep returning (p. 285); that no one is sane, that reputed ghosts may be madmen; that traffic on unknown business is heard passing; that the inhabitants though outwardly mad are brothers, 'the saddest and the weariest men on earth'; how time seems interminable (pp. 286-7); that the inhabitants all affect — and infect — one another by sharing and breathing the same air; that the cosmos has no personal attributes other than those mistakenly projected upon it by humans; how a 'River of Suicides' runs through the city; that an image of a woman overlooks the city, described as the figure of Melencolia engraved by the German artist Albrecht Durer (pp. 292-5).

The even-numbered sections refer to what the narrator saw and heard on a past visit: a man circling round visiting three places wherein, he said, had died Faith, Hope, and Love; an

open-air speaker describing the journey through a halluco-
genic landscape, when his body had split in two and he had
watched his other self being consoled by a woman who carried
her heart in her hand; people discussing how they had been
refused entrance to Hell because they had had no hope left to
abandon at the gate; others discussing how a God would have
to be vile to make such a vile world, but the world is empty of
any creator or director; the visit of a young man to a secluded
mansion to pay homage to a 'Lady of the Images' — a dead
woman lying in state; a queue of people entering a cathedral,
renouncing their previous commitments to religion, art, drugs,
politics; an orator telling the congregation there is no God or
life after death (pp. 287-9); a member of the congregation
complaining that this does not make a presently unhappy life
any happier (pp. 289-91); a man trying to find the thread that
links his present with his past, so he can go back to infancy; a
stone angel disintegrating in three stages — wings, sword,
trunk — before a sphynx (pp. 291-2).

Among the interpretations the poem can suggest is that of its
presenting a bitter reverse image to the City of God as foretold
in Revelations, and as confidently expected by such as
Thomson's mother, for whom the passage describing
Melencolia might be a kind of elegy.

from The City of Dreadful Night

PROEM

Lo, thus, as prostrate, 'In the dust I write
  My heart's deep languor and my soul's sad tears.'
Yet why evoke the spectres of black night
  To blot the sunshine of exultant years?
Why disinter dead faith from mouldering hidden?
Why break the seals of mute despair unbidden?
  And wail life's discords into careless ears?

Because a cold rage seizes one at whiles
  To show the bitter old and wrinkled truth
Stripped naked of all vesture that beguiles,
  False dreams, false hopes, false masks and modes of youth;
Because it gives some sense of power and passion
In helpless impotence to try to fashion
  Our woe in living words howe'er uncouth.

Surely I write not for the hopeful young,
  Or those who deem their happiness of worth,
Or such as pasture and grow fat among
  The shows of life and feel nor doubt nor dearth,
Or pious spirits with a God above them
To sanctify and glorify and love them,
  Or sages who foresee a heaven on earth.

For none of these I write, and none of these
  Could read the writing if they deigned to try:
So may they flourish, in their due degrees,
  On our sweet earth and in their unplaced sky.
If any cares for the weak words here written,
It must be some one desolate, Fate-smitten,
  Whose faith and hope are dead, and who would die.

Yes, here and there some weary wanderer
  In that same city of tremendous night,
Will understand the speech, and feel a stir
  Of fellowship in all-disastrous fight;
'I suffer mute and lonely, yet another
Uplifts his voice to let me know a brother
  Travels the same wild paths though out of sight.'

O sad Fraternity, do I unfold
    Your dolorous mysteries shrouded from of yore?
Nay, be assured; no secret can be told
    To any who divined it not before:
None uninitiate by many a presage
Will comprehend the language of the message,
    Although proclaimed aloud for evermore.

V

How he arrives there none can clearly know;
    Athwart the mountains and immense wild tracts,
Or flung a waif upon the vast sea-flow,
    Or down the river's boiling cataracts:
To reach it is as dying fever-stricken;
To leave it, slow faint birth intense pangs quicken;
    And memory swoons in both the tragic acts.

But being there one feels a citizen;
    Escape seems hopeless to the heart forlorn:
Can Death-in-Life be brought to life again?
    And yet release does come; there comes a morn
When he awakes from slumbering so sweetly
That all the world is changed for him completely,
    And he is verily as if new-born.

He scarcely can believe the blissful change,
    He weeps perchance who wept not while accurst;
Never again will he approach the range
    Infected by that evil spell now burst:
Poor wretch! who once hath paced that dolent city
Shall pace it often, doomed beyond all pity,
    With horror ever deepening from the first.

Though he possess sweet babes and loving wife,
    A home of peace by loyal friendships cheered,
And love them more than death or happy life,
    They shall avail not; he must dree his weird;
Renounce all blessings for that imprecation,
Steal forth and haunt that builded desolation,
    Of woe and terrors and thick darkness reared.

XIII

Of all things human which are strange and wild
    This is perchance the wildest and most strange,
And showeth man most utterly beguiled,
    To those who haunt that sunless city's range;
That he bemoans himself for aye, repeating
How time is deadly swift, how life is fleeting,
    How naught is constant on the earth but change.

The hours are heavy on him and the days;
    The burden of the months he scarce can bear;
And often in his secret soul he prays
    To sleep through barren periods unaware,
Arousing at some longed-for date of pleasure;
Which having passed and yielded him small treasure,
    He would outsleep another term of care.

Yet in his marvellous fancy he must make
    Quick wings for Time, and see it fly from us;
This Time which crawleth like a monstrous snake,
    Wounded and slow and very venomous;
Which creeps blindwormlike round the earth and ocean,
Distilling poison at each painful motion,
    And seems condemned to circle ever thus.

And since he cannot spend and use aright
    The little time here given him in trust,
But wasteth it in weary undelight
    Of foolish toil and trouble, strife and lust
He naturally claimeth to inherit
The everlasting Future, that his merit
    May have full scope; as surely is more just.

O length of the intolerable hours,
    O nights that are as aeons of slow pain,
O Time, too ample for our vital powers,
    O Life, whose woeful vanities remain
Immutable for all of all our legions
Through all the centuries and in all the regions,
    Not of your speed and variance *we* complain.

We do not ask a longer term of strife,
  Weakness and weariness and nameless woes;
We do not claim renewed and endless life
  When this which is our torment here shall close,
An everlasting conscious inanition!
We yearn for speedy death in full fruition,
  Dateless oblivion and divine repose.

XIV

Large glooms were gathered in the mighty fane,
  With tinted moongleams slanting here and there;
And all was hush: no swelling organ-strain,
  No chant, no voice or murmuring of prayer;
No priests came forth, no tinkling censers fumed,
And the high altar space was unillumed.

Around the pillars and against the walls
  Leaned men and shadows; others seemed to brood
Bent or recumbent in secluded stalls.
  Perchance they were not a great multitude
Save in that city of so lonely streets
Where one may count up every face he meets.

All patiently awaited the event
  Without a stir or sound, as if no less
Self-occupied, doomstricken, while attent.
  And then we heard a voice of solemn stress
From the dark pulpit, and our gaze there met
Two eyes which burned as never eyes burned yet:

Two steadfast and intolerable eyes
  Burning beneath a broad and rugged brow;
The head behind it of enormous size.
  And as black fir-groves in a large wind bow,
Our rooted congregation, gloom-arrayed,
By that great sad voice deep and full were swayed:—

O melancholy Brothers, dark, dark, dark!
O battling in black floods without an ark!
  O spectral wanderers of unholy Night!

My soul hath bled for you these sunless years,
With bitter blood-drops running down like tears:
   Oh, dark, dark, dark, withdrawn from joy and light!

My heart is sick with anguish for your bale;
Your woe hath been my anguish; yea, I quail
   And perish in your perishing unblest.
And I have searched the highths and depths, the scope
Of all our universe, with desperate hope
   To find some solace for your wild unrest.

And now at last authentic word I bring,
Witnessed by every dead and living thing;
   Good tidings of great joy for you, for all:
There is no God; no Fiend with names divine
Made us and tortures us; if we must pine,
   It is to satiate no Being's gall.

It was the dark delusion of a dream,
That living Person conscious and supreme,
   Whom we must curse for cursing us with life;
Whom we must curse because the life He gave
Could not be buried in the quiet grave,
   Could not be killed by poison or by knife.

This little life is all we must endure,
The grave's most holy peace is ever sure,
   We fall asleep and never wake again;
Nothing is of us but the mouldering flesh,
Whose elements dissolve and merge afresh
   In earth, air, water, plants, and other men.

We finish thus; and all our wretched race
Shall finish with its cycle, and give place
   To other beings, with their own time-doom:
Infinite aeons ere our kind began;
Infinite aeons after the last man
   Has joined the mammoth in earth's tomb and womb.

We bow down to the universal laws,
Which never had for man a special clause
   Of cruelty or kindness, love or hate:

If toads and vultures are obscene to sight,
If tigers burn with beauty and with might,
    Is it by favour or by wrath of fate?

All substance lives and struggles evermore
Through countless shapes continually at war,
    By countless interactions interknit:
If one is born a certain day on earth,
All times and forces tended to that birth,
    Not all the world could change or hinder it.

I find no hint throughout the Universe
Of good or ill, of blessing or of curse;
    I find alone Necessity Supreme;
With infinite Mystery, abysmal, dark,
Unlighted ever by the faintest spark
    For us the flitting shadows of a dream.

O Brothers of sad lives! they are so brief;
A few short years must bring us all relief:
    Can we not bear these years of labouring breath?
But if you would not this poor life fulfil,
Lo, you are free to end it when you will,
    Without the fear of waking after death.—

The organ-like vibrations of his voice
    Thrilled through the vaulted aisles and died away;
The yearning of the tones which bade rejoice
    Was sad and tender as a requiem lay:
Our shadowy congregation rested still
As brooding on that 'End it when you will.'

                         XVI

Our shadowy congregation rested still,
    As musing on that message we had heard
And brooding on that 'End it when you will;'
    Perchance awaiting yet some other word;
When keen as lightning through a muffled sky
Sprang forth a shrill and lamentable cry:—

The man speaks sooth, alas! the man speaks sooth:
  We have no personal life beyond the grave;
There is no God; Fate knows nor wrath nor ruth:
  Can I find here the comfort which I crave?

In all eternity I had one chance,
  One few years' term of gracious human life:
The splendours of the intellect's advance,
  The sweetness of the home with babes and wife;

The social pleasures with their genial wit;
  The fascination of the worlds of art,
The glories of the worlds of nature, lit
  By large imagination's flowing heart;

The rapture of mere being, full of health;
  The careless childhood and the ardent youth,
The strenuous manhood winning various wealth,
  The reverend age serene with life's long truth:

All the sublime prerogatives of Man;
  The storied memories of the times of old,
The patient tracking of the world's great plan
  Through sequences and changes myriadfold.

This chance was never offered me before;
  For me the infinite Past is blank and dumb:
This chance recurreth never, nevermore;
  Blank, blank for me the infinite To-come.

And this sole chance was frustrate from my birth,
  A mockery, a delusion; and my breath
Of noble human life upon this earth
  So racks me that I sigh for senseless death.

My wine of life is poison mixed with gall,
  My noonday passes in a nightmare dream,
I worse than lose the years which are my all:
  What can console me for the loss supreme?

Speak not of comfort where no comfort is,
  Speak not at all: can words make foul things fair?
Our life's a cheat, our death a black abyss:
  Hush and be mute envisaging despair.—

This vehement voice came from the northern aisle
  Rapid and shrill to its abrupt harsh close;
And none gave answer for a certain while,
  For words must shrink from these most wordless woes;
At last the pulpit speaker simply said,
With humid eyes and thoughtful drooping head:—

My Brother, my poor Brothers, it is thus;
This life itself holds nothing good for us,
  But it ends soon and nevermore can be;
And we knew nothing of it ere our birth,
And shall know nothing when consigned to earth:
  I ponder these thoughts and they comfort me.

XX

I sat me weary on a pillar's base,
  And leaned against the shaft; for broad moonlight
O'erflowed the peacefulness of cloistered space,
  A shore of shadow slanting from the right:
The great cathedral's western front stood there,
A wave-worn rock in the calm sea of air.

Before it, opposite my place of rest,
  Two figures faced each other, large, austere;
A couchant sphinx in shadow to the breast,
  An angel standing in the moonlight clear;
So mighty by magnificence of form,
They were not dwarfed beneath that mass enorm.

Upon the cross-hilt of a naked sword
  The angel's hands, as prompt to smite, were held;
His vigilant intense regard was poured
  Upon the creature placidly unquelled,
Whose front was set at level gaze which took
No heed of aught, a solemn trance-like look.

And as I pondered these opposèd shapes
 My eyelids sank in stupor, that dull swoon
Which drugs and with a leaden mantle drapes
 The outworn to worse weariness. But soon
A sharp and clashing noise the stillness broke,
And from the evil lethargy I woke.

The angel's wings had fallen, stone on stone,
 And lay there shattered; hence the sudden sound:
A warrior leaning on his sword alone
 Now watched the sphinx with that regard profound;
The sphinx unchanged looked forthright, as aware
Of nothing in the vast abyss of air.

Again I sank in that repose unsweet,
 Again a clashing noise my slumber rent;
The warrior's sword lay broken at his feet:
 An unarmed man with raised hands impotent
Now stood before the sphinx, which ever kept
Such mien as if with open eyes it slept.

My eyelids sank in spite of wonder grown;
 A louder crash upstartled me in dread:
The man had fallen forward, stone on stone,
 And lay there shattered, with his trunkless head
Between the monster's large quiescent paws,
Beneath its grand front changeless as life's laws.

The moon had circled westward full and bright,
 And made the temple-front a mystic dream,
And bathed the whole enclosure with its light,
 The sworded angel's wrecks, the sphinx supreme:
I pondered long that cold majestic face
Whose vision seemed of infinite void space.

XXI

Anear the centre of that northern crest
 Stands out a level upland bleak and bare,
From which the city east and south and west
 Sinks gently in long waves; and thronèd there

An Image sits, stupendous, superhuman,
The bronze colossus of a wingèd Woman,
  Upon a graded granite base foursquare.

Low-seated she leans forward massively,
  With cheek on clenched left hand, the forearm's might
Erect, its elbow on her rounded knee;
  Across a clasped book in her lap the right
Upholds a pair of compasses; she gazes
With full set eyes, but wandering in thick mazes
  Of sombre thought beholds no outward sight.

Words cannot picture her; but all men know
  That solemn sketch the pure sad artist wrought
Three centuries and threescore years ago,
  With phantasies of his peculiar thought:
The instruments of carpentry and science
Scattered about her feet, in strange alliance
  With the keen wolf-hound sleeping undistraught;

Scales, hour-glass, bell, and magic-square above;
  The grave and solid infant perched beside,
With open winglets that might bear a dove,
  Intent upon its tablets, heavy-eyed;
Her folded wings as of a mighty eagle,
But all too impotent to lift the regal
  Robustness of her earth-born strength and pride;

And with those wings, and that light wreath which seems
  To mock her grand head and the knotted frown
Of forehead charged with baleful thoughts and dreams,
  The household bunch of keys, the housewife's gown
Voluminous, indented, and yet rigid
As if a shell of burnished metal frigid,
  The feet thick shod to tread all weakness down;

The comet hanging o'er the waste dark seas,
  The massy rainbow curved in front of it,
Beyond the village with the masts and trees;
  The snaky imp, dog-headed, from the Pit,
Bearing upon its batlike leathern pinions
Her name unfolded in the sun's dominions,
  The 'Melencolia' that transcends all wit.

Thus has the artist copied her, and thus
  Surrounded to expound her form sublime,
Her fate heroic and calamitous;
  Fronting the dreadful mysteries of Time,
Unvanquished in defeat and desolation,
Undaunted in the hopeless conflagration
  Of the day setting on her baffled prime.

Baffled and beaten back she works on still,
  Weary and sick of soul she works the more,
Sustained by her indomitable will:
  The hands shall fashion and the brain shall pore
And all her sorrow shall be turned to labour,
Till death the friend-foe piercing with his sabre
  That mighty heart of hearts ends bitter war.

But if blacker night could dawn on night,
  With tenfold gloom on moonless night unstarred,
A sense more tragic than defeat and blight,
  More desperate than strife with hope debarred,
More fatal than the admanantine Never
Encompassing her passionate endeavour,
  Dawns glooming in her tenebrous regard:

The sense that every struggle brings defeat
  Because Fate holds no prize to crown success;
That all the oracles are dumb or cheat
  Because they have no secret to express;
That none can pierce the vast black veil uncertain
Because there is no light beyond the curtain;
  That all is vanity and nothingness.

Titanic from her high throne in the north,
  That City's sombre Patroness and Queen,
In bronze sublimity she gazes forth
  Over her Capital of teen and threne,
Over the river with its isles and bridges,
The marsh and moorland, to the stern rock-ridges,
  Confronting them with a coëval mien.

The moving moon and stars from east to west
    Circle before her in the sea of air;
Shadows and gleams glide round her solemn rest.
    Her subjects often gaze up to her there:
The strong to drink new strength of iron endurance,
The weak new terrors; all, renewed assurance
    And confirmation of the old despair.

Marion Bernstein

It is apparent from Marion Bernstein's *Mirren's Musings* that she wrote regularly for the *Glasgow Weekly Mail*. Her 1876 collection is not listed in the British Library Catalogue, though a copy is in the Mitchell Library Glasgow as well as Paisley Central Library (P/BERN PC 1926). The author's preface reads as follows:

> The following 'Musings' have been in a great measure, at once the solace, and the result of a long period of physical affliction, during which I was hardly capable of any greater exertion than that required for occasional reading, writing, and conversation. In consequence of this feebleness, my mind was chiefly occupied in musing over what I read or heard of the world from which I was shut out, or what I remembered of my own past experience.
>
> At times I feel deeply thankful for those calm and thoughtful years, which were not the least happy of the years I remember, in spite of physical suffering, and the natural longing for health that no human heart can quite suppress, even though able to say with the Psalmist of Israel, 'It was good for me to be afflicted.'
>
> I have to thank my stranger friends in various parts of the world for their kind letters expressing so much sympathy and good will. I am sure they will be pleased to know that my health has much improved lately. Although still quite unable to walk (through contraction of the sciatica nerve) I am no longer confined to my bed; but for many months past I have been well enough to resume my former occupation as a teacher of music, and I hope in that capacity to make the acquaintance of some of my readers, —
>
> I am, my dear Readers,
> > Yours faithfully,
> > > MARION BERNSTEIN
>
> 5 Dunrobin Place, Paisley Road,
> Glasgow, 1876

*

Woman's Rights and Wrongs

I may be wrong in opinion, but still to my mind it seems
As if Parliament, Council, or Congress could never be womanly themes.—
Touching the so-called Woman's Rights, such discussion belongs
To the tender and true in a less degree than the subject of Woman's Wrongs.

JESSIE RUSSELL

Pray, in what way is wrong redressed,
    But by conceding right?
And Woman Suffrage is the best
    For which our sex can fight.

You'd give the lash to wifebeaters,
    But surely you should know,
If women legislated, they'd
    Have had it long ago.

You speak of women's wages
    Being scandalously small;
Believe me, Woman Suffrage
    Soon would find a cure for all.

Our claims are oft misunderstood;
    We would but share with man
The human right of doing good
    In any way we can.

Why should we put our trust in men,
    Who oft betray our cause?
Let women vote away their wrongs,
    And vote for righteous laws.

A Rule to Work Both Ways

Suggested by a 'Wife-beater's' Letter

If beating can reform a wife
   It might reform a husband too,
Since such are the effects of strife—
   My sisters, I advise that you

Should try it, not with fists — Oh, no!
   For that would seem like some weak joker;
In husband-curing let each blow
   Be given with the kitchen poker!

When flagellating, let them see
   That you are not afraid to try
The very worst 'extremity;'
   Then they must yield, lest they should die.

And if you cannot cure them, 'kill!'
   As coolly teaches the Wife-beater;
In widowhood, no doubt you will
   Find your existence somewhat sweeter.

When thus bad husbands cure bad wives,
   And wives cure brutes to whom they're mated,
Soon will the plagues of many lives
   Be safely buried, or cremated.

A wife or husband 'in the way'
   You need but beat to death, or smother;
And then you may at any day
   Find better fortune with another.

Wanted A Husband

Baking and cooking, scrubbing and dressing—
Accomplishments grand, well worth the possessing;
Economy too, with wisdom discreet,
My wife must practise to make all ends meet.
                                    ELEVE

Wanted a husband who doesn't suppose,
That all earthly employments one feminine knows,—
That she'll scrub, do the cleaning, and cooking, and baking,
And plain needlework, hats and caps, and dressmaking.
Do the family washing, yet always look neat,
Mind the bairns, with a temper unchangeably sweet,
Be a cheerful companion, whenever desired,
And contentedly toil day and night, if required.
Men expecting as much, one may easily see,
But they're not what is wanted, at least, not by me.

Wanted a husband who's tender and true,
Who will stick to his duty, and never get 'fou,'
But when all his day's work he has blithely gone through,
Help his wife, 'set to rights,' till her work is done too;
Who will not absurdly, and helplessly go,
And trouble the wife about 'buttons to sew,'
On his shirt, or his gloves, or his coat, or his vest,
But will sew them himself, and not think he's oppressed.
Now, if such a lad you should happen to see,
He's wanted by many, but yet — not by me!

Manly Sports

How brave is the hunter who nobly will dare
On horseback to follow the small timid hare;
Oh! ye soldiers who fall in defence of your flag,
What are you to the hero who brings down the stag?

Bright eyes glance admiring, soft hearts give their loves
To the knight who shoots best in 'the tourney of doves;'
Nothing else with such slaughtering feats can compare,
To win manly applause, or the smiles of the fair.

A cheer for fox-hunting! Come all who can dare
Track this dangerous animal down to its lair;
'Tis first trapped, then set free for the huntsmen to follow
With horses and hounds, and with heartstirring halloo!

The brave knights on the moor when the grouse are a-drive,
Slay so many, you'd think, there'd be none left alive;
Oh! the desperate daring of slaughtering grouse,
Can only be matched in a real slaughterhouse.

The angler finds true Anglo-Saxon delight,
In trapping small fish, who so foolishly bite,
He enjoys the wild terror of creatures so weak,
And what manlier pleasures can any one seek?

Human Rights

Man holds so exquisitively tight
To everything he deems his right;
If woman wants a share, to fight
She has, and strive with all her might.

But we are nothing like so jealous
As any of you surly fellows;
Give us our rights and we'll not care
To cheat our brothers of their share.

Above such selfish *man-like* fright,
We'd give fair play, let come what might,
To he or she folk, black or white,
And haste the reign of Human Right.

A Dream

I dreamt that the nineteenth century
   Had entirely passed away,
And had given place to a more advanced
   And very much brighter day.

For Woman's Rights were established quite,
   And man could the fact discern
That he'd long been teaching his grandmamma
   What she didn't require to learn.

There were female chiefs in the Cabinet,
   (Much better than males I'm sure!)
And the Commons were three-parts feminine,
   While the Lords were seen no more!

And right well did the ladies legislate,
   They determined to 'keep the peace,'
So well they managed affairs of State,
   That the science of war might cease.

Now no man could venture to beat his wife,
   For the women had settled by law
That whoever did so should lose his life,
   Then he'd never do so any more.

There were no more physicians of either sex,
    For the schools were required to teach
The science of healing to every child
    As well as the parts of speech.

There were no more lawyers — all children learned
    The code of their country's laws;
There were female judges, and truth became
    The fashion in every cause,

All the churches attended a conference
    At which every sect agreed
That an erring opinion was not so bad
    As a false word or wicked deed.

At this I felt sure there was some mistake,
    It seemed such a *strange* idea!
My eyes opened wide, and that made me wake,
    Now wasn't the vision queer?

Married and 'Settled'

Oh! I have sighed to read
    The trials of this season;
Wife-murder seems, indeed,
    An everyday transgression.

Too oft the marriage bond
    Is one of fear and pain;
Affection true and fond
    Should link that sacred chain.

Can home appear 'sweet home'
    When 'husband' means a foe
And 'wife' a slave? — for some
    Submit to have it so.

It seems to me such wives
   Act rashly, at the least,
Like men who risk their lives
   In taming a wild beast.

Beast-taming seems to be
   Not quite a woman's mission;
The brutes might stay for me,
   In bachelor condition.

But, since you choose to wed
   And risk your limbs and lives,
Consider what I've said
   All ye unhappy wives.

Exert your common sense
   And form a combination
For mutual defence
   Against assassination.

A Song of Glasgow Town

I'll sing a song of Glasgow town,
That stands on either side
The river that was once so fair,
The much insulted Clyde.
That stream, once pure, but now so foul,
Was never made to be
A sewer, just to bear away
The refuse to the sea.
Oh, when will Glasgow's factories
Cease to pollute its tide,
And let the Glasgow people see
The beauty of the Clyde!

I'll sing a song of Glasgow town:
On every side I see
A crowd of giant chimney stalks
As grim as grim can be.
There's always smoke from some of them—
Some black, some brown, some grey
Yet genius has invented means
To burn the smoke away.
Oh, when will Glasgow factories
Cease to pollute the air;
To spread dull clouds o'er sunny skies
That should be bright and fair!

I'll sing a song of Glasgow town,
Where wealth and want abound;
Where the high seat of learning dwells
Mid ignorance profound.
Oh, when will Glasgow make a rule
To do just what she ought—
Let starving bairns in every school
Be fed as well as taught!
And when will Glasgow city be
Fair Caledonia's pride,
And boast her clear unclouded skies,
And crystal-flowing Clyde?

A Song for the Working Man

Oh! there's nothing in life so gay
　　As labour and simple fare,
If you're able to pay your way
　　Untroubled by cank'ring care.
But labour beyond one's strength
　　Turns work from joy to pain,
And tasks of a cruel length
　　May well make the brave complain.

Ye friends of the working man,
　　Who have brightened so many lives,
Now bid them do all they can
　　In striving to help their wives:
It were sin to oppress the strong—
　　But why should weak woman bear
A day's task, for man too long,
　　And seldom his leisure share?

Much good has been surely done,
　　But much still remains to do;
Then join in it every one,
　　And carry the good work through.
When the working man and his wife
　　Spend together the leisure hour,
The contentment of humble life
　　Will be sweeter than wealth or power.

Jessie Russell

Born Glasgow 1850. An article on her by A. G. Murdoch in the *Glasgow Weekly Mail* for June 18th 1881 — No. 33 in a series 'Minor Scottish Poets' — describes how she was orphaned when aged nine and taken to be brought up by her maternal grandparents in a cottage in Thorworthald, Dumfriesshire. Her grandfather was a Cameronian, and every Sunday she walked with him the nearly five miles to the Reformed Presbyterian Church in Dumfries. Her mother had hoped she would be a teacher but on the death of her grandfather Jessie entered domestic service at the age of fourteen. She subsequently learned dressmaking at which she was working when in 1873 she married a ship's carpenter and settled in Partick. Poems by her began to appear in the *Glasgow Weekly Mail* and other local newspapers, which poems were gathered in the collection *The Blinkin' o' the Fire* published in 1877. In his article of 1881 Murdoch concluded by remarking that Jessie Russell had not written any poems for a few years due to 'an increasing little family and the trials and vicissitudes of married life'.

It was Elspeth King of the People's Palace in Glasgow who drew the attention of the editor of this anthology to the work of Jessie Russell: a complete photocopy made by Elspeth King of *The Blinkin' o' the Fire* has been added to the Paisley Central Library collection.

*

Woman's Rights *versus* Woman's Wrongs

I may be wrong in opinion, but still to my mind it seems
As if Parliament, Council, or Congress could never be womanly
themes.—
Regarding the so called 'Woman's Rights,' discussion on which
belongs,
To the 'tender and true' in less degree than the subject of Woman's
Wrongs.

Woman struggling for daily bread to keep body and soul together,
Trudging to work, on a scanty meal, through all kinds of wintry
weather,
Pacing behind the shop counter, braving a thousand ills,
Stitching away at the sewing machines, or weaving the web in the
mills.

Workmen's wages have risen, but so has the price of bread,
While female work is so poorly paid, can women be clothed or fed?
Many a homeless orphan girl is mounting a stranger's stair,
Weary and sad, to the room she rents, with little of comfort there.

Many a worn-out widow, who once was tenderly cherished,
Toiling to feed her children when the winner of bread has perished,
But little she gets by her 'midnight oil', though everything else is dear,
And the rents are getting higher and higher from year to year.

And then there are slaves whom we dream not of, and many a drudge
to be found
In our city gentlemen's houses, in those kitchens underground,
She may have a wage which is better than those, nor have hunger or
cold to bode,
But throughout the year she has seldom one of the fifty days of God.

But many a one bears a greater wrong who is called by the name of
wife,
While the dogs which follow her brutal lord lead not such a wretched
life;
But a life for a life, and the murderer's hung, and we think not the law
inhuman,
Then why not the lash for the man who kicks or strikes a defenceless
woman?

A Recantation

Dedicated to Miss Marion Bernstein, who wrote to me that 'Woman's Suffrage' was the true antidote for all the evils complained of in Woman's Rights v. Woman's Wrongs.

I rather think I have been wrong,
    Upon mature reflection,
I hope to sing a different song
    The very first 'election.'

And if you'll do the eloquent
    (As Moses said to Aaron),
And plead our cause with Parliament,
    I'll vote for none but 'Marion.'

'Signs of our Times'

[The winter of 1875 in Glasgow, a time of almost unprecedented dull trade.]

Methinks that 'deep prophetic soul'
    Was 'wanting' in the cranium,
To certify us near that goal,
    A glorious grand 'Millenium.'

For still dull poortith's tempests lower
    Despite prophetic fawning,
Perchance 'tis the proverbial hour
    So dark before the dawning.

They talk o' floods in men's affairs
    An' fortune being tidal,
The present floods are floods o' cares,
    Wi' shoals o' workmen idle.

Oor leaves ha'e reached a pretty pass
    An' sair need turnin' over,
The mongrel blades o' withered grass
    Tae germinate in clover.

'The labourer's worthy o' his hire,'
    But where's the body willing
Tae draigle through the daily mire*
    When a' the hire's a shilling.

Faix, no! he'd rather starve belyve;
    But, hark! the clapper's clanging,
The only trade that seems tae thrive†
    Is 'gentlemanly' hanging.

But for St. Mungo's idle bees
    Such nectar's too appalling,‡
Better to make them 'Clyde Trustees,'
    A most 'effectual calling.'

They aften weigh the 'pros' and 'cons'
    Aboot the river's cleansing,
But, faix! I think oor wealthy 'drones'
    Are lang aboot commencing.

The grand division o' the spoil
    Is jist a wee engrossing,
But pit their brithers tae the toil,
    The men wha 'sweep the crossing.'

    The Lord Provôst's offer of a shilling a day as 'crossing sweepers', to men out of employment.
† With reference to the unusual number of executions in this district, and that 'gentleman' official, Mr Marwood.
‡ Not long ago I read a newspaper paragraph quoting some of the enormous salaries given to these gentlemen of the Clyde Trust, some as high as £1000 per annum.

The Mother's Story

Wee Teenie, who died of hydrophobia, at Govan, after suffering
great agony, May 15th 1876.

'My Teenie was but five years old,' the weeping mother said,
The while tae me the quivering voice her anguished heart betrayed,
'But oh, sae usefu' in the hoose an' sic a help tae me!
Noo oot o' nine it's pleased the Lord tae leave me only three;
I'll no rebel against His will, but oh my heart is sair.'
For twa three minutes thro' her sobs she couldna tell me mair;
I wept wi' her, an' felt as if my heart was broken tae,
The silent sympathy that words have not the power to say.
'That day I had been oot a wee, an' through the open door
A strange wee dog ran ben the hoose we never saw before,
But when I gaed tae chase it oot it managed for tae hide
Below the bed, I hadna time, an' so I let it bide.
A wee while after oot it cam', an' Teenie made to run,
It jumped up and nipped her face, as if in playfu' fun,
I thocht it only licked her mooth, the prickin' o' a preen,
The merest scratch below the nose was a' that could be seen.
A' Teenie said was, 'Mither, look!' an' gied tae grup my goon,
Syne thocht nae mair aboot it, for she was na up or doon.
    'Twas twa three weeks ere she took ill, an' then the doctors cam',
But a' their efforts failed to save my puir wee suffering lamb;
An' ower an' ower wi' childish fear, my hert was wae tae see,
My bonnie wean wad ask again, 'Ah, mither, will I dee?'
The day before she dee'd she missed her wee bit todlin' brither,
An' speering' for him, said tae me, 'Ye'll mind an' watch him mither:
It wadna dae tae let him oot, for deed it's hard tae tell
But what he micht be lost, ye ken, wi' wanderin' hissel'.'
Sae womanly the cares that filled that young but thochtfu' heed
I mind her wee auld-fashioned ways when noo she's cauld an' deed;
But at the last when sair distressed her agony grew sae wild,
I couldna bear tae look upon the death throes of my child,
I rushed oot frantic frae the hoose, away I kent na where,
In misery an' despairingly, I knelt tae God in prayer;
An' then my heart was calmed again, the Lord had strengthened me,
An' I went back tae her bedside an' saw my darlin' dee.
An' she'll never run my errands mair; but grieving 's only vain,
For Teenie's up in Glory, an' I'm sure we'll meet again.

Thomas Burnside

Born Paisley 1822. Worked as a weaver then for two years ran a small shop with a circulating library. This foundered though and he sold up at some loss and returned to weaving. He was forty-three before he started writing, having taken the notion while writing a letter to his son in Ardrossan. After this he was quite prolific. 'On occasions of agitation in the weaving trade in reference to prices and other such matters, he was always ready with a set of verses suitable to the times, some of such productions being marked with more vigour of criticism than was agreeable to those whom he satirised, and perhaps more than was necessary or strictly just. But they were signs of the fermentation that prevailed among the operatives, and were read with much avidity by his fellow tradesmen. In his later years he manifested much interest in politics, and professed to be a Radical of the most advanced type; but he was more inclined to indicate his difference of opinion with political opponents by good humoured banter than by rancorous expressions.'

He was also active in the Temperance movement. He died in 1879.

*

The Idle Weaver

The puir wabster's been lang oot o' wark,
  For the trade's been sae lang unco dull,
That he's left noo wi' scarcely a sark,
  For his loom's been sae lang staunin' still.

311

M

The shune are clean worn aff his feet,
   An' the coat on his back's jist as bad,
Rinnin' speirin' at a' he may meet,
   If they ken whaur a wab's tae be had.
      For, O, there's baith want an' distress,
        Aye when there's nae wab in the loom;
      An' naething ava in the press
        Mak's a'body thowless and grim.

But there's no ane he meets that can tell
   Whaur a thing o' the kin's to be got,
For they're a' jist as bad as himsel',
   As they canna get leese o' a shot.
But although he's sae rack't in the mind,
   He has tried Causeyside up an' doon;
Though the foremen were civil an' kind,
   Still their answer was 'No,' — roon an' roon.
      For, O, etc.

Wi' sair heart he gangs hame to the wife,
   An' the bairns ance sae canty an' crouse,
But there's noo nae mair daffing nor strife,
   For they ken there's nae meal in the house.
Then everything's gane to the pawn,
   That wud raise a bit shilling or twa;
An' the puir body hardly could stan'
   Whan he selt the auld wag-at-the-wa'.
      For, O, etc.

An' the wifie, puir body, 's gaun gyte,
   For she disna ken weel what to dae;
On the future it's waefu' to think,
   For her bed's jist a buttle o' strae;
An' she prays to the Lord for relief,
   An' for comfort in a' their distress,
For her heart's nearly broken wi' grief,
   They're sae lang oot o' wark an' opprest.
      For, O, etc.

Things are possibly noo at the warst,
　　Let us hope they may soon tak' a turn,
Then she'll talk o' this time o' the past,
　　As she birls awa' at her pirn—
An' he'll ca' through the shuttle wi' glee,
　　Wi' a heart that's baith cheery an' hale,
An' the bairns be fu' canty an' slee,
　　Wi' plenty o' parritch an' kail.
　　　　For, O, etc.

A Voice from the Workshop

By Labour's proud genius the world is fair,
　　From Labour earth's kingdoms have grown;
Yet the labourer's maligned if he asks a fair share
　　Of that which by right is his own.
'Tis the labourer upholds both the Crown an' the State,
　　And forms Britain's bulwarks so bold;
'Tis the labourer supports both the wealthy and great,
　　While he shivers himself in the cold.

Then why should we labour for pittance so small,
　　While the rich have their thousands a year,
And a small kitchen serve us for bed-room and all,
　　While they their proud mansions uprear?
And why should the wealthy have power to oppress
　　And use working men as their tools,
When true honest Union would bring us redress,
　　If we only abide by its rules?

Come then and unite into one solid band,
　　And each one a helping hand lend,
And ever remember, although we now groan,
　　That it's never too late for to mend.

To insure our success let us all organise,
    Our manhood proclaim, and unite,
And delay not till even to-morrow's sunrise,
    For our battle is Right against Might.

Though oft we may fail, never mind, try again,
    And be true to our purpose like men,
And never relax, but keep on the strain,
    And we're sure to succeed in the end:
Old Rome was not built in a day, as we know,
    Nor trees felled with one blow of the axe,
Strike then, like the woodman, hard blow after blow,
    And we'll reach yet the happy climax.

A Union Lay

I hope, dear friens, there's nae offence,
In ane wha hasna' muckle sense,
To gie a word or twa's advice,
To help to rise oor starving price,
An' a' oor mony wounds to heal,
An' raise us in the social scale,
An' bring deserters to the fold,
An' form a one and solid whole.

An' noo, dear brithren o' the shuttle,
Ye ken we've been in mony a pickle,
An' brocht to mony a waefu' crisis,
By trying to maintain oor prices
Wi' men that's void o' sense an' shame,
An' callous hearted in the main,
Wha'd starve us oot o' hoose an' ha',
To build their mansions big an' braw.

But still the truth I'm bound to tell,
There's black, black sheep amang oorsel',

That mump at nettles wi' their drover
Before they'd buy the Union clover;
But tho' they've wander'd far frae hame,
I hope to see them a' again
Established under Union laws,
An' working for oor common cause.

The kintra folks are aye a thorn—
They're here the day, awa' the morn—
When wabs are plenty, then they're wi' us,
But when they're scant, it's then they'll lea' us
To fecht the battle as we may,
While they stan' back an' view the fray,
An' watch us wi' a greedy e'e,
Tho' ready aye to turn an' flee.

And then the agents, hungry maws,
The blackest plague we hae ava,
They'll fawn an creep like sleekie mice,
For wabs they'll tak' at ony price.
If weavers wud be independent,
They'd very soon ha'e the ascendent,
They'd soon let go this cursed drag,
An' a' work thro' a general bag.

Noo, brethren, what I'd like to see
Is toon an' kintray baith agree,
Wi' honest purpose, true as steel,
An' work hard for ilk ithers weal.
Then come, my brethren, far an' near,
Come join us, for there's nocht to fear,
An' show a firm determination
By joining the Amalgamation.

Fling disputations to the win',
An' bury strife beneath the grun,
The moral sword of Justice wield,
And sweep oppressors frae the field:
Come frae the east, the wast, the north,
Come frae the south, come forth, come forth!
And let the watchword be the cry
To stand the hazard o' the die!

Never Drink Onything Stronger Than Tea

Noo friens haud yer tongue, an' I'll sing ye a sang,
At least I will try't, an' dae a' that I can;
An' the pith o' my sang is a counsel to you,
For aye to keep sober whatever ye do.

> *Chorus*
> Aye to keep sober,
> Aye to keep sober,
> An' never drink onything stronger than tea.

Just last Saturday nicht, as I daunner'd my lane,
I met Weaver Geordie gaun stachering hame;
He had na' got by me, least no very far,
When as I luck't roon he fell splash in the glaur.

> *Chorus*
> Then, oh! friens be sober,
> Aye try an' keep sober,
> An' never drink onything stronger than tea.

There's an auld frien' o' mine, an he's o' the black squad,
On the pays ne'er comes hame till he's flung owre his gab
As muckle's wud buy a new goon to the wife,
But instead o' a goon, she's to rin for her life.

> *Chorus*
> Then, oh! friens be sober,
> Aye try an' keep sober,
> An' never drink onything stronger than tea.

There's a chiel I could name, an' I ken he works sair,
But the wife drinks his pay, an' would drink sax times mair,
The ends they'll no meet let him dae what he can,
For whate'er he brings hame she whups aff to the pawn.

> *Chorus*
> Then, oh! friens be sober,
> Aye try an' keep sober,
> An' never drink onything stronger than tea.

Noo friens, if ye'd only jist tak' time to think
On the bawbees that's spent on this vile cursed drink,
Twud mak' mony hames happy wi' peace an' content,
It would buy meat an' claes, an' would aye pay the rent.

Chorus
Then, oh! friens be sober,
Aye try an' keep sober,
An' never drink onything stronger than tea.

The Good Templar movement a blessing has been—
It has done muckle guid baith to fae an' to frien,
Made mony hames happy whaur ance there was strife,
An' strife an' contention between man an' wife.

Chorus
Then, oh! friens be sober,
Aye try an' keep sober,
An' never drink onything stronger than tea.

Address to my Brither Wabsters

To you, dear brithren o' the shuttle,
    I maun address a word or twa.
The weaving trade's noo turned sae fickle,
    In fact, it's wearing fast awa;
Wee bits o' wabs no wurth the looming,
    A state o' things we a' deplore,
That keeps us ever constant grinning
    Wi' poortith never frae oor door.

Wi' selfish agents in the kintra,
    An' greedy grasping corks at hame,
The weaver's life's made cauld and wintry,
    Wi' mony a scrimpit hungry wame.

317

Come then, arise, be up an' doing,
   Let's aim at something for oorsel',
An' no our doonward course keep wooing,
   An' soundin' aye our funeral knell.

Come show the world we still are able,
   Though as a class we're sunk sae low,
To mak' the weaving trade so stable
   That comforts to our hames will flow:
Come form a strong organization,
   Let each and all assistance len'
To organised co-operation,
   An' show the world we still are men.

For what's to hinder us, as weavers,
   To manufacture for oorsel'?
Let's but keep clear o' fause deceivers,
   There's nocht ava that I can tell.
I'm sure there's plenty heads for planning,
   An' willing han's to execute,
So that wi' proper understan'ing,
   We'll sure succeed withoot a doot.

Let ilka ane, wi' brave heart struggle,
   Wi' diligence his lot pursue,
An' ne'er let envy gie him trouble,
   But 'paddle aye his ain canoe;'
And then e'er lang oor textile fabrics
   Will sure be worn by ilka frien',
Baith harness shawl an' linen cambric,
   Fit to adorn our British Queen.

In vain shall tyrants try to bend us,
   If we the golden rule pursue,
The people's love will well befrien' us,
   The many then will help the few.
Come then stand forth, be firm and truthful,
   Tho' mony doots the mind may fill,
An' wi' each ither aye be trustful,
   An' then we'll in the end prevail.

William Aitken

Born in Sorn, Ayrshire, in 1851. Although his first job at the age of ten was as a shoemaker's apprentice, it was with the Glasgow and South Western Railway that he spent his working life. By the time that the poem 'After the Accident' was published, he was known in local poetic circles as 'Inspector Aitken': the title-page of his 1893 *Echoes from the Iron Road* styles him 'Inspector Aitken, G & SW Railway, Greenock'. He later worked from St Enoch's station in Glasgow.

The point of the story in 'After the Accident' — the dangers caused by long shifts putting profit before safety in services used by the public — is summed up in the closing lines of 'Drew the Wrong Lever!' by Aitken's contemporary, Alexander Anderson ('Surfaceman') from Dumfriesshire:

'Drew the wrong lever?' 'Yes, I say!
Go tell my wife, and — take me away!'

That was what the pointsman said,
With both hands at his throbbing head.

O ye of this nineteenth century time,
Who hold low dividends as a crime,

Listen. So long as a twelve-hour strain
Rests like a load of lead on the brain,

With its ringing of bells and rolling of wheels,
Drawing of levers until one feels

The hands grow numb with nerveless touch,
And the handles shake and slip in the clutch,

So long will ye have pointsmen to say —
'Drew the wrong lever! take me away!'

After the Accident

I'm an old man, yes, I am, sir, something over sixty-one;
  I've been close on forty years about the place,
But there's no use making faces, now the mischief has been done;
  Age and service don't go far in any case.
I have tried to do my duty, and so far have done it well,
  But the sharpest man will sometimes make a fall.
It is few you'd find, I fancy, who have wrought so long a spell
  With not a single failing in it all;
It is not so much the prospect of the jail that me annoys;
  No, nor yet the vile remarks one overhears;
Nothing pains me so as parting with the dear old corduroys
  That have clad me now for more than thirty years.

For one train, when first I started as a pointsman, now there's ten;
  Everything is done in quite another style;
We'd no tall and towering semaphores to watch our welfare then
  Distant from the cabin nearly half a mile.
We'd a strange old-fashioned signal not a hundred yards away,
  That took all the strength one had to make it turn,
With one green and two red dials showing signals through the day,
  And a dim old lamp at night that would not burn;
Many a life that started with me has been crushed out long ago;
  Many a dear one's eye has filled with bitter tears;
Many a sad and mournful story it has been my lot to know
  Since I started, which is more than thirty years.

They have altered things completely from the good old-fashioned way;
  With their ringing bells and gongs and other things,
And they ring them all together, till I'm blest if you can say,
  Which of them, the 'up' or 'down' it is that rings.
There's been many a young hand started, stout and sharp-like in the
      main,
  Likely looking lads, so far as one could see,
But their smartness quickly left them when they got behind a train,
  Or were caged up in a signal-box like me;
And no wonder they got muddled, such a weight on mind and brain,
  It is not the simple work it all appears;
I should have some little knowledge of its pleasures and its pains,
  Having pulled the levers now for thirty years.

Many a time I've thought when closing with my senses dull'd and
    numb,
  And my very arms and fingers strained and sore,
After eighteen hours on duty where's the good in going home,
  I'd have almost rather stood the twenty-four;
Then you could have toppled over when the closing bell was rung,
  And awoke in time the opening ring to hear;
As it is my arms get shaky, and my nerves get quite unstrung,
  And an everlasting whistle fills my ear;
Not a single soul to speak to all the eerie drearie day,
  All alone I sit and nurse my slavish fears,
For this 'No admittance' order keeps my very friends away,
  Though I've been a pointsman more than thirty years.

That my brain was getting muddled it took no great skill to tell;
  I was getting less expert in mind and limb;
My ears were getting heavy, and I could not hear so well,
  And my eyes were getting colourless and dim.
But so long as they said nothing I was eager to remain,
  I was bound to earn an honest crust somehow;
Once you're out it's no small matter finding work to do again,
  With the frost of sixty winters on your brow.
Yes, resign! I've often thought so in my darker hours, but then—
  Rung the all important question to my ears—
Did you ever know of railways giving pensions to their men
  Though they'd wrought without a slip for thirty years?

There's no great labour in it, yet when trains are coming throng
  We are sometimes sorely puzzled what to do,
And for any small detention or when anything goes wrong,
  It's a common thing to put the blame on you.
There is scarce a single clear one all our crowd of men among,
  All in time must make their little smash and go;
I have reason to be thankful that I managed through so long,
  It is what I knew would happen long ago.
Many a shaky hour and minute in this grim old box I've passed,
  Every day and every night I had my fears
That my spell of luck would leave me; I have made a smash at last
  After sailing clear for over thirty years.

And it came about so sudden and so very simple too,
    I had nothing but the late express to come;
But I never saw it better when you're wanting early through,
    Or had set your mind on getting sooner home.
'Twas that old slow-coach, Tom Jackson, at his flukey tricks again,
    You'd to watch him like a weasel night and day;
He had only reached the crossing and was coming round his train,
When I thought he'd cleared the section right away;
And I went and drew my signals for the Mail and knew no more
    Till the thud and crash came ringing in my ears;
And an accident had happened where there ne'er was one before,
    With a pointsman on the road for thirty years.

*

And is this a prison, really? No! I'm buried in a tomb,
    Stone above, beneath, around, roof, floor, and walls;
Only one small starlike window peering down upon the gloom
    Where no glow of golden sunlight ever falls.
God! this stillness is oppressive, it will wear me out ere long,
    Even now my mind is wandering; I can feel
The floor beneath me shaking; I am perched once more among
    My polished levers gleaming clear as steel;
And the iron monster rushes like a meteor through the air,
    And his piercing whoop is ringing in my ears;
Back again I stand a pointsman in the grim old cabin where
    I have wrought the traffic safe for thirty years.

Malcolm Ferguson

Born Paisley 1838. He worked first as a carpet weaver, then was twenty years as a mechanic in R. & J. P.'s Weaving Mills, Underwood, Paisley. In 1885 he emigrated to Townsville, New Zealand, there to join his brother who had set up a house-painting business.

'The ambush of blacks' (line 12) is an interesting detail besides the rest of the poem about economic hardship. The main 'clearances' of Queensland for white occupation were in the 1840s and 1850s. Surviving aborigines were indentured for non-paid labour to white settlers. By the time Ferguson emigrated, much Chinese, Indian and Melanesian labour was also employed in Queensland, some of the first Melanesians having been brought to Australia by force. The developing white trade unions though would have nothing to do with non-whites, and by 1908 over four thousand Melanesians had been deported. (Saunders, Kay; *Workers in Bondage*; The Origins and Bases of Unfree Labour in Queensland 1824-1916 University of Queensland Press, St Lucia, London, New York, 1982, pp. 11, 20-25 and 167-172.)

*

The Emigrant's Warning

By a Paisley Man

Here are buried some human bones
　　That were found on a Queensland 'run,'
Bleached white, while the grass and the stones
　　Around them were bronz'd in the sun.

Of the people who emigrate,
　　More of their smartest fellows
Meet with this terrible fate
　　Than newsmen are able to tell us.

Sometimes it's a horseman that's lost,
　　Although he may keep on the tracks;
A-fighting, he gives up the ghost
　　In the midst of an ambush of blacks.

Sometimes it's a mortal alone,
　　A-travelling on foot — let us hush;
O God in his mercy! — he's gone!
　　He's off the track — lost in the bush.

Then round he goes, round in the woods,
　　Till, reason forsaken, he'll sink;
Then heels and hands spurning the clods,
　　He dies for want of a drink.

No doubt he had found Billy Bung,
　　A mixture of ribs, hides, and horns,
Not even a maggoty skum
　　To appease his fast rising death-storm.

Emigrationists tell you at home
　　That Queensland is all that is nice;
They should be rubbed down with a brick
　　For giving untruthful advice.

Her seaports are crowded with men
    Who long have forgotten to laugh:
Are they in employment? — not them,
    At any time more than one-half.

Let ne'er a mechanic come here;
    He's better at home in a hovel
Than enter a navvie career—
    Compete at the pick and the shovel.

Farm labourers are wanted — a trick
    That brings forth the softest chicken
For Government agents to pick,
    And then throw their bones to the dicken.

There's not in the whole of the north
    Any genuine grain-growing farms,
But counterfeits straggle its earth
    In the shape of plantation concerns.

Were it not for the gold-mining trade
    That actually keeps her in life,
North Queensland had ere this been dead,
    And standing like pillar'd Lot's wife.

A house, if containing four rooms,
    Lets at twelve 'bob' a week for the rent,
And one looks at his wages and blooms,
    For it takes away thirty per cent.

It costs sevenpence a tin for Jam
    Containing but barely a pound,
One and fourpence for Bacon Ham,
    One stone of Oatmeal for a crown.

Twopence for an Orange or an Apple—
    They don't come and go like Tomatoes;
Eightpence for two pound of Treacle,
    One and sixpence a stone for Potatoes.

One and threepence a tin for Kippers,
   And Salmon one shilling retail;
A sixpence for one glass of Bitters,
   And a sixpence one tumbler of Ale.

Three shillings per pound for the Butter,
   And eightpence the big loaf of Bread;
Thirty shillings a year for Water,
   And fourpence a spool for the Thread.

The Sugar, the Rice, and the Peas
   Are sold all at fourpence per pound,
The Barley is fivepence, and Cheese
   Is here one and fourpence all round.

Eggs, two and sixpence per dozen,
   And twopence per pound for the Salt;
Pepper, to fire up the gizzen,
   A pound for two shillings — now halt.

The wage is eight shillings per day,
   But that isn't much to be heeded;
When one gets to work right away,
   There are four that are seldomly needed.

Though the wage book's enormously big,
   It makes a deficient outrigger;
For the rent and the grocery gig
   Capsizes for want of a bigger.

The distance from Townsville to Towers,
   If you want by the railway to trip it,
Is eighty-two miles, and devours
   Ten and sixpence, the price of a ticket.

Then the soil in the town and around
   For miles upon miles is such rubbish;
An African Sahara compound
   Too poor for a carrot or cabbage.

As a proof of the truth of my say,
   And I know that big lies are big sins,
The most of their garden display
   Are grown in old kerosene tins.

Where nothing worth calling a rain
   Has rained at a stretch for three years;
Beg pardon! again and again
   'Tis watered with emigrants' tears.

Be advised, stay at home, you are well,
   Though your income but thinly be wefted
Don't come here where the devil had hell
   Once, till he got a better and left it.

             Townsville, Queensland.

John MacLeod

Reverend John MacLeod was a minister in Govan when this poem was published in *Modern Scottish Poets* (D. H. Edwards, Brechin) in 1893. There is little information provided there other than that he was born in Morven and had previously been a minister at Dunse and at Girvan. The poem was 'Written by the Rev. Dr John MacLeod of Govan on passing Morven on the first occasion after the death of his father, and the home of the family for a century had been broken up.' MacLeod's father was a minister at Morven (moderator of the church in 1851) and a poet in Gaelic. He had been introduced to Tennyson when the English poet was staying at a house nearby in Morven, and Tennyson is reported in *Modern Scottish Poets* as having afterwards told his host that 'the minister of Morven was the finest man he had ever met'.

*

Passing Morven

Down Mull's dark sound from port to port
   The vessel holds upon her way,
From green Loch Aline's wooded shore
   To yonder castle-crowned bay.

And silent 'mid a motley throng
   Of strangers — on her deck I stand
Watching with thoughts unutterable
   The glory of the gliding sand.

O land of Morven! dearer far
   To me than fairest spot of earth;
O land on which my eyes first looked,
   The land that gave my fathers birth.

Scanning to-day thy winding shores,
  Although as through a haze of tears,
I feel anew thy wondrous spell,
  Rich heirloom of a hundred years.

I see the kirk-crowned sward of Kiel,
  The old grey cross against the sky;
The eastward-ordered grassy graves
  Where holy generations lie.

I seem to see, in visions fair,
  The summer Sundays long ago;
The little church — his kingly head
  Stooping to pass its lintel low.

I hear the old familiar sounds
  That broke, but did not mar the calm;
The clear, sweet piping of the lark,
  The plaintive cadence of the psalm.

But past the shores of Achabeig
  By craggy Dhucraig—Achnahaw—
By Savary's beach and wooded knoll,
  We swiftly sweep, and nearer draw

To where, the midmost channel reached,
  Blest Fuinary I behold once more,
The double gables flanked with trees,
  The gleaming arch above the door.

And every spot on which I gaze,
  From sandy beach to cairn-topped Ben,
Islands and cottage, fields and burns,
  Green Fingal's bill, the bridge, the glen,

All—all—to-day but speak to me
  Of that bright past forever fled—
Of him, whose presence haunts them all,
  A year past numbered with the dead!

Lo! the 'Grey Isles'!—our paddles forge
  Through rushing tides, a track of foam,
The sullen shores of Mull are gained,
  And I, once more, have lost my home.

Daniel King

Born Glasgow 1844. Orphaned when four years old, he was placed with an aunt, but when aged nine he was 'provided with a little money' and left, 'having heard his relative say he was a burden in the family'.

He worked as a herd-boy in Arran, did farmwork in West Kilbride, then went to Govan and eventually got work as a shipyard apprentice. He spent the rest of his working life in shipyards, becoming a foreman riveter in Port Glasgow then in Greenock. He died in 1891.

'It is affecting to think that it was his desire to be at his post that has cut him so prematurely away. Having been laid down with an attack of influenza — that epidemic at the time being prevalent — and, returning to duty despite his doctor's orders, he was seized with inflammation of the lungs, which cut him away in ten days' illness.' (From the *Greenock Telegraph* quoted in the memoir prefacing the posthumous collection *The Auchmountain Warbler* — P/KIN PC 370.)

*

Tongue Discipline

Yer fou', oh, Robin Duff, yer fou',
　Ye haena got a fit to stan',
The smell that's comin' frae yer mou'
　Wad sicken ony sober man;
An' yet ye'll tell me to my cheek
　'Twas harmless a' the drink ye got;
Preserve us, Rab, ye canna speak,
　Ye leein', dirty, drucken sot.

I wonner what on earth ye mean,
　Wi' sic a bonnie carry-on;

330

If ye'd a wife like Bogston Jean,
  She'd smash yer nose as flat's a scone.
Turn roon! Dear me! what claes wi' glaur!
  Look at the picture o' yer coat!
Just lift yer han', man, if ye daur,
  You cruel-hearted, drucken sot.

If ye was daein' what was richt,
  Ye'd teach the bairns the fear o' God;
Ye canna, Rab, when ilka nicht
  Yer stotin' under sic a load.
Ye neither tend to wife nor bairn,
  For, haith, yer seldom aff the trot,
A feed o' drink's a' your concern,
  Ye heedless, dirty, drucken sot.

Ye tell me aft to shut my mooth,
  For fear the neebors hear me flite,
I've aften hid frae them the truth,
  But noo I dinna care a dite.
Ye've ta'en it oot me gey'n sair,
  Wi' tipplin' at the cursed tot,
An' noo ye'll bully me for mair,
  Ye greedy, dirty, drucken sot.

Mony a weary nicht I've sat,
  Aft wi' a gnawin', empty wame;
An' aften, aften, hae I grat
  To think ye made sic licht o' hame.
Your weans are nearly starved to death,
  But, Rab, ye dinna care a jot;
Oh, haud awa' frae me yer breath,
  Ye heartless, dirty, drucken sot.

I've heard ye rin the whisky doon,
  An' say it could be done withoot;
Ne'er say't again, ye drucken loon,
  Ye'd sook it through a clorty cloot.
I wish I ne'er had seen your face,
  Oh, could I only loose the knot
That's brocht me to sic black disgrace,
  Ye laithsome, dirty, drucken sot.

331

Robert Semple

Born in Broomlands Street, Paisley, in 1841. Worked as a weaver's drawboy then as a pattern designer. The family into which he was born became known as 'the singing Semples' for their musical and church choir activities, and Robert conducted the choir of the Paisley Orpheus Society. He became very involved in the Temperance movement and moved to Belfast to work as a lecturer with the Irish Temperance League before emigrating to Australia in 1888 to take up a similar post in New South Wales.

*

A Sober Saturday Night

When day is past and work is o'er,
   And night comes on the scene,
We gladly hail, ere morning comes,
   The hours that intervene;
But when the day comes to its close,
   And Sunday comes in sight,
How sweet to spend with loving hearts
   A sober Saturday night!

     A sober Saturday night, my friends,
      For you, for all is right;
     And a right good Sunday we will have
     From a sober Saturday night.

When summer's glories deck the fields,
    I ramble forth to view
The charming scenes around me spread,
    And find them ever new;
I gather ferns in hidden dells,
    They make my home more bright,
And mutely teach me how to spend
    A sober Saturday night.

When winter's barriers, cold and gray,
    Forbid that I should roam,
I turn to taste the perfect joys
    That wait me in my home;
My loving ones, my pleasant books,
    Afford me rare delight;
And all combine that I may spend
    A sober Saturday night.

I would not give a night at home,
    When Saturday comes round,
For a hundred years of sinful joys
    Within the drink-shop found.
O leave the darkness of the drink,
    And seek the Temperance light,
And we will teach you how to spend
    A sober Saturday night.

Robert Tweedale

Born near Ballymoney, County Down, in 1832. He came to Johnstone with his parents in 1841, and learned the trade of a shoemaker there. In 1859 he moved to Paisley and subsequently was employed as a shoemaker with the Co-operative Society at Shieldhall in Glasgow.

*

Co-operation: The Brotherhood of Man

Dedicated to the Directors of the Scottish Co-operative Wholesale Society, Limited

> 'It's coming yet for a' that,
> That man to man the world o'er,
> Shall brithers be an' a' that.'

Arise, ye bards, your muse awake,
    Why in a stupor dream?
Come sing the brotherhood of man,
    For that's a noble theme.

'Twas sung by angels long ago
    From starry worlds on high,
So raise it on the footstool now
    And ring it to the sky.

Behold, Co-Operators march
    From north, south, east, and west,
They're coming to St. Mungo
    Attired all in their best.

334

They come with fraternal greetings;
   Long may they tell the tale
Of the major celebrations
   Of Scotia's great Wholesale.

They come when summer decks the vale
   With gems at nature's call,
To feast 'midst rural grandeur,
   At beautiful Shieldhall.

Come sing of Rochdale pioneers
   Who taught the simple plan—
How Co-Operative union could
   Exalt the working-man.

Their fame is now in all the land
   And over oceans wide;
Their seed is yielding golden fruit
   Upon the banks of Clyde.

May success attend the enterprise
   That's dear unto us all;
May honour crown each brow that has
   An interest in Shieldhall,

Where labour, trade, and capital,
   Together do unite,
To banish all monopoly,
   And give each one his right.

Away with fleets and armies,
   Which impoverish the nation,
And speed the time when men shall join
   One great Co-Operation.

For why doth poverty prevail
   Beneath the British Crown?
The millions that are squandered
   Must keep the people down.

We will fortify Britannia
  On the Co-Operative plan—
Of giving share of wealth and power
  To each industrious man.

The orphan bairns and drooping age
  Shall always have our care,
To invalids of every grade
  A portion we will spare.

We'll give no quarter to the drones
  Who fatten on the spoil;
But those who work with hand or brain
  Shall reap the fruit of toil.

To-day we meet in unity,
  As brothers let us part;
Altho' we differ in detail,
  We'll still be one in heart.

Let us trust our noble leaders,
  Assist them all we can,
To solve the glorious problem—
  The Brotherhood of Man.

22nd June, 1889

Hugh Kilpatrick

Born Smith Street, Charleston, Paisley, in 1823. A weaver, he set up business as a manufacturer then emigrated to America where he worked for seven years after his Paisley business had foundered. He returned to Paisley in 1869, paid his creditors and set up business again. Once again though he was unsuccessful and Kilpatrick 'became a collector of accounts for various business men, from which he made an adequate, if somewhat precarious livelihood'. He died aged 85 in 1909.

*

The Social and Reform club

A BURLESQUE

Ye wha wad ken the charms o' drinking,
Tae join a club are maybe thinking,
Hear me, sin' I've turn'd teetotal,
An' even hate a hair-ile bottle.
I gaed ance wi' a jolly core,
And left Reflection's solid shore;
Amang the breakers I got toss'd
An' common-sense in drink was lost.
It's true my stock was sma' o' sense,
An' wit was scarcer than my pence,
Yet some I thocht still waur than me,
If possible that some could be.
But noo I'll tell ye the occasion
That brocht aboot my reformation;
I'll tell ye o' the wild hub-bub
That drove me frae the Social Club.

337

A chiel I kent had sense afore,
A wag noo turn'd, a perfect bore,
Sang, danc'd, and rapped on the table,
An' made the place a perfect babel—
Tae better show his wit an' sense,
His learnin' an' his eloquence,
Insisted tae get on a chair,
That he micht show his graces there.
But ane, wha thocht himsel' mair able,
The Socrates threw 'neath the table,
An' there, 'mang spittoons lying glorious,
Was swearin' still he'd be victorious,
Till ane, wha wi' a tankard fill,
The whole contents let on him spill,
Near blinded his cat-starin' een,
An', nearly droon'd, he lay between
Twa raws o' feet, like horses rampin',
Or, like the deil's ane, legions trampin'.
The victor claimèd noo a hearin',
But only met wi' shouts o' swearin',
Tae ance the jug was fill'd again,
He micht as weel socht joy frae pain,
Or grace frae Beelzebub below,
Wha ne'er was kent tae come or go.
The bell-pull hangin' 'gainst the wa'
Was clean torn frae the crank awa',
An' he wha pull'd fell aff his chair,
An', sprachlin' lay upon the flair.
The door was battered wi' a bottle—
Some swore the landlord they would throttle.
The landlord noo stood at the door,
But swore he'd bring them in no more;
Syne the chairman said, wi' thunderin' roar,
'Ye'll fill the jug or square the score.'
'Mang thunderin' roars, but wi' a hanker,
He slunk awa' an' fill'd the tankar'.
Then in he cam' tae lay it doon,
But couldna for the crood aroon',
Wha press'd him sae again' the wa',
His breath was nearly clean awa'.

Some on the table got an' stamped,
Ithers curs'd an' swore an' ramped;
The gas was turn'd oot for a lark,
An' noo the glorious scene was dark.
Some bor'd an' sprachl'd for the door,
An' through the crood they tried tae bore,
But fell amang a sea o' slime,
An' there lay sprachlin' jist like swine.
The police noo wad clear the room,
An' tried tae shine their lanterns roon,
But syne got mix't up wi' the chairs,
An' some o' them nae doot, got scares,
An' weel were served for a' their flurry
Tae scale the club in sic a hurry,
Which was for love an' drink notorious,
An' huggin' ane anither glorious.

William Sharp

Born in Garthland Place, Paisley, in 1855. He was the son of a wealthy Paisley textile manufacturer and the grandson of that William Sharp to whom Alexander Wilson (q.v.) had dedicated his poem 'The Shark' which had led to Wilson's prosecution and imprisonment.

William Sharp the poet entered a lawyer's office after education at Glasgow University, then went to Australia for a short period after some poor health; he travelled extensively throughout his life — America, Europe, North Africa. He became a prominent literary figure in London, prolific in prose and verse, though his editorship of the pocket *Canterbury Poets* series was probably his most significant practical contribution to literature. Under the pseudonym 'Fiona MacLeod' — an alter ego whose true identity he preserved until his death — Sharp published plays, stories and poems of the Celtic Twilight. These included the verse-drama *The Immortal Hour* on which Routland Boughton based his once-popular opera of the same name. The poems here are early, and written under the poet's own name.

Sharp died in Sicily in 1905.

*

from Transcripts from Nature

A Green Wave

Between the salt sea-send before
  And all the flowing gulphs behind,
  Half lifted by the rising wind,
Half eager for the ungain'd shore,
A great green wave of shining light
Sweeps onward crowned with dazzling white:

Above, the east wind shreds the sky
With plumes from the grey clouds that fly.

*

Moonrise (November)

The first snows of the year lie white
  Upon the branches bending low;
  A surging wind the flakes doth blow
Before the coming feet of Night—
Half dusk, half day, betwixt the pines
Green-yellow the full moon reclines:

Green-yellow, and now wholly green,
While faint the windy stars are seen.

Charles Nicol

Born Pollokshaws 1858. After his father's death when Charles was aged ten, Charles worked three years in a weaving factory, then was employed in the engraving department of a printworks. At the time of publication of his *Poems and Songs* he was working as a traveller on behalf of a Glasgow draper and house furnisher's.

*

A Mither's Lecture Tae Her Ne'er-dae-weel Son

Ye thochtless tyke, what time o' nicht
    Is this for tae come hame?
Whan ither decent fouk's in bed—
    Oh! div ye no think shame?
But shame's no in ye, that I ken,
    Ye drucken ne'er-dae-weel!
You've mair thocht for the dram-shop there—
    Aye, that ye hae, atweel!

Ye drucken loon, come tell me quick
    Whaur ye hae been, ava?
I'm shair it's waefu' that frae drink
    Ye canna keep awa.
An' bidin' tae sic 'oors as this,
    When ye should be in bed;
I doot there's something in this wark;
    Come, tell the truth, noo, Ted?

Can ye no speak? What's wrang wi' ye?
    Ye guid-for-naething loon,
Yer gettin' jist a fair disgrace,
    An' *that* ye'll be gey soon.
Noo, dinna stan' there like a mute—
    The truth I want tae ken,
Sae tell me noo the *truth* for aince,
    It's nae too late tae men'.

You've been wi' twa-three bosom freens
    At Bob Broon's birthday spree;
Aweel, aweel, if *that's* the case,
    You this time I'll forgie.
But mind, sic wark as this, my man,
    Will never, never dae;
Ye maun gie up that waefu' drink,
    Aye, frae this very day!

Oor Wee Liz

(For Music)

Was there e'er sic a lassie kent
    As oor wee Liz?
On fun and mischief she's aye bent,
    Is oor wee Liz.
Frae early morn to late at e'en
    She's always in a biz—
I think the equal ne'er was seen
    O' oor wee Liz.

When she is wanted by her ma—
    Oor wee Liz—
She's off wi' other bairns awa',
    Is oor wee Liz.

343

N

And when we get her back again
    Ma speers her whaur she wis?
She says 'Awa a walk her lane,'
    Roguish wee Liz.

She's up to a'maist everything,
    Is oor wee Liz;
An' jist yestreen she dune something,
    Did oor wee Liz.
She ran awa', an' ye can guess,
    We were a' in a fiz;
An' whaur was she?—but in the press,
    Roguish wee Liz.

When she's kept in the days it rains,
    Then oor wee Liz,
She hauds a skule amang the weans,
    Dis oor wee Liz.
Syne at nicht, the daurlin' lammie,
    Fair wearied oot she is;
Then fu' snug beside her mammie
    Rests oor wee Liz.

A Kitchen Lecture

Eh, losh preserve us a'! what's wrang?
    Whaur hae ye been this nicht, Johnnie?
Awa' I've nae doot, wi' that gang
    Wha made ye leave a faithfu' cronie.
But, by my certies, you will yet
    Live to rue sic a carry-on;
Sic wark as this I'll no forget,
    An' that's as sure as your name's John.

Ye guid-for-naething senseless fule,
   Come tell me quick whaur ye hae been;
Noo mind yersel'—don't coup the stool—
   Losh me! yer like I've never seen.
You've been wi' Tam M'Luckie, hae ye?
   He's a fine ane to ca' a mate;
Aweel, aweel, guid forgi'e ye,
   An' that's whaur ye hae been sae late?

Haud aff o' that, ye drucken loon;
   Ye're getting jist a fair disgrace;
You'll be the talk o' a' the toon,
   If ye keep gaun at sic a pace.
You'll be the death o' me ye will,
   An' o' my puir negleckit weans;
I'm shair o' grief I've got my fill,
   An' that's a' I get for my pains.

You'll be a better man, you say;
   Aweel, aweel, John, time will tell;
If ye reform noo frae this day,
   'Twill be a bliss for me an' yersel'.
But ye hae promised oft before;
   I trust you'll keep this promise noo;
An' if you never taste drink more,
   A happy hame we'll hae, I voo.

John Davidson

Born Barrhead 1857, he was the son of a minister in the Evangelical Union Church. His father moved church to Greenock, where at the age of 13 the boy started work in a sugar factory. Then the young John Davidson had a job as an assistant in the Greenock town analyst's office, before he returned to his old school in Greenock, the Highlander's Academy, where he worked as a pupil-teacher from 1872 to 1876.

A year at Edinburgh University studying Latin and Greek was followed by a succession of schoolmaster jobs over ten years in Glasgow, Perth, Paisley, Crieff and again in Greenock. There was a break from teaching in 1884 after he married, when he worked for the year as a clerk in the Glasgow office of a thread manufacturer. Clerking he disliked, as teaching he disliked. The bitterest attack in Scottish Literature on corporal punishment in schools is contained in his unjustly neglected short story 'The Schoolboy's Tragedy' (in *The Pilgrimage of Strongsoul and other Stories*, Ward & Downey Ltd., London 1896, PCL Ref F/DAV PC 481).

In 1889 he went to London to attempt to make his living from writing. He had already written two novels, a number of plays, short stories, and the greater part of his first collection of poetry, *In A Music Hall*. He did journalistic work for *The Speaker* as well as the *Glasgow Herald*, and the success of his poetry — *Fleet Street Eclogues* (1893) and *Ballads and Songs* (1894) — gave him some literary standing in the London literary world, and in the Rhymers' Club, to which he belonged.

But it did not bring him enough money. He had to support his mother and sister in Scotland as well as his wife and the two sons born in 1887 and 1889. He did not have good health, and after his mother's death the strain on his nerves required him to leave London to live in Shoreham in Sussex for a while before returning again to the city. A series of commissions and translations for the stage then were not successful, and his long subjective-philosophical poems, or 'Testaments' as he called them, did not have the success, or the wider appeal, of his earlier work. Moved to Penzance, he suffered from asthma and bronchitis, and in 1910 he believed that he had contracted cancer. In March that year he disappeared, and a prefatory note to his last manuscript beginning 'The time has come to make an end', has usually been taken to indicate that his death was by suicide. His body was washed up three months after his disappearance; in accordance with the will he had made the previous year, he was formally buried at sea off Land's End.

The first poem in the selection of Davidson's work here, 'Selene Eden', is from the sequence *In a Music Hall* that formed the title-piece of Davidson's first poetry collection. The verse prologue states that the poems are descriptions of artists the narrator knew when, as a clerk in Glasgow in 1884, he went to a music hall 'night after night'.

The description of the harbour in ' A Ballad in Blank Verse' can be taken as a description of Greenock.

*

from In a Music Hall

5: Selene Eden

My dearest lovers know me not;
  I hide my life and soul from sight;
I conquer all whose blood is hot;
  My mystery is my mail of might.

I had a troupe who danced with me:
  I veiled myself from head to foot;
My girls were nude as they dared be;
  They sang a chorus, I was mute.

But now I fill the widest stage
  Alone, unveiled, without a song;
And still with mystery I engage
  The aching senses of the throng.

A dark-blue vest with stars of gold,
  My only diamond in my hair,
An Indian scarf about me rolled:
  That is the dress I always wear.

And first the sensuous music whets
  The lustful crowd; the dim-lit room
Recalls delights, recalls regrets;
  And then I enter in the gloom.

I glide, I trip, I run, I spin,
  Lapped in the lime-light's aureole.
Hushed are the voices, hushed the din,
  I see men's eyes like glowing coal.

My loosened scarf in odours drenched
  Showers keener hints of sensual bliss;
The music swoons, the light is quenched,
  Into the dark I blow a kiss.

JOHN DAVIDSON

Then, like a long wave rolling home,
  The music gathers speed and sound;
I, dancing, am the music's foam,
  And wilder, fleeter, higher bound,

And fling my feet above my head;
  The light grows, none aside may glance;
Crimson and amber, green and red,
  In blinding baths of these I dance.

And soft, and sweet, and calm, my face
  Looks pure as unsunned chastity,
Even in the whirling triple pace:
  That is my conquering mystery.

from From Grub Street

Rondeau

My love, my wife, three months ago
  I joined the fight in London town.
I haven't conquered yet, you know,
And friends are few, and hope is low;
  Far off I see the shining crown.

I'm daunted, dear; but blow on blow
With ebbing force I strike, and so
I am not felled and trodden down,
      My love, my wife!

I wonder when the tide will flow,
Sir Oracle cease saying 'No,'
    And Fortune smile away her frown.
    Well, while I swim I cannot drown;
And while we sleep the harvests grow,
    My love, my wife.

Roundel

My darling boys, heaven help you both!
    Now in your happy time of toys
Am I to die? How I am loth,
    My darling boys!

My heart is strong for woes or joys;
My soul and body keep their troth,
    One in a love no clasping cloys.

Why with me is the world so wroth?
    What fiend at night my work destroys?
Has fate against me sworn an oath,
    My darling boys?

Villanelle

On her hand she leans her head,
  By the banks of the busy Clyde;
Our two little boys are in bed.

The pitiful tears are shed;
  She had nobody by her side;
On her hand she leans her head.

I should be working; instead
  I dream of my sorrowful bride,
And our two little boys in bed.

Were it well if we four were dead?
  The grave at least is wide.
On her hand she leans her head.

She stares at the embers red;
  She dashes the tears aside,
And kisses our boys in bed.

'God, give us our daily bread;
  Nothing we ask beside.'
On her hand she leans her head;
Our two little boys are in bed.

from Rail and Road

March Many-weathers, bluff and affable,
The usher and the pursuivant of Spring,
Had sent his North wind blaring through the world—
A mundane wind that held the earth, and puffed
The smoke of urban fire and furnace far
Afield. An ashen canopy of cloud,
The dense immobled sky, high-pitched above
The wind's terrestrial office, overhung
The city when the morning train drew out.
Leaping along the land from town to town,
Its iron lungs respired its breath of steam,
Its resonant flanges, and its vertebral
Loose-jointed carcase of a centipede
Gigantic, hugged and ground the parallel
Adjusted metals of its destined way
With apathetic fatalism, the mark
Of all machinery. — From Paddington
To Basingstoke the world seemed standing still:
Nothing astir between the firmaments
Except the aimless tumult of the wind,
And clanging travail of the ponderous train
In labour with its journey on the smooth,
The ineludible, the shining rails.

  But prompt at Basingstoke an interlude
Began: a reckless youth, possessed with seven
Innocuous devils of self-consciousness
Primeval, bouncing in irruptively,
Lusty-Juventus-wise, annexed the whole
Compartment — as a pendant to the earth,
Already his! Wind-shaven, ruddy; hunched
And big; all knees and knuckles; with a mouth
That opened like a portal; fleshy chops
And turned-up nose widespread, the signature
Of jollity; a shapeless, elvish skull;
His little pig's eyes in their sockets soused
But simmering merrily; just twenty years;
One radiation of nervous energy;

A limber tongue and most unquenchable,
Complacent blaze of indiscretion, soft
As a night-light in a nursery. 'Where away?'
Quoth he; and 'Hang the weather! I've seen worse,
In my time for the season.' Then: Did we think
The train was doing thirty or forty miles
An hour? Sometimes, by instinct, he could tell
To a mile the rate at which a train went.
This morning, for a wonder, he couldn't trust
His judgement in the matter; — annoying! — still
A man's form varied, and we must excuse
His inability to gauge our speed.
Good golf about here, — very! Did we play?
And, by the bye, talking of golf, he did
A brilliant thing just now: — missing the train
At Farnham on the other line, instead
Of waiting for the next, he tramped across
To Basingstoke, — some decent tale of miles;
His destination being Winchester,
Either line suited, — see? The weather, — yes,
The weather; healthy, of course; — your moist cold kills;
Your dry cold cures; — to-day it seemed as cold, —
But that must be the wind; in sheltered roads
It smelt like Spring; — to-morrow, — who could tell
To-morrow's weather? — a funny climate, ours!
Was that a cow there, or a — Yes, a cow.
He didn't know how we regarded it,
But he, for his part, took it that the hand
That rocked the cradle ruled the world; to drop
A signature into a ballot-box
Would make no earthly! (Slang, elliptical.)
Although we must remember, all of us,
This rocking of the cradle was out of date;
But that he wouldn't canvass; — we were to mind
There must be no mistake: women were women
All the world to nothing; and — mark him — if
They *had* political enfranchisement,
No one could say — no one at all! — what might
And mightn't happen: not a doubt of that.
Getting along more quickly; forty miles,
He thought; or less, perhaps. He meant to lunch
At Winchester; then hire a trap and drive . . .
'Instanter to the devil,' someone sighed.

All this, and further, an infinitude
Of dislocated prattle, with a smile
Indelible, and such a negligent
Absorbition in self that no appeal,
Except a sheer affront, abuse or blow,
Could have revealed remotely any gleam
Or shade, to him apparent, of his own
Insipid and grotesque enormity!
When time, distemper or disaster sap
Such individuals, and they see themselves,
In facets of disrupted character,
As others see them, stupid and absurd,
How bad the quarter of an hour must be!
Natheless there are extant a hearty breed,
Incorrigibly cheerful, who behold
Themselves for ever in the best of lights.
And by the pipe and bowl of Old King Cole
They have the best of it! To see ourselves
As others see us may be good enough;
But to love others in their vanities,
And to portray the glorious counterfeit—
In sympathetic ink that sympathy
Alone can read aright, — why, that's a gift
Vouchsafed to genius of the rarest strain!

from A Ballad in Blank Verse

His father's house looked out across a firth
Broad-bosomed like a mere, beside a town
Far in the North, where Time could take his ease,
And Change hold holiday; where Old and New
Weltered upon the border of the world.

'Oh now,' he thought — a youth whose sultry eyes,
Bold brow and wanton mouth were not all lust,
But haunted from within and from without
By memories, visions, hopes, divine desires —
'Now may my life beat out upon this shore
A prouder music than the winds and waves
Can compass in their haughtiest moods. I need
No world more spacious than the region here:
The foam-embroidered firth, a purple path
For argosies that still on pinions speed,
Or fiery-hearted cleave with iron limbs
And bows precipitous the pliant sea;
The sloping shores that fringe the velvet tides
With heavy bullion and with golden lace
Of restless pebble woven and fine spun sand;
The villages that sleep the winter through,
And, wakening with the spring, keep festival
All summer and all autumn: this grey town
That pipes the morning up before the lark
With shrieking steam, and from a hundred stalks
Lacquers the sooty sky; where hammers clang
On iron hulls, and cranes in harbours creak
Rattle and wing, whole cargoes on their necks;
Where men sweat gold that others hoard or spend,
And lurk like vermin in their narrow streets:
This old grey town, this firth, the further strand
Spangled with hamlets, and the wooded steeps,
Whose rocky tops behind each other press,
Fantastically carved like antique helms
High-hung in heaven's cloudy armoury,
Is world enough for me. Here daily dawn
Burns through the smoky east; with fire-shod feet
The sun treads heaven, and steps from hill to hill

355

Downward before the night that still pursues
His crimson wake; here winter plies his craft,
Soldering the years with ice; here spring appears,
Caught in a leafless brake, her garland torn,
Breathless with wonder, and the tears half-dried
Upon her rosy cheek; here summer comes
And wastes his passion like a prodigal
Right royally; and here her golden gains
Free-handed as a harlot autumn spends;
And here are men to know, women to love.'
His father, woman-hearted, great of soul,
Wilful and proud, save for one little shrine
That held a pinch-beck cross, had closed and barred
The many mansions of his intellect.

'My son,' he said — to him, fresh from his firth
And dreams at evening; while his mother sat,
She also with her dingy crucifix
And feeble rushlight, praying for her boy —
'My son, have you decided for the Lord?
Your mother's heart and mine are exercised
For your salvation. Will you turn to Christ?
Now, young and strong, you hanker for the world;
But think: the longest life must end at last,
And then come Death and Judgment. Are you fit
To meet your God before the great white throne?
If on the instant Death should summon you,
What doom would the Eternal Judge pronounce —
"Depart from me" or "Sit on My right hand"?
In life it is your privilege to choose,
But after death you have no choice at all.
Die unbelieving, and in endless woe
You must believe throughout eternity.
My son, reject not Christ; he pleads through me;
The Holy Spirit uses my poor words.
How it would fill your mother's heart and mine,
And God's great heart with joy unspeakable,
Were you, a helpless sinner, now to cry,
"Lord I believe: help Thou mine unbelief".'
He clenched his teeth; his blood, fulfilled of brine,
Of sunset, and his dreams, boomed in his ears.

A vision rose before him; and the sound
Husky and plaintive of his father's voice
Seemed unintelligible and afar.
He saw Apollo on the Dardan beach:
The waves lay still; the winds hung motionless,
And held their breath to hear the rebel god,
Conquered and doomed, with stormy sobbing song,
And crashing discords of his golden lyre,
Reluctantly compel the walls of Troy,
Unquarried and unhewn, in supple lines
And massive strength to rise about the town.

*

Wasted and sad with wantonness, and wan
With fantasy — a furnace seven times hot,
Wherein he tried all things; and wrung with woe
To see his father dying for his sake,
And by the memory of his mother's death,
He yielded tamely and professed himself
Convinced of sin but confident in Christ.

Then to the table of the Lord he went,
Ghastly, with haunted eyes that shone, and limbs
That scarcely bore him, like a heretic
Led to the chamber where tormentors stood
Muffled and silent, earnest to explore,
With cunning flames and cords and engines dire,
The sunken wells of pain, the gloomy gulfs
Obscurely wallowing in the souls of men.

In solemn tones, the grey-haired presbyter —
'This is My body which is given for you,
This do in memory of Me.'

                    The boy,
Whose blood within him clamoured like a storm,
Uttered a smothered cry and rose, but lo!
The happy triumph on his father's face!

357

'Why do I not die now? like husks of corn,
The bread, like vitriol the sip of wine!
I eat and drink damnation to myself
To give my father's troubled spirit peace.'
The stealthy elders creaked about the floor,
Guiding the cup and platter; looking down,
The children in the gallery smirked and watched
Who took the deepest draught; and ancient dames
Crumpled their folded handkerchiefs, and pressed
With knuckly fingers sprays of southernwood.

Ah! down no silver beam the Holy Grail
Glided from Heaven, a crimson cup that throbbed
As throbs the heart divine; no aching sounds
Of scarce-heard music stole into the aisle,
Like disembodied pulses beating love.

But in the evening by the purple firth
He walked, and saw brown locks upon the brine,
And pale hands beckon him to come away,
Where mermaids, with their harps and golden combs,
Sit throned upon the carven antique poops
Of treasure-ships, and soft sea-dirges sing
Over the green-gilt bones of mariners.

*

Our ruthless creeds that bathe the world in blood
Are moods by alchemy made dogmas of —
The petrifaction of a metaphor.
No creed for me! I am a man apart:
A mouthpiece for the creeds of all the world;
A soulless life that angels may possess
Or demons haunt, wherein the foulest things
May loll at ease beside the loveliest;
A martyr for all mundane moods to tear;
The slave of every passion; and the slave
Of heat and cold, of darkness and of light;
A trembling lyre for every wind to sound.

I am a man set by to overhear
The inner harmony, the very tune
Of Nature's heart; to be a thoroughfare
For all the pageantry of Time; to catch
The mutterings of the Spirit of the hour
And make them known; and of the lowliest
To be the minister, and therefore reign
Prince of the powers of the air, lord of the world
And master of the sea. Within my heart
I'll gather all the universe, and sing
As sweetly as the spheres; and I shall be
The first of men to understand himself . . .

Patrick Magill

Born Glenties, Donegal, in 1891, he worked from childhood as a farmhand then came from Derry to Scotland when he was fourteen. He worked for seven years as 'farmhand, drainer, tramp, hammerman, navvy, plate-layer or wrestler', and published *Gleanings from a Navvy's Scrapbook* when he was nineteen. It sold 8,000 copies. He was with the Caledonian Railway Company at Greenock when he left Renfrewshire and headed south to join the *Daily Express* in London in 1911. He published *Songs from the Dead End* in 1912. His best-known novel is the autobiographical *Children of the Dead End*. Others include *The Rat-Pit, Moleskin Joe* and *Lanty Hanlon.*

*

Have You

(On the road to Kinlochleven, 1908)

Have you tramped about in Winter, when your boots were minus soles?
Have you wandered sick and sorry with your pockets full of — holes?
Have you wondered which was better, when your capital was light,
A plate of fish and taters, or a hammock for the night?
Have you smelt the dainty odour of some swell refreshment shop,
When you'd give your soul in barter for a single mouldy chop?
Have you sought through half the kingdom for the job you could not get?
Have you eyed the city gutters for a stump of cigarette?
Have you dossed in drear December on a couch of virgin snow
With a quilt of frost above you and a sheet of ice below?

These are incidental worries which are wrong to fuss about;
But God! they matter greatly to the man who's down and out.

Have you sweltered through the Summer, till the salt sweat seared
    your eyes?
Have you dragged through plum-dead levels in the slush that reached
    your thighs?
Have you worked the weighty hammer swinging heavy from the
    hips,
While the ganger timed the striking with a curse upon his lips?
Have you climbed the risky gang-plank where a bird might fear to
    stop,
And reckoned twenty fathoms would be hellish far to drop?
Have you swept the clotted point-rods and the reddened reeking cars
That have dragged a trusty comrade through the twisted signal bars?
Have you seen the hooded signal, as it swung above you clear,
And the deadly engine rushing on the mate who didn't hear?

If you want to prove your manhood in the way the navvies do,
These are just the little trifles that are daily up to you.
And if you haven't shared the risk, the worry and the strife,
Disappointment, and the sorrow, then you know not what is life.

Have you padded through the country when the Summer land was
    fair,
And the white road lay before you leading on just anywhere?
Have you seen the dusk grow mellow, and the breaking morn grow
    red,
And the little diamond dew-drops come to sentinel your bed?
Though your clothes were rather shabby, and your toes and knees
    were bare,
The little silly birdies sure they didn't seem to care;
But just sang to cheer your journey, as they would to cheer a prince,
For they saw old Adam naked, and they know no better since.

Have you slouched along the meadows, have you smelt the new-
                                        mown hay?
Have you smoked your pipe and loved it as you plodded on the way?
Have you bummed your bit of tucker from the matron at the door
And blessed the kindly woman who had pity on the poor?
A pipe of strong tobacco (if you get it) after meals
And there's many a scrap of comfort for the man who's down at
    heels.

Have you felt your blood go rushing, and your heart beat strangely
  high,
As the smoke of your tobacco curled upwards to the sky,
When lying 'neath a spreading tree that shaded from the sun
The happiest mortal in the land, it dared not shine upon.
If you haven't shared the pleasure, that follows after strife,
You do not know the happiness that fill's a navvy's life.

from Padding It

You speak of the road in your verses, you picture the joy of it still,
You of the specs and the collars, you who are geese of the quill,
You pad it along with a wine-flask and your pockets crammed with
  dough,
Eat and drink at your pleasure, and write how the flowers grow—
If your stomach was empty as pity, your hobnails were down at the
  heels,
And a nor'easter biting your nose off, then you would know how it
  feels,
A nail in the shoe of your bluchers jagging your foot like a pin,
And every step on your journey was driving it further in,
Then, out on the great long roadway, you'd find when you went
  abroad,
The nearer you go to nature the further you go from God.

Played Out

As a bullock falls in the crooked ruts, he fell when the day was o'er,
The hunger gripping his stinted guts, his body shaken and sore.
They pulled it out of the ditch in the dark, as a brute is pulled from
  its lair,
The corpse of the navvy, stiff and stark, with the clay on its face and
  hair.

In Christian lands, with calloused hands, he laboured for others'
    good,
In workshop and mill, ditchway and drill, earnest, eager and rude;
Unhappy and gaunt with worry and want, a food to the whims of
    fate,
Hashing it out and booted about at the will of the goodly and great.

To him was applied the scorpion lash, for him the gibe and the
    goad—
The roughcast fool of our moral wash, the rugous wretch of the road.
Willing to crawl for a pittance small to the swine of the tinsel sty,
Beggared and burst from the very first, he chooses the ditch to die—
. . . Go, pick the dead from the sloughy bed, and hide him from
    mortal eye.

He tramped through the colourless winter land, or swined in the
    scorching heat,
The dry skin hacked on his sapless hands or blistering on his feet;
He wallowed in mire unseen, unknown, where your houses of
    pleasure rise,
And hapless, hungry, and chilled to the bone, he builded the edifice.

In cheerless model and filthy pub, his sinful hours were passed,
Or footsore, weary, he begged his grub, in the sough of the hail-
    whipped blast,
So some might riot in wealth and ease, with food and wine be
    crammed,
He wrought like a mule, in muck to the knees, dirty, dissolute,
    damned.

Arrogant, adipose, you sit in the homes he builded high;
Dirty the ditch, in the depths of it he chooses a spot to die,
Foaming with nicotine-tainted lips, holding his aching breast,
Dropping down like a cow that slips, smitten with rinderpest;
Drivelling yet of the work and wet, swearing as sinners swear,
Raving the rule of the gambling school, mixing it up with a prayer.

He lived like a brute, as the navvies live, and went as the cattle go,
No one to sorrow and no one to shrive, for heaven ordained it so—
He handed his check to the shadow in black, and went to the misty
    lands,
Never a mortal to close his eyes or a woman to cross his hands.

As a bullock falls in the rugged ruts
  He fell when the day was o'er.
Hunger gripping his weasened guts,
  But never to hunger more—
They pulled him out of the ditch in the dark,
  The chilling frost on its hair,
The mole-skinned navvy stiff and stark
  From no particular where.

La Basée Road

(Cuinchy, 1915)

You'll see from the La Basée Road, on any summer's day,
The children herding nanny-goats, the women making hay.
You'll see the soldiers, khaki clad, in column and platoon,
Come swinging up La Basée Road from billets in Bethune.
There's hay to save and corn to cut, but harder work by far
Awaits the soldier boys who reap the harvest fields of war.
You'll see them swinging up the road where women work at hay,
The straight road, — La Basée Road, — on any summer day.

The night-breeze sweeps La Basée Road, the night-dews wet the hay,
The boys are coming back again, a straggling crowd are they.
The column's lines are broken, there are gaps in the platoon,
They'll not need many billets, now, for soldiers in Bethune,
For many boys, good lusty boys, who marched away so fine,
Have now got little homes of clay beside the firing line.
Good luck to them, God speed to them, the boys who march away,
A-singing up La Basée Road each sunny summer day.

The Listening-Patrol

With my bosom friend, Bill, armed ready to kill,
  I go over the top as a listening-patrol.
Good watch we will keep if we don't fall asleep,
  As we huddle for warmth in a shell-shovelled hole.

In the battle-lit night all the plain is alight,
  Where the grasshoppers chirp to the frogs in the pond,
And the star-shells are seen bursting red, blue, and green,
  O'er the enemy's trench just a stone's-throw beyond.

The grasses hang damp o'er each wee glow-worm lamp
  That is placed on the ground for a fairy camp-fire,
And the night-breezes wheel where the mice squeak and squeal,
  Making sounds like the enemy cutting our wire.

Here are thousands of toads in their ancient abodes,
  Each toad on its stool and each stool in its place,
And a robin sits by with a vigilant eye
  On a grim garden-spider's wife washing her face.

Now Bill never sees any marvels like these,
  When I speak of the sights he looks up with amaze,
And he smothers a yawn, saying, 'Wake me at dawn,'
  While the Dustman from Nod sprinkles dust in his eyes.

But these things you'll see if you come out with me,
  And sit by my side in a shell-shovelled hole,
Where the fairy-bells croon to the ivory moon
  When the soldier is out on a listening-patrol.

Marching

(La Basée Road, June, 1915)

Four by four, in column of route,
By roads that the poplars sentinel,
Clank of rifle and crunch of boot—
All are marching and all is well.
White, so white is the distant moon,
Salmon-pink is the furnace glare
And we hum, as we march, a ragtime tune,
Khaki boys in the long platoon,
Ready for anything—anywhere.

Lonely and still the village lies,
The houses sleep and the blinds are drawn,
The road is straight as the bullet flies,
And we go marching into the dawn;
Salmon-pink is the furnace sheen.
Where the coal stacks bulk in the ghostly air
The long platoons on the move are seen,
Little connecting files between,
Moving and moving, anywhere.

Alphabetical list of poets with names of books from which the poems have been taken, and their references in Paisley Central Library

[Note: A source given as *Paisley Poets* refers to Brown, Robert: *Paisley Poets, With Brief Memoirs of Them and Selections from their Poetry*, 2 Vols J. & J. Cook Paisley Vol 1, 1889; Vol 2, 1890. *Paisley Pamphlets* refers to collections of pamphlets bound chronologically and numbered under this title, in Paisley Central Library.
N.D. = No Date of Publication   N.P. = No Publisher given]

ANON (**'B.O.P.'**)   The Renfrew Volunteers: undated sheet No. 18 in volume bound as *Songs, Poems and Poem Broadsheets* 080 PC 2954.

ANON   (**'Candidus'**) Teetotalism versus Intemperance — *Tee-Totalism versus Intemperance, Humbly Inscribed to All Whom It May Concern by Candidus*, printed by J. Neilson, Paisley, 1838. In Paisley Pamphlets Vol. 23 (1838) PC 282.

ANON   The Deluge of Carnage at Length Has Subsided — *Report of the Meeting Held at Paisley, in the Saracen's Head Inn, on the 31st of October 1822, in celebration of Mr Hunt's Release from Ilchester Bastille, Containing Speeches, Songs, Toasts Etc.* J. Neilson, Paisley, 1822. (PC 800, bound as *Hunt's Release from Ilchester Bastille, 1822*.)

ANON   The Honest Farmer's Declaration: *The New Paisley Repository* No. 3, January 1st 1853. (In *Paisley Repository* 050.REN PC5440).

ANON   The Hour of Retribution's Nigh: *Report of a Soiree in Honour of the Rev. Patrick Brewster, one of the Ministers of the Abbey Church, Paisley, for his Exertions in the Cause of Freedom, on Monday Evening, Nov. 12, 1838, with Two of the Songs Sung on the Occasion*, J Caldwell & Son, Paisley, 1838. (In *Paisley Pamphlets* Vol. 23 PC 282.)

ANON   Memento Mori — undated sheet No. 23 bound in volume titled *Songs, Poems and Broadsheets*, Ref no. 080 PC 2954.

ANON   Paisley Politics: Rab and Pate — in *Paisley Poets* Vol. 2, pp. 147-152. (821.08 PC 900)

ANON   (**'A Working Man'**) Lorne and Louise: A Republican Rhyme — *Lorne and Louise: A Republican Rhyme* by a Working Man *Dedicated to Our Scottish Representatives in Parliament*, David Glassford, Paisley. n.d. In Paisley Pamphlets Vol. 43 (1869) PC 302.

AITKEN, **William**   After the Accident — *Lays of the Line* by Inspector Aitken, St Enoch's Station, Glasgow. John Menzies & Co., Edinburgh & Glasgow, 1883 (P/AIT PC 3318)

ANDREW, John   Address to the Dundee Microscopical Society — in *Modern Scottish Poets* (4th Series), ed. D. H. Edwards, pp. 297-298. Brechin, 1882. (821.08 PC 3714)

BARR, John   A Twa Handit Crack; Rise Oot Yir Bed; Tam Maut; There's Nae Place Like Otago Yet; When To Otago First I Came: *Poems and Songs Descriptive and Satirical.* W. P. Nimmo, Edinburgh, 1861 (P/BAR PC 1924).

BERNSTEIN, Marion   Woman's Rights and Wrongs; A Rule to Work Both Ways; Wanted a Husband; Manly Sports; Human Rights; A Dream; Married and 'Settled'; A Song of Glasgow Town; A Song for the Working Man: *Mirren's Musings,* A Collection of Songs and Poems. McGeachy, 93 Union Street, and M. Bernstein, 5 Dunrobin Place, Paisley Road, Glasgow, 1876 (P/BERN PC 1926).

BOOG, Robert   *Excursion Through the Starry Heavens, North Pole Elevated about 55 Degrees* Pamphlet. N.D. In *Paisley Pamphlets* Vol. 26, 1841 (PC 285). Also in *Paisley Poets* Vol. 1, pp. 31-36 (821.08 PC 899).

BORLAND, Alexander   The Brown Cleuk On — in *Paisley Poets* Vol. 1, pp. 274-275 (821.08 PC 899).

BROWN, David   When Johnnie Was Gi'en to the Weeting His Mou': In *Minstrelsy of My Youth.* Caldwell & Son, Paisley 1845. In *Paisley Pamphlets* Vol. 30 (1845-46) PC 289.

BURNSIDE, Thomas   The Idle Weaver; A Voice from the Workshop; A Union Lay; Never Drink Onything Stronger Than Tea; Address to My Brither Wabsters: *Lays from the Loom.* J. & J. Cook, Paisley, 1889 (P/BUR PC 2422).

CAMERON, W. C.   Epitaph: Here Lies Wee Jamie Brucklebreeks — *Mall Jamieson's Ghost, or The Elder's Dream, founded on fact,* with other Poems, J. Motherwell, John Mitchell, J. Bowie, Paisley, 1844 (P/CAM PC 1146).

CLARK, Robert   Song: O come sweet dearest lass — *Original Poetical Pieces, Chiefly Scottish.* Caldwell & Son, Paisley, 1836 (P/CLE PC 1125).

CRICHTON, Thomas   The Library (exc.) — *The Library, A Poem Etc.,* printed by J. Neilson for R. Smith, Bookseller, Paisley, 1803 (P/CRI PC 770).

DAVIDSON, John   Selene Eden; From Grub Street: *In a Music Hall and Other Poems.* Ward and Downey, London, 1891 (P/DAV PC 5257). Rail and Road (exc.); A Ballad in Blank Verse (exc.); *The Poems of John Davidson* (2 Vols.), ed. Turnbull, A., Scottish Academic Press, Edinburgh & London, 1973. Vol. 2 (P/DAV PC 5392).

ELDER, **William** To the Defenders of Things as They Are — in *An Address Delivered by William Elder on the Evening of Monday, 7th March 1870, at the Soiree of the Eclectic Mutual Improvement Class, Meeting in the Trades Hall, Paisley. S. Mitchell in the Chair*. Printed at the 'Herald' Office, by Wm. B. Watson, Paisley. N.D. In Paisley Pamphlets Vol. 45 (1870) PC 304.

FERGUSON, **Malcolm** The Emigrant's Warning — in *Paisley Poets* Vol. 2, pp. 321-324 (821.08 PC 900).

FINLAYSON, **William** Weaver's Lament; Geordie's Marriage; On Three Children in the Eastwood Churchyard — 1814: *Simple Scottish Rhymes*, printed by S. & A. Young, Paisley, 1815 (821.08 PC 5440).

FISHER, **James** The Queer Folk in the Shaws — in Murdoch, A. G. (ed.): *Recent and Living Scottish Poets*. Porteous Bros., Glasgow. N.D. The copy in PCL is the second edition, and Fisher's poem has been omitted.

GRAHAM, **William** My Ain Toun: *The Wild Rose, Being Songs, Comic and Sentimental*. John Neilson, Paisley, 1851 (P/GRA PC 882).

HAMILTON, **John** *The Lay of the Bogle Stone, An Erratic Poem by the Author of* Revivalist Letters *Etc. Etc. Etc.* Part First N.P. London, 1869. In Paisley Pamphlets Vol. 59 (1879) PC 318.

KENNEDY, **William** Och! While I live, I'll Ne'er Forget — *Fitful Fancies*, Oliver & Boyd, Edinburgh & G. B. Whitaker, London, 1827 (P/KEN PC 369).

KILPATRICK, **Hugh** The Social and Reform Club: *The Death of Wallace or The Spectre of Elderslie and Other Poems* by Hugh Kilpatrick ('Eagle Eye'). Wm. Lochhead, Paisley, 1909 (P/KIL PC 507).

KING, **Daniel** *Tongue Discipline — in Modern Scottish Poets* (9th Series), ed. D. H. Edwards, Brechin, 1886, pp. 246-247 (821.08 PC 3179). This is preferable to the version as amended in the posthumous collection *The Auchmountain Warbler*. J. & R. Parlane, Paisley, 1893 (P/KIN PC 370).

LAIRD, **Margaret Thomson** *Anniversary Lines on the Death of my Only Son — Memorial Volume of Poems* by the late Mrs Margaret Thomson Laird McLeod. Printed for Private Circulation, Alex Gardner, Paisley, 1893. The copy in the Paisley Central Library has been bound as *Poems by Margaret McLeod* (P/McL PC 2039).

LORIMER, **John** Instructions for the Police — *Poems and Songs with Memoir and Notes* by George Masson, Oakshawside. J. & J. Cook, Paisley, 1889 (P/LOR PC 1983).

MacDONALD, **Hugh**   The Trysted Hour; Young Spring; For Gudesake Let's Agree: from *Poems and Songs with a Memoir of the Author* William Love. Glasgow, 1863 (P/McD PC 6233).

MacGREGOR, **John**   The Tories Treat Us With Disdain — in Collection of Newspaper Cuttings bound as *Fugitive Pieces Chiefly Local* (941.41 RENI PC 2174).

McGILVRAY, **Alex**   Of Whig and Tory we can see; When I wi the Laird did enlist: in *The Town's House on the Market Day A Poem in Two Cantos*. Caldwell & Son, Paisley, 1840. In Paisley Pamphlets Vol. 25 (1840) PC 284. An Address Delivered by a Certain Gallant Gentleman — *Poems and Songs Satirical and Descriptive, Bearing on the Political, Moral & Religious Character of Man*. Wm. Gilchrist, Glasgow, 1850 (P/McG PC 2911). What Deil has gane wrang with the true holy kirk — *Epistle to Mr James Lee, Stanly Green, detailing The Exploits of the Renowned Governor of Stanley Castle During One Day's Ramble in Paisley; with his opinion of the clergy in general, and the town council in particular*. Caldwell & Son, Paisley, 1843. In Paisley Pamphlets Vol. 28 PC 287.

MacINDOE, **George**   Nelson's Monument, Glasgow Green; from 'The Vision of Inanimates', in *The Wandering Muse, A Miscellany of Original Poetry*, Printed by Stephen & Andrew Young, Paisley 1813. In Paisley Central Library this is found in *Poems and Songs by Various Authors* Vol. 2. (080 PC 1394)

McLACHLAN, **Alexander**   The Log Cabin; Young Canada: *The Poetical Works of Alexander McLachlan*. William Briggs, Toronto, 1900 (P/McL PC 1215).

MacLEOD, **John**   Passing Morven: *Modern Scottish Poets* (15th Series), ed. D. H. Edwards, Brechin, 1893, pp. 432-433 (821.08 PC 3185).

McNEIL, **Duncan McFarlane**   When I was a Drawboy; The Three Elders; Auld Watty: *The Reformed Drunkard or The Adventure on the Muir with Other Poems and Songs*. John Reid, Paisley, 1860 (P/McN PC 511).

MAGILL, **Patrick**   Have You; from 'Padding It'; Played Out: *Songs of the Dead End*, F. W. Dean & Sons, The Year Book Press Ltd., London, 1920 (P/McG PC 4833). La Basée Road; The Listening-Patrol; Marching: *Soldier Songs*, Herbert Jenkins, London, 1917 (821.08 PC 1372).

MARSHALL, **Charles**   A Poor Victim; Stick to Your Last; Scotland's Curse: *Lays and Lectures for Scotia's Daughters of Industry*. Published for the author by Sutherland and Grove, Edinburgh, 1853; Paisley Ref. 824 PC 1355.

MAXWELL, James   The Divine Origin of Poetry Asserted and Proved (exc.): *The Divine Origin of Poetry Asserted and Proved, The Abuse of it Reproved, and Poetasters Threatened. To Which is Added. A Meditation on May, or, The Brief History of a Modern Poet. Two Moral Essays by* James Maxwell *Poet in Paisley.* Printed by J. Neilson for the Author. Paisley, 1790. (In PCL package marked *Broadsides by James Maxwell, Poet, Presented by David Semple* P/MAX PC 2046).
On the Divine Attributes of God: Introduction: *On the Divine Attributes of God, a Sacred, Philosophical and Poetical Essay, by* James Maxwell, *Poet in Paisley.* Printed by John Neilson, Paisley, 1793. In *Scottish Miscellanies* 080 PC 470.)

MITCHELL, John   *Cautious Tam or How to Look a Foe in the Face* by Somebody, G. Caldwell, Paisley, 1847. In Paisley Pamphlets Vol. 28 (1843) PC 287. Title page of Paisley Central Library copy inscribed 'John Mitchell' under 'by Somebody'.
The Third Class Train Respectfully inscribed to the Weavers of Paisley by a Third Class Man. Published by J. Mitchell, Bookseller, Paisley, 1840. Copy in Paisley Pamphlets vol. 25, 1840 (PC 284). PC 284, 1840. Title page of Paisley Central Library copy inscribed 'by John Mitchell, Paisley'.
A Braid Glower at the Clergy by Ane not o' Themsel's, W. & W. Miller, Glasgow, 1843. In Paisley Pamphlets Vol. 28 (1843) PC 287. Title page has 'John Mitchell, Paisley' handwritten in pencil at author's name position.

MOTHERWELL, William   Jeannie Morison; I Am Not Sad! O That This Weary War of Life!: *The Poetical Works of William Motherwell with Memoir by James McConechy Esq,* 3rd edition, David Robertson, Glasgow, 1849 (P/MOT PC 2129).

MUTRIE, Robert   The Shilling in the Puir Man's Pouch — *Poems and Songs Dedicated to the West-End Callans Association.* N.P. Paisley, 1909 (P/MUT PC 826).

NICOL, Charles   A Mither's Lecture Tae Her Ne'er-dae-weel Son; Oor Wee Liz; A Kitchen Lecture: *Poems and Songs Chiefly in the Scottish Dialect.* McLaren & Bruce, Edinburgh. N.D. (P/NIC PC 1758).

NOTMAN, Peter   Lines on Mechanism — *Small Poems and Songs,* by 'Petrus', J. Neilson, Paisley, 1840. 'Peter Notman' written in ink on title page in Paisley Central Library (P/NOT PC 804).

PICKEN, Joanna   An Auld Friend wi a New Face; The Death Watch: *The Poems and Poetry of Scotland from the Earliest to the Present Time* (2 Vols.), ed. by James Grant Wilson, Blackie & Son, London, Glasgow & Edinburgh. N.D. Vol. 2, pp. 174-175. (821.08 P 507)

POLIN, **Edward**   Married the Morn — in *Paisley Poets* Vol. 1, pp. 59-60. In The Days When We Were Radicals; John Henderson My Jo: in *Councillors In Their Cups, or the Reformed Transformed; a Lyrical Laughterpiece*. Caldwell & Son, Paisley, 1842. In Paisley Pamphlets Vol. 27 (1842) PC 286. This copy has 'E Polin' written under the preface signed 'THE AUTHOR'.

POLLOK, **Robert**   *The Course of Time* A Poem in Ten Books, Blackwood, 7th edition, Edinburgh, 1828 (P/POL PC 5434).

PYPER, **Mary**   Epitaph — A Life: *Sacred Poems* with an Introductory note by the Very Rev. E. B. Ramsay, Dean of Edinburgh. Andrew Elliot, Edinburgh, 1865 (P/PYP PC 3165).

RICHMOND, **Daniel**   Subject Matter of the Books of the Bible: in *Paisley Poets* Vol. 1, pp. 474-475 (821.08 PC 899).

ROBERTSON, **John**   The Toom Meal Pock: two undated pages (as from a broadsheet) bound into *Paisley Miscellanies 1813-1851* Vol. 1, Paisley Central Library, Ref. No. 080 PC 6263. The song also appears in *The Poets and Poetry of Scotland*, ed. Wilson, J. G., Vol. 2, p. 536 (821.08 PC 508). In *Paisley Poets* Vol. 1, pp. 60-61 (PC 899) the word 'just' in the third line of the last verse has been altered to 'them'.

RUSSELL, **Jessie**   Woman's Rights *versus* Woman's Wrongs, A Recantation, 'Signs of Our Times', The Mother's Story: *The Blinkin' o' the Fire* & Other Poems, Cossar, Fotheringham & Co. Glasgow 1877. (PC 3040)

SEMPLE, **Robert**   A Sober Saturday Night: *Paisley Poets* Vol. 2, p. 364 (821.08 PC 900).

SHARP, **William**   Transcripts from Nature: *The Human Inheritance*, Elliot Stock, London 1882 (P/SHA PC 538). The PCL copy is signed by Sharp 'To my friend A.H. Palmer', and contains two annotations by the poet.

SMITH, **Alexander**   Glasgow: A Boy's Poem (exc.): *City Poems,* Macmillan & Co., Cambridge, 1857 (P/SMI PC 3164).
Blaavin: *The Poetical Works of Alexander Smith* (ed. Sinclair, W.), Nimmo, May & Mitchell, Edinburgh, 1909. (Not in PCL.)

TAIT, **Alexander**   A Ramble Through Paisley (exc.): *Poems and Songs,* printed for and sold by the author, Paisley, 1790 (P/TAI PC 3199).

TANNAHILL, **Robert**   The Braes O Gleniffer; When John an' Me War' Married; O Are Ye Sleeping Maggie; Lang Syne, Beside the Woodland Burn; W.——'s Recipe; Ode to Jealousy; The Moralist; A Resolve; The Trifler's Sabbath Day; Bonnie Wood o' Craigie-Lee: *The Soldier's Return, A Scottish*

Interlude in Two Acts, with Other Poems and Songs, Chiefly in the Scottish Dialect. Stephen Young, Paisley, 1807 (P/TAN PC 1260).
The Simmer Gloamin': *The Scots Magazine and Edinburgh Literary Miscellany* Vol. LXXII, January 1810, Constable & Co., Edinburgh.
'Gloomy Winter's Now Awa'', *Written by R. Tannahill with Symphonys & Accompaniment by R. A. Smith*. Printed & Sold by J. McFadyen, Glasgow. N.D. National Library of Scotland, Ref. MH 299 (52). This is catalogued as c. 1810. Mitchell Library, Glasgow, has a copy Ref. 784.4941, bound in a collection of airs published by McFadyen (786.4552) and noted as from 1790-1826.

THOMSON, James   *The City of Dreadful Night and Other Poems*. P. J. & A. E. Dobell, London 1922. (P/THOM PC 9389).

THOMSON, **Robert Burns**   The Flae Affair: Quoted in the biographical introduction to a selection of Thomson's work in *Modern Scottish Poets*, 7th Series, pp. 151-160, D. H. Edwards, Brechin, 1884 (821.08 PC 3177).

TWEEDALE, **Robert**   Co-Operation: The Brotherhood of Man: in *Paisley Poets* Vol. 2, pp. 355-357 (821.08 PC 900).

WEBSTER, David   Song: Wha Wadna Be Blyther; Tak it Man Tak it; Paisley Fair; Droll Will Dunbar: *Original Scottish Rhymes with Humorous and Satirical Songs*, Caldwell & Son, Paisley, 1835 (P/WEB PC 3990).

WILSON, **Alexander**   Hollander, or Lightweight; The Insulted Pedlar: *The Hollander or Lightweight with Other Poems and Songs*, J. Caldwell, Paisley, 1829 (P/WIL PC 793).
Daybreak: *Poems*, J. Neilson, Paisley, 1790 (P/WIL PC 591).
The Shark (exc.): *Lang Mills Detected*, R. Smith, Paisley, 1832 (P/WIL PC 1123).
Rab and Ringan; The Teacher: *Poems Chiefly in the Scottish Dialect*, Longman, Hurst, Rees, Orme and Brown, London; Gale and Fenner, Constable & Co., Edinburgh; J. Smith & Son, Glasgow; T. Stewart, Greenock; H. Crichton and T. Auld, Paisley, 1816 (P/WIL PC 5828).
Watty and Meg or The Wife Reformed, To Which Is Added, The Ladies' Petition to the Doctor, Glasgow, printed for the booksellers. N.D. N.P. (080 P/WIL PC 35).

WILSON, **John**   Turn Ye to Me: in Hopkins, K. & Roekel, R. van — *John Wilson/Christopher North: A Biographical Sketch*, Renfrew District Libraries, Paisley, 1979 (P/WIL PC 7390).

WILSON, **William**   Lines on Looking at the Picture of a King — *Poetical Pieces Composed by a Young Author*, G. Caldwell, Paisley, 1842. In Paisley Pamphlets Vol. 27 (1842) PC 286.

RADICAL RENFREW

WINGATE, David   A Miner's Morning Song; The Collier's Ragged Wean;
Wha'll Buy My Linties?: *Poems and Songs,* Blackwood & Sons, Edinburgh
& London, 2nd edition, 1863 (P/WIN PC 708).
A Day Amang the Haws; Annie Weir; The Birdie; The Sin O Sang; The
Better Land: *Annie Weir and Other Poems,* Blackwood & Sons, Edinburgh
& London, 1866 (P/WIN PC 1741).

YOOL, James   *The Rise & Progress of Oppression, or The Weavers'
Struggle for their Prices, A Tale,* Stephen and Andrew Young, Paisley, 1813
(P/YOO PC 471).
O! If Ye Hae a Heart Tae Spare — *The Poems and Songs and Literary
Recreations of James Yool, Collected and Collated for the Paisley Burns
Club by William Stewart, and an Obituary Notice of the Author from the
'Renfrewshire Independent' of the 15th December 1860,* Glasgow, May
1883. Single handwritten volume of 213 quarto pages bound in leather,
Paisley Central Library no. PC 3982.

Glossary

abreed	widely	blether	bladder
aiblins	maybe	blow't	fart, suddenly dis-
airls	a deposit as earnest		charge faeces
	of more to come	blue	whisky
airn	iron	blue deils	delirium tremens
ase	ashes	bodle	small coin, two
atweel	assuredly, indeed		pence Scots
ava	at all	bools	marbles
awee	a wee while	boonmost	uppermost, nearest
ayont	beyond		the surface
bachals,	slippers, down-at-	boor-tree	elder-tree
bauchles	heel shoes	boost	box
bag	stomach, jilt, kitty	bor'd	pressed, shoved
baint (raw)	boned (raw-)		through
bang't	hurried, dashed	braid	broad
bear	aggressive, pugna-	braird	barley, first sprout-
	cious person		ing of barley
beild	shelter	braws	good clothes,
belly-flaught	headlong, hastily		Sunday best
ben	in, to the parlour	breckans	brakes, ferns
bere	barley	brent	burnt
bethankit	(God) be thanked	brunt	burnt
bicker	cup, beaker	brussen	snatched, hasty
biel	shelter	buckl't	fastened, wrapt up
biel'less	unprotected	buckled	married
bien; bienly	comfortable, well-	bummers	bagpipers
	off; comfortably,	buneuchs	diarrhoea
	cosily, liberally	bung	throw violently,
big; biggin'	build; building		forcibly
billy	fellow, comrade	burrel	ridge in ploughed
bink	bench		field, barrel
binna	be not, don't be	busk	dress, make ready
binweed	bindweed	buskit	decorated
birkies	conceited people,	buttle	sheaf, bundle
	stout, smart folk	caft	bought, purchased
birks	birches	cairnies	pyramids
birls	spins	callan	lad, youth, old
birsled	broiled; scorched,		man (affect.)
	toasted	caller	clear
bitch	man or woman	camseugh	stern-faced,
	(contempt)		crooked, surly
blate	backward, bashful	cankert	bad-tempered

cantie	cheery	corning	feed
capernuitie	intoxicated	Corse	Cross (Paisley)
cappy	small drinking cup	corse	course
carle	man, fellow	coup'd	drank off, emptied
carlin	old man, woman		by tilting up
carritch	catechism	crack	instant
carry	sky	craigie	crag; throat, gullet
cauldrife	cold, indifferent	crannie	little finger, pinkie
caup	wooden drink cup	cranreugh	hoar, frost, rime
certies,	by my troth,	crave	payment demand,
by my	assuredly		invoice
chafts	cheeks	croodles	makes pigeon noise,
cheek	side		'coos'
chiel	man, person	croon	wail, lament
chincough	whooping cough	crouse	bold, cosy
chirl	sound, make cry	cuffets	blows, buffets
chirt	gnash, teeth-clench;	cushat	wood-pigeon
	hug	daffin',	having fun; idle
chirts	strains, presses	daffing	talk
chittering	shivering, with	darg, dark	the day's work
	chattering teeth	daunert	dandered, sidled
clachan	village	deaved	worried, bothered;
claiver'd	blethered, gossiped		annoyed with talk,
clash, clashin	gossip, gossiping		bored
clatter	gossiping, chatter	deavin'	deafening
clavering,	gossiping, gossip	dichting	wiping away
clavers	nonsense	dight (dicht)	wipe clean or dry
cleed	clad	dinsome	noisy
cleuk	cloak	dirl	vibrate, rattle
clishmaclavers	gossip, nonsense	dite, care a	care a wipe
cloot	cloth	divor	debtor, rogue,
clorty	filthy, clatty	(dyvour)	good-for-nothing
cockernony	woman's piled-up	douf	dull, spiritless
	hairstyle	dover	to be half-asleep,
cog	measure, fourth		in a dottery state
	part of a peck	dowie	sad, mournful
cogie	wooden vessel, pail,	doxes	sweethearts
	licquor	doyt	copper coin worth
condies	conduit, drain		one-twelfth of a
coosten	cast		penny
core, cores	company, crew;	draff	dregs of brewed
	cronies, mates		malt, grain
cork	employer of	drag	hindrance, toil,
	weavers, 'manufac-		encumbrance
	turer'; supplied	drappie (the)	drink, whisky
	cloth, sometimes	dreepends	fat income, perks
	hired out looms and		(roast drippings)
	premises	drouket	drenched

376

drouth	thirst, parched craving for alcohol	gaffin'	guffawing
drover	sheep driver	gart	made, compelled
drucken	drunken	gate	way, direction, distance
drummock	mixture of meal and water	gaucie	plump, pleasant, jolly
Dryster	man in charge of drying grain	gauntet	yawned
duddy;	ragged, tattered;	gavil	gable, wide open door
duddies	ragged, everyday clothes	gawpish	feeling like yawning, getting bored
dumfunert	dumbfounded	geer (gear)	possessions
dunt	knock, thump	gell, on the	on a binge, spree
dyvour	bankrupt, troublesome person	gin	ere, before, if, by the time that
ebber	shallower, nearer the surface	girn, girnan, girning	grimace, grinning, grimacing, snarling
eerie	dismal	glaur	mud, muck
eidantly	industriously	gleg	quick-witted, attentive pressing
eident, eydent	industrious, attentive	glib-gabbet	fluent, smooth-tongued
eldrin	elderly	glint	look
Embro	Edinburgh	gloits	dull, stupid, lazy people
ettled	strove, tried to		
fash	vex, cause worry to	gooldies	goldfinches
fecht	fight	gowan	daisy
fee	servant's wages	gowk	cuckoo
felt	worn out pasture land	graith	business effects, tools of the trade
flate	scolded (p.p. flyte)	gree	live in harmony, be friends
flee'd	excited (especially through drink)	grumphan	grumbling, complaining
flite	scold, quarrel, rebuke	gumstick	child's teething stick
flow	small quantity of powder, of grain	gunk, gie the	throw over, give the heave to
flyting	scolding, rebuking	gyte	mad
fore-doors	front doors of buildings	had	hold
		haffits	sides of the head, temples
fung,	a blow, wallop		
fushonless	lacking nourishment, pithless	hainches	haunches
		haith's	exclamation (e.g. 'In faith it's')
fykes	fidgets, restless moods		
gab	incessant talk, mouth	hale sale	wholly alone, just myself
gab, flung owre	drank, hurled back	halflins	partly, almost

hallen	partition wall between door and fireplace	ingle cheek	fireside, chimney corner
hallow	hollow	jaunering	jokingly talking
hanker	hesitation, loitering	jaur (verb)	quarrel, jar
hans'ling	handseling, first taste or experience of	jaut	jaunt
		jimp	dainty, sparing, scanty
hap	shelter from the elements	jum'le	jolt, jumble
		kail	cabbage broth
happer	mill hopper	kail-yard	cottage or kitchen garden
happit	wrapped in; clothed	kame	comb, coxcomb, crest
harl	drag, haul; move with difficulty; amass (money)	karry (carry)	sky
		keek	peep
harnishes	harness weaving, harness plaids, shawls	keel	measure mark on warp sent to weaver
		kibbock	cheese
harns	brains	kill	kiln
hash	mess, person (contempt.)	kimmer's (cummer's)	wife's, gossip's
haud, hauding	hold, keep, check; holding	kintra	country
		kippl't	coupled, married
haveral	half-wit, fool, blether	kist	chest, box
		knowe	knoll
haw-tree	hawthorn tree	knowt	cattle
haws	hawthorns	kookit	peeped, keeked
hearst	harvest	kuits	ankles
heigh	high, big	kye	cattle
het	hot	laigh	low
hil't	held, raised	lair	lore, learning
hinnied	honeyed	lampin, lampit	striding, taking long strides; strode purposefully
hizzie	housewife, a woman not 'genteel'		
horn	drinking vessel	lang-kail	dish of Scotch cabbage
horn, auld in the	old and wise, long in the tooth	lash	looped string fastened to raise groups of warp-thread in a loom together
howden	hodden		
hower	hollower, deeper		
howkit	delved		
howlets	owl, owlet	lave	bale, scoop the water from; the remainder
hue	small portion of		
hunkered	squatted, crouched on haunches		
		laverock	lark
hurdies	buttocks, haunches	lawn	land
hurlin	rumbling, gurgling like rushing water	lay	pasture, lea, bit of loom
ilk, ilka	each, every	leal	loyal, genuine, true

378

leese	divisions of threads in warp before put on loom	nail't	clinched in agreement
lift	sky	nettles	puzzles
limmers	rascals, prostitutes, mistresses	nieve	fist
		noddle	temper, the head
lingle	shoemaker's thread	nowt (knowt)	cattle; stupid fellow
linn	waterfall, cascade, pool at bottom of such		
		painches	bowels
		pairtricks	partridges
linties	linnets	pash	the head
listet	enlisted	pea strae	pea straw, used usually as animal bedding
lone	lane		
loof	palm of hand		
loon	bloke, rogue; boy, fellow	pease-meal	flour made of ground pease
louping	leaping	peery	spinning-top
lowe	light, flame	peesweep	lapwing
lowse	loose	pensie	responsible, possessing forethought
lug	ear		
mae	more, others	pirn	bobbin, reel
mailin'	farm, holding, rent from such	playrife	playful
		pleugh	plough
maukins	hares	plides	plaids
maun	must	pock	bag, poke
mavis	thrush	Poortith	poverty
maw	mouth	pouket	plucked, picked
mawing	mowing	pouney	pony
meikle	much, great	pouther	powder
mid-room lums	chimneys in room between the but and the ben	pree	prove, attain, kiss
		racket	stretched
		raggy	ragged, poorly clothed
millin's	crumbs of bread		
minnie	mother	ramped, rampin'	stamped, beat on the floor; stamping
mirk	dark		
monie−plies	ruminants' third stomach; a dish of such	rape	rope
		rattons	rats
		ravelins	broken loose ends of thread
mump	mutter peevishly as if under the breath		
		raw'd	set up, arranged in a line
murphies	potatoes	rax't	stretched
muter	multure; proportion of grain exacted from someone grinding at a mill, by its owner or tenant	red wud	stark raving mad
		redd	cleared debris and rubble
		reivers	robbers
naigie	horse, pony	rive	pull apart, pull to pieces

roos'd	praised, boasted, flattered	shoon, shune	shoes
roupit	auctioned, sold off as in warrant sale	short syne	not long ago
		shot	single movement of shuttle carrying weft across web
rout	rolled, twisted and turned		
routh	abundance, plenty	siccan	such a, an
row't	wrapped in	sicker	cautious, certain
rowting	bellowing	skail't	dispersed
rug	pull, tug	skirls	shrieks of laughter, of enjoyment
rump	cut, clip		
rumple	rump, buttocks, bum	slaisterin'	splashy, sloppy, pail-spilling
rung	stout stick, cudgel	sleekie, sleekit	crafty, deceitful; plausible, sly
sairt	served		
sark	shirt	slocken, sloken	quench, slake
saughs	willows		
sca't	scabby, scruffy	snell	sarcastic, tart
scaddin'	scalding	snood	hair ribbon-tie
scamber, scamb	burner, burn, scorch	snoovt	moved at a steady pace
scar	scare	snuffy	sulky
scarts	scratches	sook	suck
scawlin	railing at, abusing	sough	sound of the wind, sigh
scogies	scullions, kitchen maids	spaewife	fortune teller
scourin' thing	domestic metal display object needing regular polishing or cleaning; one of 'the brasses'	spavie	rheumatic disease of horses, jokingly applied to people
		speel, speil	climb, ascend
scowth	room to range, abundance	speering	asking
		spenticle	bespectacled
screigh	whisky	splores	sprees, binges
scrimp, scrimpit	cut down, restrict; pinched	spoulin'	spoiling, marring
		sprachlin'	sprawling
scrunt	worn-down stub of pen or pencil	spraul	struggle (sprachle)
		spurtle	thrash, struggle, stir limbs
sculk	avoid		
Seestu	Paisley	squake	squawk, make harsh cries
sharney	cowdung-besmeared	squashes	cascades, dashes of water, urine
shaw	small wood, thicket		
shearing	first vertical cutting at the mineface	squatter	splashing agitation, like a duck thrashing
shift	own devices	stabs, stobs	(fences with) stakes, posts
shods	shoes		
shoen	shoeing, cobbling	starn	star

staucher'd	staggered	thrapple	throat, windpipe
stauns	stands	thraw	twist, wring
steek	shut, shut up, confine; quick pace, blow	threep	maintain, contend, pipe up
		thrift	work, industry
steeket	shut, fastened	throssil	thrush
steerin'	busy	throttle	throat; strangle
stent	rates	thrum-keel	final mark on the web which indicates end of the work
stey	stay, check, steep		
stirk	a steer; oaf, stupid person; stout man		
stoited	stumbled (through drink)	thrums	scraps of waste thread
stooks	sheaves, shocks of corn	tint	lost
		tints	taints
stoup	drinking vessel, flagon, decanter	tirl	move causing rustling noise, scrabble
stourie, stoury	dusty, restless, bustling	tittlin'	having small talk
		tod	fox
strae	straw	token	badge
straun	gutter	toom, toum	empty, lean
strave	strove	towmont	year, twelvemonth
striddle, striddlen	stride, step out; straddling	traikin	trekking
		trig	tidy, smart, trim
strussel	struggle	trottin	flowing briskly, chuckling
study, studdie	anvil		
stumpin'	hobbling, walking heavily	trow	feel sure, warrant
		tume's	empty as
suchin'	of such a manner	twines	bonds, i.e. handcuffs
sumphs	oafs, sulks		
swack	hard blow	twinna	it will not
sweert	lazy, slow, reluctant	tyne, tyneing	lose, losing
swither	hesitation, hesitate	unco	uncommon, very great
syne	ago, since, then		
tack	stitch, pin	voo	vow
tail	horizontal section of cords in harness of a draw loom	wab	web
		wae	sorrowful
		wag-at-the-wa'	uncased pendulum clock
tanle	blaze, bonfire		
tap	top, head, crest	wair, wair't	spend, spent; laid out as expense
tawny	a bully		
tawpies	foolish girls or boys	wame	stomach
teen	at e'en, night	wat, weel a	well I know
theekit	roofed, hatched	wauket	hardened, calloused
thowe	thaw	waukrife	wakeful, light-sleeping
thowless	energyless		
thrang, thranging	busy, thronging	weet	wet
		whalps	whelps

whang	thick slice	yate	gate
wheesles	wheezes, asthma, bronchitis	yaummer	lament
		yeldrins	yellow-hammers
whilk	which	yett	gate
whum'le	reversal of luck, upset, overturning	yill	ale, beer
		yirth	earth
winnock-brods	window-boards, shutters	yokit	set vigorously about
		yorlin's	yellow-hammers
winnocks	windows		
wins	earns a living, harvests		